SUPREME
COURT
APPOINTMENTS

SUPREME COURT

APPOINTMENTS

Judge Bork and the Politicization of
Senate Confirmations

Norman Vieira and Leonard Gross

Southern Illinois University Press
Carbondale and Edwardsville

Library of Congress Cataloging-in-Publication Data

Vieira, Norman.
    Supreme court appointments : Judge Bork and the politicization of Senate
confirmations / Norman Vieira and Leonard Gross.
        p. cm.
    Includes bibliographical references and index.
    1. United States. Supreme Court—Officials and employees—Selection and
appointment—History. 2. Judges—Selection and appointment—United
States—History. 3. Bork, Robert H. 4. Political questions and judicial
power—United States.   I. Gross, Leonard, 1951-   . II. Title.
    KF8742.V54 1998
    347.73'2634—dc21   98-15735
        ISBN 0-8093-2204-8 (cloth : alk. paper)   CIP

CONTENTS

PREFACE

This volume on Supreme Court appointments grew out of the controversy surrounding President Reagan's nomination of Judge Robert Bork to succeed Justice Powell on the Supreme Court. Because few knowledgeable observers questioned Judge Bork's professional qualifications, opposition to Bork quickly focused on his judicial philosophy. The focus on ideology raised a crucial issue as to whether it was proper for the Senate to reject for ideological reasons an otherwise qualified nominee. This book analyzes the Bork proceedings and the role of judicial ideology in the confirmation process. It also examines all of the post-Bork appointments to the Supreme Court. In these endeavors, we have relied on interviews with major participants in the confirmation process, as well as on traditional primary materials like committee hearings and Senate debates. We are grateful for the help of Gregg Walters, Nancy Stanley, and other research assistants.

It is significant that the fallout from the Bork confirmation battle has not abated in more than ten years following the event. Indeed, the impact of the Bork precedent has now reached beyond Supreme Court appointments to affect the nomination of judges for all federal courts and even the selection of candidates for cabinet and subcabinet positions. Just this year, the *Washington Post* reported that "[n]early 10 percent of the 846 seats on the federal bench are now empty, and the Senate has confirmed only 53 judicial nominees over the past two years," compared with 101 confirmations in 1994 alone. Chief Justice Rehnquist has warned that "vacancies cannot remain at such high levels indefinitely without eroding the quality of justice" (*Washington Post*, Jan. 3, 1998, A20). But Senator Orrin Hatch, who chairs the Senate Judiciary Committee, responded that the problem stems from President Clinton's nomination of "activist judges," and other Republican senators have said that they would strongly oppose the confirmation of judicial nominees who hold "activist views." It is apparent, therefore, that the issue of ideological qualification for service on federal courts has lost none of its vitality in the years following the Bork proceedings.

PART ONE

THE BORK NOMINATION

I
EXIT JUSTICE POWELL

Powell's clerks were surprised, but not shocked.[1] For several years, Justice Powell had been rumored to be in ill health. He had undergone major surgery three times since coming to the Court, including most significantly, surgery for prostate cancer in 1985. Moreover, he had told President Nixon at the time of his appointment that he did not expect to stay on the Court for more than ten years. In fact, Powell had thought seriously about leaving the Court in 1982, but his children persuaded him to stay.[2] Now, as he approached his eightieth birthday, it was time to reconsider.

Powell called his clerks into his office as the Court was about to end its 1986 Term and, without fanfare, quietly announced that he had decided to retire and assume senior status. None of his clerks believed that Powell was under any outside pressure to leave or that, if there had been any pressure, it would have made any difference to him. His clerks thought Powell "left with a great deal of regret. He was still mentally and intellectually capable. He loved his job so much, and he wanted to go out while he was on top. Yet, he thought it was in the best interest of the Court for him to retire."[3] In his farewell press conference, Powell expressed concern that he might handicap the Court if he experienced a recurrence of serious health problems.[4]

In the past, some justices had tried to time their resignations so as to maximize the chance that a successor would be appointed who would carry forward their views. Chief Justice Earl Warren tendered his resignation to President Johnson in June 1968 "effective at your [Johnson's] pleasure"[5] in an apparent attempt to give Johnson, a fellow liberal, the opportunity of appointing his successor.[6] Warren was unsuccessful because conservative senators blocked Johnson's appointment of Abe Fortas to be chief justice.

Similarly, Justice William O. Douglas tried to postpone his retirement in order to deny President Ford the opportunity to name his successor.[7] However, Douglas's ill health prompted the Court to order reargument in any case in which his vote was decisive, an order tantamount to refusing to count his vote when it mattered most. That action eventually induced Douglas to retire.[8] A few years later, Justice Stewart, then about to leave the Supreme Court, told Vice President Bush that other justices contemplating retirement were watching to see what kind of appointments the newly elected president would make.[9] More recently, Justice Brennan made known his reluctance to retire during the administration of a conservative president, but a series of strokes forced him to change his plans.

In each of these instances, a retiring justice hoped to time his departure from the Court to give a president who shared his views the opportunity to nominate a like-minded person to the Court. Justice Powell apparently did not have the selection of a successor uppermost in his mind, though one of his law clerks remarked that "the Justice felt that anybody who succeeded him should have been like him."[10] Yet in Powell's case, the appointment of a like-minded successor seemed particularly important to some observers because of the position he held at the ideological center of the Supreme Court. Powell had supplied the crucial fifth vote on many of the social issues confronted by the Court. In the 1986 Term, the Court had decided forty-six cases by a vote of 5 to 4, and Powell was the justice most often in the majority—thirty-five times. Although Powell has frequently been characterized as a "moderate," his voting record placed him much closer to the Court's conservative wing than to its liberal wing. For example, in 1986, Powell voted with Chief Justice Rehnquist 86.1 percent of the time, but he voted with Justice Brennan only 56.3 percent of the time. Similarly, in 1985, he voted with Rehnquist 87.7 percent of the time but with Brennan only 55.8 percent of the time.[11] Nevertheless, Powell was viewed as a centrist who was "fiercely independent, with an abiding faith in precedent and judicial self-restraint."[12]

Powell voted with the majority in *Roe v. Wade*,[13] upholding a woman's right to an abortion. He cast the decisive fifth vote in the *Bakke* case, holding that a white male applicant for admission to medical school had been subjected to illegal discrimination by the school's special admissions program for minorities. On church-state matters, Powell had supplied the fifth vote to strike down a major federal program aiding parochial schools[14] and to uphold a city-sponsored nativity scene in Pawtucket, Rhode Island.[15] In the criminal justice area, where Powell usually sided with the conservative bloc, he cast the decisive vote to uphold capital punishment, despite the charge that it was being applied in a racially discriminatory manner.[16] Not surprisingly, litigants in the Supreme Court would frequently frame their argument with a view to securing Justice Powell's vote. "You would be going for two or three people in the middle and Powell was the key," said Washington lawyer Benjamin W. Heineman Jr.[17]

Because of Powell's position as a swing vote on many important issues, the selection of his successor was viewed as critical both by the administration and by groups on the left and right of the political spectrum. Liberal groups did not view Powell as one of their own, but they believed they had some chance to get his vote. After Powell's retirement, these groups expressed concern that they would not fare well with a successor appointed by President Reagan. Their concerns seemed well founded in light of the history of judicial appointments under Reagan. That history made it clear that the president would not search for a judicial centrist as a replacement for Justice Powell. His effort would be aimed at changing, not maintaining, the balance on the Supreme Court.

The effort to alter the direction of federal courts began during the first year of the Reagan administration. In October 1981, Attorney General William French Smith criticized federal judges for usurping the power of elected officials on issues like abortion, school prayer, and pornography. He said that Reagan would appoint judges who would be more "attuned to the 'groundswell of conservatism evidenced by the 1980 election.'"[18]

The first step in reshaping the federal judiciary was to change the way in which lower court judges were selected. The Office of Legal Policy was established by Attorney General Smith in 1981. During Reagan's two terms, that office was successively headed by Jonathan Rose, Tex Lezar, James M. Spears, and, finally, Stephen J. Markman.[19] The central role of the office was to screen potential judges. Markman boasted that the Reagan administration "has in place what is probably the most thorough and comprehensive system for recruiting and screening federal judicial candidates of any administration ever."[20]

First, a candidate's records were scrutinized and compared with those of possible competitors through the use of computer data banks that contained published speeches, articles, and judicial opinions of various candidates.[21] Then the candidates were interviewed to determine whether they were committed to a policy of judicial restraint. They also were asked how they would approach a wide variety of issues like federalism, separation of powers, statutory interpretation, criminal law, and constitutional interpretation. Stephen Markman asserted that no judicial candidate was ever subjected to ideological litmus tests by any Justice Department interviewer in the Reagan administration.[22] However, some individuals who went through the process have said they were asked their views on such issues as abortion, affirmative action, and criminal justice.[23] Bruce Fein, an assistant attorney general during Reagan's first term, was quoted as stating that prospective judicial nominees were asked if they thought *Roe v. Wade* was correctly decided.[24] Grover Rees, who also was involved in the judicial selection process during Reagan's first term, thought *Roe v. Wade* was an appropriate litmus test but believed it soon became worthless because prospective nominees realized that they had to criticize *Roe* in order to be seriously considered.[25]

During Reagan's first term, Attorney General William French Smith and Jonathan Rose, the director of the Office of Legal Policy, compiled an "A" list of conservative candidates whom they wanted to place on the federal court of appeals. Rose is reported to have said that the names on that list included Robert Bork, Antonin Scalia, Richard Posner, Frank Easterbrook, Ralph Winter Jr., Kenneth Starr, Alex Kozinski, Lino Graglia, and J. Harvie Wilkinson III. All, except Graglia, were eventually appointed to the court of appeals.[26] Ed Meese chaired regular meetings of White House and Justice Department attorneys to discuss possible lower court nominees who would adhere to what Meese called the "jurisprudence of original intent"—interpreting the Constitution in accordance with the original understanding of the Framers. After lawyers at the Office of Legal Policy had interviewed various candidates, the attorney general would select one candidate to recommend to the Federal Judicial Selection Committee. That committee was chaired by the attorney general, and it included the deputy attorney general and the assistant attorney general for the Office of Legal Policy. After review by the FBI and the American Bar Association (ABA), the candidate's name would be forwarded by the attorney general and the White House counsel to President Reagan for formal nomination.[27]

Melanne Verveer of People for the American Way noted that the Justice Department was less insistent on ideological tests for trial judges than it was for appellate judges. Verveer stated that, in the case of trial judges, senators from the president's party were still permitted to propose the persons they wanted nominated. But whereas senators might have been able in the past to select a single individual whom they would propose to the president, now they were asked to submit three possible nominees so that the Justice Department could determine which one was philosophically most acceptable.[28]

The Reagan administration was quite successful in selecting nominees whose judicial philosophy was consistent with the president's requirements.[29] Although some of Reagan's nominees were only marginally more conservative than those selected by previous Republican presidents, a small group including Bork, Scalia, and Richard Posner was highly conservative. Reagan was equally successful, as will be seen, in choosing conservative justices for the Supreme Court. Of course, there is nothing sinister or unusual about nominating justices who share the president's judicial philosophy. Prior to the Reagan presidency, there was a long history, dating back to the first days of the Republic, of presidential consideration of ideology in deciding whom to appoint to the Supreme Court. President Washington selected only avowed Federalists for service on the Court. Franklin Roosevelt even went so far as to try to expand the size of the Court from nine justices to fifteen in order to guarantee that a majority would be favorably disposed to his New Deal legislation. Although Roosevelt failed in his court-packing scheme, he later succeeded in placing eight nominees on the Supreme Court, all of whom passed his ideological test of support for the New Deal.[30]

In making appointments to the Supreme Court, the Reagan administration tried to avoid the mistakes of previous administrations. It closely scrutinized each nominee with a view toward reshaping the Court's approach to constitutional interpretation. In order to reduce the risk of surprise, all nominees were drawn from the federal court of appeals except for Sandra Day O'Connor, whose nomination basically represented the fulfillment of Reagan's campaign pledge to put a woman on the Supreme Court.[31] The practice of drawing nominees from lower federal courts gave attorneys at the White House and the Justice Department an opportunity to review the opinions of the candidates to determine the nature of their ideological commitment.

This is not to suggest that O'Connor was not herself examined for ideological reliability. One high administration official stated that O'Connor was questioned on such matters as the exclusionary rule and "whom she felt closest to" on the Supreme Court. Abortion was another topic on which O'Connor was apparently questioned. O'Connor had been sharply criticized by Jerry Falwell and the National Right to Life Committee for cosponsoring a bill in the Arizona legislature that made "all medically acceptable family planning methods and information available to anyone who wanted it." Falwell argued that this bill demonstrated that O'Connor favored abortion, and he urged that she not be given the nomination. At that point, President Reagan questioned her on the subject, and she told him that she was personally opposed to abortion. In a press conference on July 8, 1981, Reagan said that after interviewing her, he was "completely satisfied with her views on that issue."[32] Another administration official stated that O'Connor "really made it easy. . . . She was the right age, had the right philosophy, the right combination of experience, the right political affiliation, the right backing."[33]

In Reagan's second term, the Justice Department was asked to compile a list of possible Supreme Court candidates in case the White House got an opportunity to make another nomination.[34] Assistant Attorney General W. Bradford Reynolds assembled a group of attorneys from the White House and the Justice Department who put together a list of about twenty names, consisting mostly of judges on the federal court of appeals. The candidates were then subjected to lengthy interviews.[35]

Ed Meese said the candidates were asked what they thought the proper role of a federal judge was. Meese stated that the interviewers were attempting to find out what the judge's approach to judicial decision making might be.[36] However, according to Terry Eastland, the nominees were also questioned about specific cases. He remembered in particular a lengthy discussion with candidates about the decision in *Ollman v. Evans*,[37] concerning the extent to which the First Amendment right of free speech would limit a defendant's liability under state libel laws.[38] When told of Eastland's statement about *Ollman v. Evans*, Meese acknowledged that specific cases were discussed, but he said they were used basically for illustrative purposes—to learn the candidate's general philosophy rather than to determine how he or she would vote on a particular issue.[39] Yet, an aggressive search for the proper judicial philosophy could easily slide into a search for proper rulings in cases likely to come before the Court.

On May 27, 1986, Chief Justice Burger, who was approaching his eightieth birthday, informed President Reagan that he would retire at the end of the Court's term a month later.[40] At the urging of Chief of Staff Donald Regan, the President kept Burger's decision secret while Attorney General Meese and White House Counsel Peter Wallison began a search for Burger's successor.[41]

Terry Eastland said that the two candidates who were "head and shoulders above the rest were Scalia and Bork." The decision to rank those two above the rest was not based on their confirmability or the politics of the situation but "on the merits," meaning that Bork and Scalia were intellectually the strongest candidates. Equally important, their legal philosophy was exactly what the Reagan administration was seeking. Legal philosophy was determined mainly by an analysis of their judicial opinions, although some attention was also paid to their speeches and other writings.[42]

The question then came down to whether Bork or Scalia should be picked to fill the vacant slot. Since Burger had been chief justice and since neither Bork nor Scalia was inclined toward administrative work, a decision was quickly made to nominate Rehnquist to be chief justice and to "back fill" from there. Scalia was viewed somewhat more favorably than Bork from an ideological perspective. Scalia had come down on the "conservative" side and Bork on the "liberal" side in the *Ollman* case, for example.[43] *Time* reported that some of Scalia's colleagues at the court of appeals thought that he wrote strongly worded dissents and concurring opinions to reinforce his conservative credentials and advertise his agreement with President Reagan.[44] Nevertheless, conservatives like Pat Buchanan, former White House communications director, pressed hard for Judge Bork.[45]

In the end, the decision to choose Scalia over Bork in 1986 was a pragmatic one. Almost everyone in the administration felt that Bork would be more difficult to confirm than Scalia because of Bork's firing of Archibald Cox as Watergate prosecutor and because Bork had spoken out vigorously on many conservative issues. In addition, Scalia had the political advantage of being born of Italian-immigrant parents, thereby attracting an ethnic base of support that Bork lacked. Despite the consensus that Scalia was more easily confirmable, Peter Wallison pushed for Bork, wisely perceiving that by the time the Senate got done wrangling over Rehnquist's nomination, Bork would sail through quite easily and that Scalia could fill a later vacancy on the Court. However, White House Chief of Staff Donald Regan argued successfully against nominating Bork on the heels of Rehnquist's promotion to chief justice on the ground that "waving two red flags before the enraged liberal bloc on the committee would be too much."[46] In the end, the fact that Scalia was readily confirmable and eight years younger than Bork tipped the scales in Scalia's favor.[47] Meese and Assistant Attorney General Brad Reynolds were not sure that they would get an opportunity to make another appointment, and they decided to go with the younger nominee.[48] A year later, with the retirement of Justice Powell, it was time to rethink the possibility of appointing Judge Bork to the Supreme Court.

2
ENTER JUDGE BORK

When Justice Powell retired, President Reagan asked the Justice Department to put together a complete list of potential nominees. He specifically asked that Judge Bork be included on the list, since Bork had been a candidate earlier and had lost out narrowly when Scalia was nominated. A list was prepared, containing about ten names.[1]

White House Chief of Staff Howard Baker showed the list to Senate Majority Leader Robert Byrd and Judiciary Committee Chairman Joseph Biden. Administration sources said that the list was submitted *pro forma* and that the real purpose of the consultation was to determine whether Bork would receive serious opposition in the Senate.[2] Although Biden indicated that a Bork nomination would cause problems, the White House decided that he would still be confirmable. When asked whether consideration had been given to the difficulty of confirming Bork, Meese remarked that "it was discussed but [was] not decisive."[3]

The list of ten candidates was quickly narrowed to three or four.[4] All of the candidates on the short list were then interviewed by Justice Department and White House personnel. On July 1, 1987, Bork was interviewed by Presidential Counsel A. B. Culvahouse. According to Bork, no legal issues or cases were discussed. The interview consisted basically of an attempt to update the FBI background check and to determine whether there were any skeletons in Bork's closet. Later that day, Bork received a telephone call from Howard Baker, who asked him to come over to see the president. At the White House, Bork talked about the confirmation process with Baker, A. B. Culvahouse, and others. Again, no substantive issues were discussed; but no discussions were necessary, given Bork's widely known views on public issues.[5]

Shortly thereafter, Bork met with President Reagan in the Oval Office. Reagan told Bork that he proposed to nominate him to fill Justice

Powell's seat on the Court and asked Bork what he thought. Bork told him that he had "been thinking about the idea for the past five or ten minutes and decided . . . [that he] liked the idea."[6] A few minutes later, with Bork at his side, Reagan held a press conference to announce that Bork would be nominated to the Supreme Court.

It is apparent that Bork was always the leading candidate for the appointment, even though Bork had told one of his colleagues at the court of appeals that he did not expect to be nominated. John Bolton, a Justice Department liaison to Congress, remarked that "these things have a pecking order to them."[7] Bork had labored in the vineyards for years, and it was now his turn. Bork had the strong backing of Ed Meese, of Presidential Assistant Ken Cribb,[8] and of President Reagan, so convincing evidence of Bork's confirmation difficulties would have been needed to prompt a reconsideration of the nomination. The White House view was that Bork had impeccable credentials, having served as solicitor general and having been a distinguished professor at Yale Law School.[9] Although the Justice Department believed that Bork's role in firing Archibald Cox as Watergate special prosecutor might present some problems, it was thought that Elliot Richardson's willingness to give Bork a "clean bill of health" would defuse that issue. What Meese and others did not foresee was Bork's vulnerability on questions of ideology and the lengths to which the opposition would go to exploit those vulnerabilities. In order to understand the strong feelings that Bork generated, both among his opponents and among his supporters, it may be useful to examine Bork's early background, his political evolution from liberal to conservative, and his record of public service.

THE FORMATIVE YEARS

Robert Bork was born in Pittsburgh and raised in Ben Avon, an upper-middle-class suburb. He was an only child of a former schoolteacher and of a father who worked as a purchasing agent for a steel company. Bork's mother helped to develop his interest in books by reading to him every night. Bork relates that once his mother read *Tom Sawyer* to him and stopped at a very exciting point in the book. Bork picked up the book and finished reading it. He then became a voracious reader.[10] Bork's mother also helped to develop his intellectual curiosity by arguing with him "far into the night about all kinds of things" until, finally, his father would yell down to them: "This is not a debating society; go to sleep."[11]

In high school, Bork became president of his class, editor of the school paper, and a champion boxer. At that time, he was enamored with socialist ideals, an interest that stemmed in part from his father's experience as "a union sympathizer who had taken repeated pay cuts during the Depression."[12] Bork was a truculent youth who liked to engage people in provocative argument. As a high school sophomore, Bork had read the essays of British Marxist John Strachey and discussed his ideas with anyone who would listen.

In 1943, Bork transferred to a prep school in Lakewood, Connecticut, for his senior year. He had a more difficult time adjusting there, in part because the students came from wealthier families than the students he had known previously. After graduating from high school in 1944, Bork enlisted in the marine corps. He studied to be a Japanese language translator, but as Bork testified before the Senate Judiciary Committee, after "they dropped the bomb . . . they did not need Japanese language specialists any more. So instead, they sent me to China with a rifle to guard Chiang Kai-Shek's supply lines."[13]

After the war ended, Bork enrolled at the University of Chicago, largely because of the great books program instituted by the university chancellor, Robert Maynard Hutchins. Chicago offered a stimulating intellectual atmosphere, and Bork has said that he received a good education there, much of it outside the classroom, where he argued with other students late into the night.[14] Bork's political views at that time were basically those of a liberal Democrat, and in 1952 he handed out campaign literature for Adlai Stevenson.[15]

While in college, Bork met Claire Davidson, whom he married soon after graduation.[16] Although Claire was Jewish and Bork had been raised a Protestant, those differences presented no problem since neither of them dwelled on religion or on their different backgrounds. At that point in his life, Bork wanted to be a journalist. He applied to the Columbia School of Journalism but was rejected.

At the suggestion of Robert Maynard Hutchins, Bork enrolled at the University of Chicago Law School because he was convinced that it was a school of jurisprudence and not a traditional nuts-and-bolts law school.[17] There, he came under the influence of Aaron Director and other free-market economists. Although initially he found their approach counterintuitive, he soon became a true believer.[18] It was under Aaron Director that Bork began his intellectual odyssey from liberal Democrat to libertarian and, later, conservative Republican. Bork stayed at Chicago for a year after graduation from law school in order to work with Director as a research assistant. During that year, Bork wrote a paper with Director, arguing that vertical integration—the union within a single company of two or more successive stages of production, such as producing pig iron and then converting the iron into steel—was not necessarily monopolistic but might be just an example of economic efficiency.[19] The paper won considerable recognition for Bork among antitrust experts.

In 1954, Bork became an associate at the New York law firm of Willkie, Owen, Farr, Gallagher & Walton (now Willkie, Farr & Gallagher), but he worked there for only a few months.[20] In 1955, Bork joined the Chicago firm of Kirkland & Ellis, where he specialized in antitrust law. While he was an associate at Kirkland, a Jewish attorney named Howard Krane interviewed for a position with the firm.[21] Bork took a liking to Krane, who was, like himself, a protégé of Aaron Director.[22] After learning that Krane would not receive an offer because of a policy at the firm against hiring Jews, Bork discussed the matter with his friend and fellow associate Dallin Oaks.[23] Bork decided that he should take a stand, and together with Oaks, he urged several senior partners to consider Krane on his merits.[24] The partners did, in fact, reconsider and gave Krane a job. After that, Krane and Bork became good friends.[25]

Both Bork and Oaks had serious apprehensions about going to the senior partners, although they were secure enough in their positions to believe they would not lose their jobs. What was threatening was the possibility that by challenging the firm's hiring policy, the two might become known as troublemakers. That kind of reputation could have an impact on their standing with the firm and, ultimately, on their chance of becoming partners.[26]

After a few years, Bork began to grow frustrated with the lack of intellectual fulfillment in the practice of law. He wondered whether he would be happy remaining at the firm for forty years, "doing the same kind of thing over and over again."[27] Bork thought he might be happier teaching law or writing for a national magazine. He and Dallin Oaks discussed the possibility of forming a conservative think tank to do research and provide spokesmen for the points of view they thought were not adequately represented in the legal profession. But those casual musings never came to fruition. In 1961, Oaks told Bork that he was leaving the firm to join the University of Chicago law faculty, news that evidently came as a blow to Bork.[28] In the following year, Bork, who was then a partner, left the firm, where he was earning $40,000 a year, and joined the Yale law faculty at a salary of less than $15,000.

Bork's early years are revealing. They show a young man with great intelligence, strong commitments, and a tendency to be aggressively outspoken. These are characteristics common to some of the most able judges who have served on the federal bench. But they are also characteristics that are highly threatening in a judge whose views challenge the conventional legal orthodoxy. Thus, both Justice Brandeis and Justice Rehnquist encountered serious confirmation problems, despite their obvious qualifications, because they posed a threat—one from the left and the other from the right—to the prevailing fashion in judicial decision making. Bork would trigger many of the same reactions as Brandeis and Rehnquist but with dramatically different results.

POLITICAL EVOLUTION

Life in academia gave Bork an opportunity "to think things through." Dean Guido Calabresi of Yale Law School said that when Bork "came on, he immediately made an impact because he was so bright and ornery in terms of being willing to argue with everybody about everything. He loved to sit around with people in the lounge and argue."[29] Calabresi added that academic life gave Bork an opportunity to test his emerging libertarian notion that the government should keep out of almost everything.

Bork had running arguments with Alexander Bickel, his close friend and mentor at Yale, concerning Bork's view that any coercion of the individual had to be justified by a principle that would not lead government into various kinds of undesirable coercion. In 1963, Bickel, who frequently wrote for the *New Republic*, urged Bork to write an article expressing his views on a federal civil rights bill. Bork prepared an article in which he harshly criticized the public accommodations provision of the bill. Bork wrote: "Of the ugliness of racial discrimination there need be no argument. . . . But the principle of [this] legislation is that if I find your behavior ugly by my standards, moral or aesthetic, and if you prove stubborn about adopting my view of the situation, I am justified in having the state coerce you into more righteous paths. That is itself a principle of unsurpassed ugliness."[30] Ten years later, during hearings on his nomination to be solicitor general, Bork acknowledged that he no longer held the views taken in the article and that he "was on the wrong tack altogether."[31] In the hearings on his nomination to the Supreme Court, Bork amplified his position:

> I now take what I would call—at least what Bickel described as—the Edmund Burke approach, which is, you look at each measure—this is a political matter, not a judicial matter—you look at each measure and ask whether it will do more good than harm.
>
> Had I looked at the civil rights proposals in that way, I would have, as I later came to, recognize that they do much more good. In fact, they make everybody much happier and they help bring the nation together in a way that otherwise would not have occurred.[32]

Soon after writing his article for the *New Republic*, Bork began paying his political dues. In 1964, he sent a longer version of his critique of the Civil Rights Act to Barry Goldwater, the Republican presidential nominee. Also, at the urging of Aaron Director, he joined a group called Scholars for Goldwater. The group supported Goldwater because of his position favoring diminished government control over the economy and a reduction in the size of government. At one meeting of the group, Bork advised Goldwater to show a stronger commitment to civil rights while still challenging some parts of the 1964 Civil Rights Act.[33]

In 1968, Bork took a more overt political posture when he wrote an article for the *New Republic*, praising Richard Nixon.[34] Later in the year, Bork wrote a piece for *Fortune* magazine in which he tried, from a libertarian perspective, to find a way to safeguard individual liberties like the right of privacy, which were not specifically protected by the terms of the Constitution.[35] But by 1970, Bork's libertarian views had shifted dramatically. He came to understand Bickel's argument that one could not uniformly apply economic arguments to all fields of social intercourse. Bork's emerging philosophy of "original intent" could best be described as majoritarianism. He believed, and continues to believe, in judicial deference to legislative determinations, except where there is a specific constitutional guarantee of individual rights.

In the spring of 1971, Bork delivered a lecture at the Indiana School of Law in Bloomington, setting forth his views on the Supreme Court's role in interpreting the Constitution. His remarks were published by the *Indiana Law Journal* in an article entitled "Neutral Principles and

Some First Amendment Problems." In Bork's view, value choices made by individual judges, which represent only their own preferences, are not entitled to public acceptance, because such a system of constitutional interpretation lacks legitimacy. Judicial legitimacy and popular acceptance of Supreme Court decisions rest, in Bork's opinion, on the premise that judges are merely interpreting the Constitution in a manner consistent with the intent of the Framers. In that way, the justices' own predilections will be circumscribed, and popular acceptance of judicial decisions will increase.[36] It was this commitment to original intent and to majoritarian control that made Bork such an attractive candidate to the Reagan administration. But it was also this commitment, and the intellectual strength to carry it forward, that generated such intense political opposition to Bork's nomination.

YEARS OF PUBLIC SERVICE

In 1972, Bork joined Academics for Nixon and began to advise the president on federal legislation designed to limit bussing in school desegregation cases.[37] Nixon was so impressed with Bork's advice and, more generally, with Bork's views on the threat posed by what Bork called the "imperial judiciary" that he instructed his aides to call Bork and ask whether he would be interested in serving as solicitor general. Bork met with Nixon at Camp David, where "Nixon gave me a remarkably thoughtful lecture on judicial restraint."[38] Nixon then personally offered Bork the position of solicitor general, and Bork jumped at the opportunity. He was reported to have viewed the position as a stepping-stone to the Supreme Court. Indeed, three solicitors general—William Howard Taft, Robert Jackson, and Thurgood Marshall—had gone on to become Supreme Court justices. Bork himself came close to achieving this goal in 1975, when President Ford considered him for the Supreme Court. But in the end, Ford was advised by Attorney General Edward Levi that Bork would be too controversial,[39] and he decided to nominate Judge John Paul Stevens instead.

A. Raymond Randolph, who served as deputy solicitor general under Bork for almost three years, testified before the Senate Judiciary Committee that Bork had been an outstanding solicitor general. Randolph, now a close personal friend of Bork, said that he had not known Bork when he began serving under him. He had been advised by his friend

Lawrence Wallace, an attorney in the solicitor general's office, to evaluate Bork on his performance, particularly his performance in civil rights cases.

Randolph found Bork to be quite open minded. In an interview, Randolph stated that, as Solicitor General, Bork exercised independence and did not take strident positions. "He favored incremental change. With respect to civil rights, he expressed the appropriate amount of sensitivity." Randolph said he saw Bork everyday for almost three years, attended meetings Bork held with civil rights groups, and was impressed with the way Bork handled himself.[40]

Jewel LaFontant, a black woman who served as deputy attorney general under Bork, agreed with Randolph's assessment. LaFontant told the Senate Judiciary Committee that Bork placed her in charge of the entire civil division. When attempts were made to exclude her from meetings that other deputies regularly attended, she reported this to Bork, who was appalled. The next day, and thereafter, LaFontant was included in all relevant meetings and was literally bombarded with information. LaFontant, like Randolph, believed that Bork was open minded and that he was firmly committed to equal rights for women and minorities. LaFontant was particularly impressed with Bork's support for the Federal Women's Program of the Department of Justice, which was aimed at eliminating sexism in the recruitment and hiring of women in the department.

Bork loved the job of solicitor general. At the time, he commented that this was the best job he had ever had. He was particularly enamored with the opportunity to assist the Supreme Court in developing legal doctrine. He said: "The elaboration of principle that the Court undertakes is an enormously difficult task, seeking to create stability and continuity in the law in times of crises and changing values. This is an intellectual task of almost monumental proportions, but I think the effort to accomplish it is alone what legitimates the Supreme Court's power to govern us all."[41]

After leaving the solicitor general's office in 1977, Bork briefly joined the American Enterprise Institute, a conservative think tank in Washington, D.C. Shortly thereafter, he returned to Yale as Chancellor Kent Professor of Law, the chair formerly held by Alexander Bickel, who had died in 1974 at the age of fifty. In 1978, Bork completed his highly regarded book, *The Antitrust Paradox*. Some of the students at Yale had called his course in antitrust law "pro-trust," because of Bork's argument that mergers and acquisitions often promoted, rather than impeded, consumer welfare.[42] Nevertheless, Bork's book has been widely praised and has had great influence on antitrust law. In his prepared statement to the Senate Judiciary Committee, James T. Halverson, former director of the Bureau of Competition of the Federal Trade Commission and now a partner with the New York law firm of Shearman & Sterling, termed *The Antitrust Paradox* "perhaps the most important single work written in this field in the past twenty-five years."[43] Halverson pointed out that Bork's book had been cited by six of the nine justices on the Supreme Court. Halverson said that in Bork's view, the antitrust laws are designed to enhance consumer welfare, and the best way of promoting consumer welfare is to allow American firms to enhance their efficiency through intensely competitive activity. "Active and intense competition which increases output and lowers prices for the American consumer is to be encouraged even if some inefficient firms suffer in the process."[44]

But things were not the same at Yale, when Bork returned in 1978. Bickel had died, and Bork's wife, Claire, was suffering from a malignant tumor that would take her life two years later. Because he needed to earn money for Claire's medical bills and also hoped to buy a house in the country in the event that Claire recovered, Bork began doing more consulting work on antitrust matters. Students found Bork no longer to be intellectually stimulated by the teaching process. It seemed that Bork basically put in his hours teaching class at the Law School and then went home to take care of Claire. Interestingly, the one issue on campus that aroused the old passion in Bork was a proposal to prohibit recruiting at Yale by law firms that discriminated against homosexuals. Bork took a strong stand against the proposal, believing that it was designed to induce the faculty to express approval of homosexuality. The proposal was adopted, despite opposition from Bork and from other faculty members, both liberal and conservative.

After Claire died in 1980, Bork wanted to get away from New Haven. He had never been particularly fond of the town. New Haven, he once remarked, "is the Athens of America—if you like pizza."[45] He missed Washington, D.C., which, he now thought, had many more interesting people. Bork told an old friend: "It's tough enough living in New Haven. Imagine doing it as a widower."[46] Bork contacted his old friend Howard Krane, who had become the managing partner at Kirkland & Ellis, and they agreed that Bork would rejoin the firm, working in its Washington office at a salary of $400,000 a year.

At one point during Bork's early years in teaching, Bickel had half-jokingly advised Bork to "wreak himself upon the world"—the same advice that Justice Holmes had given to Felix Frankfurter and that Frankfurter had given to Bickel. Bork took the advice to heart. Earlier in his career, he had tried to influence public policy through articles in popular journals. In 1976, Bork began making speeches on matters of public policy, repeating a few major themes. Bork's most popular theme involved his "wave theory" of constitutional law. He spoke about how different waves of antitrust theory had revolutionized the law in that field and said the same thing was happening in constitutional law. Bork argued that after World War II, the courts addressed social problems without regard to any recognizable theory of constitutional interpretation, thereby shattering the tradition of looking to original intent. Constitutional theorists and academics began to rationalize what the courts were doing. Bork said: "That wave has become a tsunami and its intellectual and moral excesses are breathtaking. Like the first wave theorists of antitrust, these theorists exhort the courts to unprecedented imperialistic adventures." Bork argued that, as in antitrust theory, a second wave was rising that, he predicted, would bring an escape from judicial imperialism and a return to the Framers' vision of the Constitution.[47] Shortly after Bork rejoined Kirkland & Ellis, he was offered an appointment to the federal court of appeals for the District of Columbia. Bork clearly saw the position as another stepping-stone to the Supreme Court. Over the next few years, Bork continued to "wreak himself upon the world" through speeches and articles. These appearances had the effect of keeping him in the limelight and of enhancing his conservative credentials. In 1981, although Bork was on the White House list of possible nominees, he was not given serious consideration. Instead, Reagan kept his campaign promise to name a woman to the Court, nominating Judge Sandra Day O'Connor. In 1985, Bork reached the list of finalists but was ultimately passed over in favor of Antonin Scalia.

By the spring of 1987, Bork was bored with the court of appeals and was giving some thought to stepping down in the near future. Bork's caseload was heavy, and he did not find the work particularly interesting. The routine regulatory matters often before the Court were tiresome for Bork. He complained that he had too little contact with other judges and too little time to reflect on broader issues.[48] As late as July 1987, Bork still had not chosen his law clerks for the next year. He decided that if he stayed on the court, he would hire his clerks the next spring.[49] It was at this point that Justice Powell announced his retirement from the Court, and lightening struck Robert Bork.

3
BATTLE LINES FORM

The Bork nomination provoked strong reactions from both ends of the political spectrum. The left saw Bork as a threat to the gains that had been achieved in legal rights. Women's groups thought Bork would vote to overturn *Roe v. Wade*, and civil rights groups believed he would undermine affirmative action programs for minorities. Finally, civil libertarians were worried that Bork would read free speech guaranties too narrowly and that he would reduce the wall of separation between church and state. Perhaps as much as his vote, liberals feared the influence that Bork's intellectual power might have over other members of the Court.

The right saw Bork's ascension to the Court as a culmination of the Reagan revolution. Conservatives believed Judge Bork would be a forceful advocate for the values they cherished. In particular, Bork had long railed against the decision in *Roe v. Wade*, which he termed an "illegitimate" usurpation of power by the Supreme Court. More generally, conservatives recognized that although Bork did not necessarily share their underlying beliefs on abortion or other social issues, he was fiercely resistant to "judicial activism" and would be a powerful force for upholding the authority of elected public officials.

DELAY AND THREATS OF FILIBUSTER

A crucial part of the strategy against the Bork nomination was to delay the start of the confirmation hearings. Historically, delays have worked to the detriment of the nominee, especially when approaching the end of the president's term of office. A delay in Bork's case would give opponents time to prepare an ideological attack and to mount a grassroots campaign to "educate" the public and the Senate on Judge Bork's record.

Early in the process, there had even been talk among Democrats of a prolonged debate in the Senate, which prompted one White House staffer to
predict that "once we get through the hearings there clearly will be an
attempt to stall, to filibuster."[1]

But many senators were reluctant to pay the political price that a filibuster would entail. Senator David Pryor remarked that "[t]he President
has a right to have his nominee considered." There was also some feeling
that the use of a filibuster might be more threatening to the Democratic
majority than to the Republican minority. Senator John Breaux thought
that "[a] filibuster would cause long-range damage for our party. . . . The
majority ought to be able to work its will. . . . Life goes on."[2] A delay in
the start of the hearings was clearly more attractive than a filibuster, and
it was this strategy that Bork's opponents decided to use.

Even before Bork was nominated, Senator Biden, chair of the Judiciary Committee, and Robert Byrd, the Senate majority leader, had threatened to postpone consideration of a Bork nomination until September.[3]
President Reagan responded by urging the Senate to "expedite its consideration of the nomination." In his weekly radio address to the nation,
Reagan said that in order "to maintain the independence of the judiciary,
I hope we can keep politics out of the confirmation process and promptly
schedule hearings."[4]

On July 7, 1987, Senate Minority Leader Robert Dole and Strom
Thurmond, the ranking Republican on the Judiciary Committee, took
the Senate floor to urge Democrats to complete the confirmation process
before the start of the Supreme Court session in October. The next day,
Biden announced—after meeting with Senators Kennedy, Metzenbaum,
and Cranston—that hearings would begin on September 15 and would
take at least two weeks. Mark Goodin, a spokesman for Senator Thurmond, said that Republicans on the committee would tentatively accept
the September 15 date "provided that a written agreement . . . [can] be
reached on a broad package of timetables and deadlines. . . ."[5] Goodin
favored a timetable that called for hearings to end in September and for
a vote to be taken in early October. But while Biden was willing to agree
in principle to a timetable, he was initially unwilling to commit to any
firm deadline, saying only that the hearings together with committee de-
liberations would take about two weeks.[6]

Senator Dole was not satisfied. He stated that "there is absolutely no
substantive reason why we have to wait more than two months to begin
nomination hearings." He also said that he would seek a meeting with

Thurmond and Biden "to see if there isn't some way we can push the schedule up." Dole added that Bork was ready to testify and that Senate Republicans were willing to hold hearings during the August recess.[7] Other Republicans also urged Biden to fix a "date certain" for the committee vote on Bork. White House spokesman Marlin Fitzwater expressed regret that Biden had "chosen to politicize the hearings. . . ."[8] And Senator Humphrey pointed out that the average delay between nomination and the start of hearings was seventeen days and the longest delay was forty-two days, whereas the hearings on Bork's nomination would not begin for seventy days under the proposed timetable. Still, Biden refused to accede to the demand for a time certain for the committee vote, although he did say on July 15, 1987, that he expected the nomination to be ready for consideration by the full Senate by October 1. He added that "we have no intention to hold up this nomination," a statement that few of Bork's supporters found very reassuring in light of Biden's earlier pronouncements on the subject.[9]

By August, the momentum that usually accompanies a Supreme Court nomination seemed to be lost. The loss of momentum could be partly attributed to the White House failure to campaign hard for Bork's confirmation. But it was also attributable in part to Biden's announcement that he would lead the opposition, which opened the resources of the Judiciary Committee to the anti-Bork forces. Biden, who was in the middle of a campaign for the Democratic nomination for president, found himself in a delicate position. Because he had been slow to oppose Rehnquist's nomination for chief justice, civil rights groups warned him that he would have no political future if he did not strongly oppose Bork. On the other hand, his need for support from Southerners and independents required him to conduct the hearings fairly or at least with an appearance of fairness.

THE THREAT OF A RECESS APPOINTMENT

In a speech in Indianapolis on July 27, Senator Dole accused Senate Democrats of putting a "Biden stall" on the nomination. He decided to give Biden "some food for thought" by reminding him that the Constitution authorizes the president to make recess appointments to the Court when the Senate is not in session. Under this procedure, which had not been used for some thirty years, Bork could be appointed without the need for confirmation and would be able to serve through the next session of Congress.[10] Senator Strom Thurmond, ranking Republican on the Judiciary Committee, was able to use the threat of a recess appointment as a lever to get Biden to set a definite date for a committee vote on the nomination.[11]

Dole's remarks were part of a Republican strategy to focus on the unfairness of the confirmation process; other Bork supporters said that Senator Biden should not preside over the hearings because he had already announced his opposition to Bork.[12] But Dole's suggestion of an interim appointment was ultimately rejected for a number of practical reasons. First, there was no precedent for making a recess appointment after the president had already nominated someone to the Supreme Court.[13] Second, the last recess appointment, involving the nomination of Potter Stewart, had led to a heated battle. Southern Democrats, who opposed Stewart because of his support for *Brown v. Board of Education*, relied on his recess appointment as a reason for denying his confirmation when President Eisenhower eventually nominated him. Senators Olin Johnston of South Carolina and James Eastland of Mississippi argued in the Judiciary Committee that one way for the Senate to discourage the practice of recess appointments was to refuse "to confirm the subsequent nomination of any such recess appointee, without regard to the qualifications of the appointee."[14] In 1960, the Senate passed a nonbinding resolution stating that recess appointments to the Supreme Court should not be made except under unusual circumstances.[15]

There were also some tactical reasons for not making a recess appointment. It is clear that the White House did not want to give the anti-Bork forces an opportunity to reject Bork on the basis of procedural issues. In addition, there was concern that delaying the battle until the fall of 1988 might enable Senate Democrats to filibuster the nominee, thereby denying President Reagan the opportunity of making any appointment at all. Finally, Bork's supporters were understandably concerned about antagonizing undecided senators by making a recess appointment. In response to Senator Dole's suggestion of a recess appointment, Senator Byrd stated that such an appointment would be a "circumvention of the people's branch" and that "we've seen too much of that for the last few months. . . . "[16] Similarly, Senator Dennis DeConcini of Arizona, who was considered a swing vote on the Judiciary Committee, told Reagan in a letter that a recess appointment "would subvert the checks and balances among the branches of government established by the Constitution." DeConcini added that a recess appointment "would almost certainly adversely affect a final vote on Judge Bork's appointment to the Court." He suggested that such an appointment would antagonize senators and make it harder for Bork to be confirmed.[17]

ATTACK FROM THE LEFT

It was apparent from the beginning that the anti-Bork forces would hit the ground running. Since Bork was known to be the leading candidate, his opponents were able to get started even before the nomination was officially announced.[18] An initial strategy session, held on the weekend before the announcement, was attended by Senator Biden, his staff, and a group of outside advisers that included Washington attorney Kenneth Bass and law professors Walter Dellinger, Philip Kurland, and Susan Prager. The group discussed Bork's speeches, judicial opinions, and scholarly writings. They believed that they understood the candidate and how he would react to specific issues when he was on the bench and, significantly, when he went before the Senate Judiciary Committee.

On that same weekend, Senator Kennedy and his staff worked on a speech in which Kennedy would viciously attack Bork on the very day the nomination was announced. The speech was riddled with exaggeration and distortion, but it set the tone for the campaign against Judge Bork. Kennedy said:

> Robert Bork's America is a land in which women would be forced into back alley abortions, blacks would sit at segregated lunch counters, rogue police could break down citizens' doors in midnight raids, school children could not be taught about evolution, writers and artists could be censored at the whim of government, and the doors of the federal courts would be shut on the fingers of millions of citizens for whom the judiciary is—and is often the only—protector of individual rights that are at the heart of our democracy.[19]

There was scarcely a truthful word in this parade of horrors that was widely quoted in the mass media. Bork had never advocated racial segregation, and there was no risk that his confirmation would lead to segregated lunch counters in "Robert Bork's America." Moreover, Bork had neither opposed the teaching of evolution nor supported midnight raids by rogue police. Judge Bork had, of course, opposed *Roe v. Wade*, which established a constitutional right to abortion. But a decision to overrule *Roe* was more likely to drive women into legislative halls, or perhaps across state lines, than into back alleys.[20] Kennedy's speech, as Ethan Bronner observed, had "shamelessly twisted" Bork's views,[21] and yet no one attacked Kennedy's misrepresentations. Bork's supporters made the crucial mistake of assuming that the excesses in the speech would be self-defeating. As a result, Kennedy succeeded in his effort "to sound the alarm and hold people in their places" so that they would not commit themselves in favor of Bork.[22] What was needed from Bork's supporters was not silence in the face of distortion but a vigorous response that would "sound the alarm" for Bork and alert his opponents that the White House was prepared to fight for its nominee and to exact a price for unwarranted political attacks. No such response was forthcoming.

A week later, Senators Kennedy, Metzenbaum, and Biden met to devise a strategy. Their first major decision was to postpone the Bork hearings until after the August recess in order to give themselves more time to fight the nomination.[23] The group then put together a list of the undecided senators and determined which member of their group would have the most influence with particular senators. Kennedy's staff collected all of Bork's provocative writings and speeches into a binder and circulated copies to a number of senators during the August recess.

Senator Kennedy then began organizing liberal public-interest groups into a large coalition that would oppose the Bork nomination. He hired Anthony Podesta, a lobbyist and founding president of People for the American Way, to help organize the opposition. Kennedy personally called the leaders of various liberal groups to ask them to assist in grass-roots efforts by contacting their members and urging them to lobby senators in opposition to the nomination. Kennedy phoned Reverend Joseph Lowery at the annual convention of the Southern Christian Leadership Conference (SCLC). Lowery "turned the entire day's meeting into an anti-Bork strategy session." From that meeting, the issue made its way into black churches throughout the country.[24]

The annual conferences of the National Association for the Advancement of Colored People (NAACP) and the National Education Association (NEA) were also used as platforms to advocate rejection of the Bork nomination. At the NAACP convention, several Democratic presidential candidates, including Senator Al Gore, Congressman Richard Gephart, and former Governor Bruce Babbitt, spoke out against Bork's confirmation. Although Howard Baker argued that the NAACP should give Bork "an opportunity to be heard," his voice was overwhelmed by those who argued that Bork would "turn back the clock" on civil rights.[25]

The liberal interest groups were able to organize so quickly because previous Supreme Court nomination struggles had laid the groundwork for the Bork battle. Estelle Rogers, who was then the executive director of the Federation of Women Lawyers, remarked that "we had done a lot of work on the Rehnquist nomination" and "Rehnquist was a dress rehearsal for Bork."[26] Similarly, Ken Kemmerling of the Puerto Rico Legal Defense and Education Fund said that the fighting over the nominations of William Rehnquist to be chief justice and of Brad Reynolds to be assistant attorney general for civil rights "gave us hope that the Senate Judiciary Committee would act in a strong way against Bork." Kemmerling explained that the level of questioning by the Senate in the Rehnquist hearings "raised people's hopes and expectations."[27] More important, the opposition was now better prepared because of the previous confirmation battles. Melanne Verveer of People for the American Way had testified during the hearings on Justice Rehnquist's nomination to be chief justice and had submitted a lengthy memorandum, arguing that the Senate's role should be coequal with that of the president in the appointment process. The arguments made in that memorandum were identical to those later raised in connection with the Bork nomination.[28]

The Leadership Conference on Civil Rights, a coalition of numerous civil rights groups, played a pivotal role in bringing together hundreds of organizations under a loose umbrella. Ralph Neas, executive director of the Leadership Conference, had a reputation as an effective advocate for liberal causes and was credited by Assistant Attorney General Brad Reynolds with torpedoing his nomination to be associate attorney general.[29] Neas had come to Washington as an aide to Senator Ed Brooke of Massachusetts and later served as chief legislative aide to Senator David Durenberger of Minnesota. In 1979, Neas was stricken with Guillain-Barre's syndrome, became paralyzed from the neck down, and almost died. His health eventually improved, and he went back to work on Durenberger's staff. Later, after an extended trip to Europe, he returned to Washington to take a position with the Leadership Conference on Civil Rights. Neas made his mark by becoming a leading expert on civil rights legislation and by helping to draft a compromise on the Voting Rights Extension Act of 1982.[30]

The Leadership Conference held numerous meetings after the Bork nomination was announced. The group included Benjamin Hooks, president of the NAACP, Eleanor Smeal of the National Organization of Women (NOW), and civil rights veteran Joseph Rauh. The Leadership Conference decided that it needed to focus on a few major areas—the media, grassroots organizing, and research and lobbying. The anti-Bork forces then made a crucial decision to concentrate on obtaining the support of uncommitted members of the Judiciary Committee, and of "swing votes" in the Senate, by targeting the home states of key senators. Irene Natividad, chair of the National Women's Political Caucus, generated rallies in each state that was represented on the Judiciary Committee, and other members of the coalition engaged in similar local activity.[31]

The Judicial Selection Project of the Alliance for Justice also played an important role in the coalition. According to George Kassouf, director of the organization, the Judicial Selection Project evaluates all nominees to the federal bench. "We make phone calls to attorneys in the nominee's community just to get a feel for the person. If those calls are troubling from our perspective, we go further." Kassouf said that his organization also trades information with other evaluation groups, like Supreme Court Watch.[32] The information is then given to the Judiciary Committee or to senators friendly to the concerns of the Alliance for Justice.

The early research by the anti-Bork forces was to pay off handsomely at the confirmation hearings. Whenever Bork's testimony appeared to diverge from positions he had previously taken on issues like free speech or gender discrimination, position papers were brought out overnight by the American Civil Liberties Union (ACLU), the National Abortion Rights Action League (NARAL), or the Leadership Conference on Civil Rights. They described how "the new Bork" contradicted "the old Bork," thereby raising concerns about whether Bork's testimony could be trusted.[33] The research was also used to feed questions and information to senators during the confirmation hearings.[34]

Several of the public interest groups, including People for the American Way, the NAACP Legal Defense and Education Fund, the ACLU, and Ralph Nader's Public Citizen Litigation Group, also prepared lengthy reports describing Bork's conservative judicial philosophy. These reports portrayed Bork as an early opponent of civil rights legislation, whose narrow view of constitutional freedoms would be harmful to women and minorities.[35] One of the most frequently quoted of these studies had reported that in nonunanimous decisions Judge Bork consistently ruled in favor of the government when suit was brought by public interest groups but ruled against the government when suit was brought by business interests. William B. Schultz, who directed the study on behalf of the Public Citizens Litigation Group, claimed that in close cases "Judge Bork's votes can be predicted with almost 100 percent certainty simply by identifying the parties to the case."[36] There were significant flaws in this study, including (1) its small sample, which ignored 86 percent of Bork's decisions because they involved unanimous rulings, (2) the way "public interest" groups were defined, and (3) how it was determined whether a decision had been "pro-business or pro-consumer." But, of course, the conclusions of the study received far more attention than its flawed methodology.

Significantly, the anti-Bork coalition was able to attract many interest groups that traditionally had not participated in the judicial selection process. Estelle Rogers said the Bork opposition grew "almost as a matter of spontaneous combustion. . . . We'd pass out a list that said 'internal use only' . . . and it just grew." Rogers added that "even the ACLU, which usually doesn't do judicial selections, made an exception in this case."[37] Similarly, Common Cause, a group that had never lobbied against a Supreme Court nominee, decided to oppose Bork, stating that "Judge Bork's nomination . . . [represents] a radical rejection of much of the Court's work. . . . "[38] Interestingly, Archibald Cox, chair of Common Cause, apparently took no part in the organization's decision, because he had been fired by Bork as Watergate special prosecutor under instructions from President Nixon.[39]

Some of the less well-known groups also entered the fray. Mike Martinez, president of the Hispanic Bar Association, said that his organization had never taken a formal stand against a Supreme Court nominee but that the Bork nomination was different. Initially, the group received calls from members saying that "we ought to investigate [Bork] and find out where he stands." Martinez said they did a thorough analysis—producing twelve three-ring binders—much of which came from the NAACP Legal Defense and Education Fund. Before long, people were demanding that the organization take a position. The Hispanic Bar Association became the first civil rights organization to oppose Bork's confirmation. Like a number of other interest groups, the Association found that the work it did against Bork enhanced its credibility. Martinez noted that "in the process, and since, we've become the de facto attorneys for a number of non-legal Hispanic groups. It's helped us progress." He added that they had matured as a group "because of the credibility we had from presenting a professional position on Bork."[40]

Durwood Zaelke of the Sierra Club Legal Defense Fund had planned to sit out the Bork nomination, as he had the nomination of William Rehnquist to be chief justice. Although organizers of the anti-Bork coalition asked Zaelke to join the group, he thought the Sierra Club should maintain its traditional neutrality on judicial nominations. But eventually Zaelke reconsidered after receiving numerous calls from Sierra Club members. Zaelke concluded, after studying Bork's decisions, that Bork would be hostile to environmental claims, and so the Sierra Club joined the coalition.[41]

Richard Nugent of the Government Affairs Unit of the Epilepsy Foundation of America stated that most organizations like his try not to get involved in "political issues of this kind." But Nugent decided to take a position after reading about some of Bork's "opinions about the appropriate role of the courts in prisons and institutional care. We found these quite disturbing because the courts have been involved in improving institutions for the mentally retarded."[42]

The anti-Bork forces were highly effective in lining up support from groups that were not viewed as traditionally liberal. This helped to broaden the coalition and to avoid the appearance that it consisted only of "left wing" groups. Thus various health organizations, such as the Association for Retarded Citizens, the National Mental Health Association, the Epilepsy Foundation, and United Cerebral Palsy, lined up solidly against Bork. Leonard Rubenstein of the Mental Health Law Project noted that these organizations were "mainstream groups which cannot be characterized as liberal interest groups by anyone's definition."[43]

Although the various groups in the coalition had different interests, they cooperated remarkably well, subordinating their individual goals to the common goal of defeating Judge Bork. Many compromises were necessary because each group had its own agenda. Ralph Neas played a key role in ironing out differences among the groups and in keeping the coalition focused on its objective of defeating Bork.[44]

Another important element of the strategy was to downplay the more controversial positions of group members and adopt a low-key approach. During a weekend retreat from August 1–3, 1987, about twelve hundred organizations of consumer, civil rights, feminist, environmental, and public interest groups heard Ralph Neas and Ricki Seidman, the legal director of People for the American Way, urge their allies to de-emphasize issues like abortion and affirmative action—the so-called "a-words"— and instead criticize Bork's overall record of "radical activism." Neas added that they should avoid being heavy handed, and Seidman told the group that many senators would feel the need to "appear" to be even handed until after the hearings, so they should "push but not pressure."[45]

In sum, although opponents of Supreme Court nominees in the past had used some of the tactics that were applied against Bork, the anti-Bork coalition was more broadly based and better organized than opposition forces had previously been. And the tools the coalition used most effectively—polling, television ads, computer data bases—were the weapons of modern political campaigns. Five years later, the White House was well prepared when a similar campaign was mounted against Clarence Thomas, but it reacted slowly and ineffectively when the campaign was directed against Judge Bork.

RESPONSE FROM THE RIGHT

The reaction of Bork's supporters to the attack from the left was limited and tentative. To a large extent, the nominee was simply left to plead his own case, with occasional help from friendly members of the Senate Judiciary Committee. Judge Bork's main focus was on persuading uncommitted senators, particularly the members of the Judiciary Committee.[46] Bork spoke personally to each senator on the committee, in the senator's office. Although such courtesy visits have been considered fairly routine for Supreme Court nominees, many of Bork's visits were far from routine. In his sessions with Senator Specter, Bork spent hours engaged in substantive discussions on a number of legal topics, all at Specter's request.[47] When he met with Senator Packwood, a strong advocate of abortion rights, Packwood asked for assurances that Bork would not vote to overturn *Roe v. Wade*. When Bork responded by telling Packwood about articles he had read on fetal pain and euthanasia, Packwood decided to vote against his confirmation.[48]

Tom Korologos, a Washington lobbyist and a veteran of many Supreme Court confirmations, was enlisted by the White House to assist Judge Bork. He accompanied Bork on courtesy calls and, according to Bork, "was a great support."[49] In addition, Bork was assisted by law clerks and by friends and former colleagues. A. Raymond Randolph, a former assistant to Bork in the solicitor general's office and now a judge on the federal court of appeals, provided advice to Bork and helped recruit prominent attorneys and other private individuals to write letters of support for Bork. Randolph, together with Assistant Attorney General John Bolton and Lloyd Cutler, former White House counsel to Jimmy Carter, gathered for a so-called "murder board" session in a conference room in the Old Executive Office Building and for a second session in Bork's dining room. These sessions, which resembled mock committee hearings, consisted of a discussion of a wide range of constitutional issues. The participants asked Bork anything they thought might be the subject of committee questioning.[50] Randolph said that the private session at Bork's house worked better and that it provided a good review for Bork.[51]

Korologos thought that perhaps he should have tried to get Bork to agree to more of these murder board sessions, but at the time, he did not press the issue because Bork was adamantly opposed to the idea.[52] Bolton did not think that more sessions would have been helpful in any event. He said Bork was highly experienced, and it would have been impossible "to make him over."[53] Randolph agreed that further preparation would not have helped. He said Bork was an honest person who did not view the confirmation process as a popularity contest and was not enamored with the prospect of trying to appeal to voters.[54]

Bork decided not to give television or radio interviews because he did not want to politicize the process further. Although he was willing to give newspaper interviews, he declined to discuss any substantive issues that might be raised by the Judiciary Committee. At the confirmation hearings, Bork decided that he had no choice but to respond to substantive questions, because there was so much material already in the public record—much of it misleading—on which the Committee seemed prepared to convict him.[55]

Bork received some grassroots support, but there was far less activity on the pro-Bork side than on the anti-Bork side. Dan Casey, executive director of the American Conservative Union, said his group "led the 'charge' for Bork from the grass roots." His efforts included contacting the sixty thousand members of his organization by mail and appealing for funds and general support for Judge Bork. Later, Casey made some targeted mailings and placed a few radio advertisements in states like Arizona, Louisiana, and Alabama, states whose senators seemed to be undecided.[56] Other groups focused their energy on lobbying and on running newspaper ads in the home states of undecided senators. The Conservative Caucus looked for ways to have some impact without spending a great deal of money. But while the pro-Bork forces were heavily involved in telephone and direct-mail campaigns, they were less visible and much less effective than the anti-Bork forces.[57]

Dan Casey also sent packets of press mailings to newspapers throughout the country. The packets were sent once a month, beginning in July and ending in October 1987. They contained endorsements from various celebrities, as well as newspaper editorials from around the country. Casey's group made many telephone calls and gave interviews at a rate of twenty per month over a three-month period.[58] Casey admitted that the pro-Bork forces were severely hampered by a shortage of money, which he blamed directly on the White House.[59] He said that President Reagan never raised any money to support Judge Bork although, as he noted, Bork's nomination was used as a vehicle to raise money for Republicans and for conservative causes. For example, the Christian Voice and the Moral Majority used the Bork issue to solicit contributions, but the solicited funds were used in large part for the general purposes of the organization and not for the Bork campaign. Similarly, Charles Orndorff of the Conservative Caucus said that his organization urged its members to make donations and to contact their senators in support of Bork, but the money went into the general fund of the caucus, and only a portion of it was used to buy ads for Bork.[60]

Some conservative groups seemed to blame White House failures for much of Bork's confirmation trouble. Pat McGuigan said that presidents seem "honestly to believe that quiet dinners and gentle conversation in the halls of Congress [can] somehow overcome an all-out partisan assault, and persuade liberals and moderates to support conservative judicial nominees."[61] Phyllis Schlafley of the Eagle Forum encouraged her members to unite and speak to their senators, but her role was very limited. She criticized the White House for underestimating the campaign "by Teddy Kennedy and others, such as the pro-abortionists." She said the White House "should have recognized early on what Kennedy was doing—running a political campaign."[62] Bork was also deprived of the support of the National Rifle Association (NRA), one of the country's most powerful conservative lobby groups, in part because the White House was opposed to NRA participation until the very end. In his book *Ninth Justice*, Pat McGuigan writes that Wayne L. Pierre, president of the NRA, told him that the White House "started out saying 'we don't need you guys, you will only make it tougher. You guys are gonna polarize this issue.'"[63]

Although a more strident approach by the White House might not have succeeded, there is reason to believe that the Bork nomination was mismanaged. During August, President Reagan took his customary month-long vacation together with his senior staff, so not much could be accomplished by the White House during this period. Sam Donaldson of *ABC News*, who was hardly a friend of the nominee, was moved to quip that the Bork nomination was lost in August on the beaches of southern California.[64] Other Bork supporters also did little to counteract the early campaign against Judge Bork.

The pro-Bork forces had several reasons for taking a rather passive approach to the Bork nomination. First, there was a high level of confidence at the White House that Bork would ultimately be confirmed. After all, as Terry Eastland noted, Bork "was a top scholar and had written a book on antitrust. And, really, there never had been a political campaign of this kind for [a] Supreme Court confirmation. No one could quite conceive that this would happen. Consequently, they thought: let's do the campaign the old fashion way." Eastland noted that in the past there had been some nominees who had been opposed because of their judicial philosophy, but never before had the campaign been waged like an election, using all the techniques of modern politics.[65] Dan Casey agreed that "time got away" from the pro-Bork side. "Nobody thought there was a problem with Bork until August, and then it was too late."[66]

In part because of this overconfidence, conservatives were unable to raise as much money as liberals for the confirmation battle. This meant that the pro-Bork forces would later be unable to run television ads to counteract the negative ads run by People for the American Way. By the latter part of September, Bruce Eberle, a direct-mail consultant, had mailed one million letters, which raised $300,000 for the pro-Bork side, while Arthur Kropp of People for the American Way found an "outpouring of support" from a direct-mail campaign that enabled his organization to buy $2 million of media time to oppose Bork. Eberle said that "Bork has become a better issue for the left than for the right because conservatives have minimized the Bork opposition."[67] For example, Sandra McPherson of the National Conservative Political Action Committee is reported to have made only one mailing to 450,000 people. In late September 1987, McPherson said: "We're not doing any further mailings on it primarily because the signs are showing up that Bork will be successful. We feel pretty confident."

A second major reason for a low-key approach to confirmation was the unwillingness of the White House to expend valuable political capital on Judge Bork. President Reagan's popularity had ebbed as a result of the Iran-Contra disclosures. Since Bork was viewed as something of a political liability, the White House was fearful that he could damage the president and undermine the Republican Party's chances in 1988.[68]

The final reason for a passive approach was the belief, promoted by Howard Baker and others, that Bork's best chance for success would be to keep the nomination low key and appeal to moderate senators. David G. Sanders, national field director of the Conservative Caucus, criticized the "touchy-feely approach" taken by the White House, and Pat McGuigan of the Conservative Coalition for America chided Tom Korologos for not letting Bork's true conservative colors come out.[69] But Korologos felt there was no need to sell Bork to the right wing, and he concentrated his efforts on winning over the moderates. President Reagan, in a radio speech to the National Law Enforcement Council, pointed out that none of Judge Bork's four hundred decisions for the court of appeals had been reversed.[70] The White House then released a briefing paper called "Materials on Robert H. Bork," which portrayed Judge Bork as part of the "mainstream tradition of such Justices as Lewis Powell and John Harlan." The White House briefing paper argued that the Senate should focus on Judge Bork's judicial record rather than on his academic record, which criticized various Supreme Court opinions, because such criticism is merely something "that law professors do" and had little relevance to the Senate's inquiry.

Korologos indicated that his strategy was to "humanize" Bork and make him available to everyone, particularly the press. But Korologos "had two criteria: [Bork] was not to talk about anything specific, as far as legal issues or cases. He was to talk about his life and his times and his favorite color. . . . And it worked. We showed he wasn't the right-wing kook they were trying to paint him as."[71] Korologos explained that they were not fighting "a battle for Miss America or Miss Congeniality." All they had to have was eight votes in the Judiciary Committee and fifty in the Senate, "and the votes they needed were from the moderates."[72] In short, the strategy was to try to limit the Senate's inquiry to legal qualifications and, failing that, to package Bork as a "moderate" in the judicial mainstream. It soon became clear that both of these strategies would fail.

4
THE FIRST CRUCIAL ISSUE

Few knowledgeable observers doubted the professional qualifications of Robert Bork. By any of the conventional standards applied to judicial nominations, Judge Bork was superbly qualified for service on the Supreme Court, perhaps, as former Chief Justice Burger would say, better qualified than any other nominee in the twentieth century.[1] It is hardly surprising, then, that opponents quickly focused on Bork's judicial philosophy, rather than his professional qualifications, as the basis for denying confirmation. This focus on ideology raised a crucial issue as to whether it was proper to reject an otherwise qualified nominee for ideological reasons. Senator Biden, chairman of the Judiciary Committee, which was to conduct the confirmation hearings on Judge Bork, assumed responsibility for making the case that advice and consent to judicial nominations could properly be denied on the basis of a nominee's judicial philosophy.

On July 23, Senator Biden delivered an important speech, attempting to define the terms of the confirmation debate. Biden argued that constitutional history and Senate precedents supported the rejection of Supreme Court nominees on ideological grounds. More specifically, he said that "in case after case" the Senate has "rejected technically qualified candidates whose views it perceived to clash with the national interest."[2] In order to assess Biden's argument, it will be necessary to review the various nominations rejected by the Senate to determine whether the rejections were based on ideology. However, a few points may be made preliminarily.

First, it is clear that while a number of nominees have been rejected for political reasons, it was rarely the candidate's judicial philosophy that triggered the political reaction. Of the twenty nominations rejected or withdrawn during the nineteenth century, fully one-third were submitted to the Senate after a presidential election in which the president making the nomination had been denied reelection. It is scarcely surprising that when the president-elect is awaiting the administration of his oath of office, the Senate may be reluctant—for reasons quite independent of a nominee's ideology—to confirm a lame-duck nomination to the Supreme Court.

Second, in several cases a negative political reaction was triggered by invoking "senatorial courtesy."[3] One should not, however, dignify these rejections of Supreme Court nominees by characterizing them as having been based on philosophical considerations. Senator David Hill, who killed the nominations of William Hornblower and Wheeler Peckham during the Cleveland administration, came closer to the mark when he candidly stated that "every Democrat whose name has been sent to the Senate will be confirmed if he loyally supports the Democratic ticket this Fall. No others have any claim on the party."[4] Because Hornblower and Peckham had failed this test of party loyalty by exposing the political chicanery of Senator Hill's allies, their nominations to the Court were condemned by Hill and rejected by the Senate.

Finally, in a significant number of cases, it was opposition to the president that caused the rejection of Supreme Court nominees. President Tyler, who accounts single-handedly for 25 percent of the rejections in the nineteenth century, and Andrew Johnson, who was impeached and barely escaped conviction, were unable even to get cabinet officers confirmed. The rejection of their Supreme Court nominees had little or nothing to do with the legal philosophy of the nominee.

This leaves a handful of cases in which nominees have been rejected for reasons related to ideology, and Senator Biden understandably emphasized those cases. He discussed Rutledge (opposed for his intemperate criticism of the Jay Treaty), Woolcott (opposed for vigorously enforcing the embargo and nonintercourse laws, as well as for incompetency), Taney (opposed for removing government deposits from the U.S. Bank), and Parker (opposed for alleged antilabor and racist views). Senator Biden might also have mentioned Ebenezer Hoar, who was rejected because he had the temerity to support civil service reforms, to insist on merit-based appointment of federal judges, and to oppose the impeachment of President Johnson.

Yet, even in these cases, it is important to note the nature of the ideological objections. Rutledge, Woolcott, Taney, and Hoar may have been rejected in large part because of their political views, but those views were not likely to be the subject of Supreme Court litigation. Accordingly, the Senate's action in these cases provides no support for rejecting a Supreme Court nominee because of the way he or she is likely to vote as a member of the Court. These nominees were rejected not because of their *judicial* philosophy but because of their unpopular political positions. So far as the historical record discloses, the president could have secured the confirmation of candidates embracing the same judicial views as Rutledge, Woolcott, Taney, and Hoar, provided that the nominee was unencumbered by similar political baggage. It is difficult to see how these cases could bear significantly on the confirmation of Judge Bork, who was attacked for his legal philosophy and whose rejection on that ground should presumably have barred other candidates holding the same legal philosophy.

This leaves only Judge Parker as a case of rejection based largely on judicial philosophy. Judge Parker, who was denied confirmation by the narrowest of margins, continued to serve with distinction on the federal court of appeals. His rejection, like that of Ebenezer Hoar, reflects more unfavorably on the Senate than on the nominee. Cases like these should serve not as examples to be emulated but as a reminder of the importance of avoiding a politicization of the confirmation process.

John Rutledge

The first Supreme Court nominee to be denied confirmation by the Senate was John Rutledge, who was nominated by President Washington in 1795 to be chief justice of the United States. Because the nomination came so soon after the ratification of the Constitution and because six members of the Constitutional Convention were then sitting in the United States Senate,[5] the confirmation proceedings for John Rutledge have been thought to reflect the Framers' intent and, hence, to warrant close scrutiny.

John Rutledge was one of the most prominent attorneys of his time. He had been a principal architect of the United States Constitution and had written the constitution of South Carolina. Rutledge had also served as governor of South Carolina, chancellor of the southern district of South Carolina, chief justice of the South Carolina Supreme Court, and delegate to the first and second Continental Congresses. Perhaps equally important to Washington was that Rutledge had been instrumental in his selection as commander in chief of the continental army.[6]

Washington first nominated Rutledge to be associate justice in 1789. Following his confirmation, Rutledge served on the Supreme Court until 1791, when he resigned to become chief justice of the Supreme Court of South Carolina. In June 1795, Rutledge learned that John Jay would resign his position as chief justice of the United States to become governor of New York. Rutledge promptly wrote to Washington, expressing his interest in being the next chief justice of the United States. On July 1, 1795, one day after receiving Rutledge's letter, Washington nominated Rutledge to be the next chief justice and named him acting chief justice.

On July 12, 1795, Rutledge delivered an impassioned speech in opposition to the Jay Treaty at a meeting in Charleston, South Carolina. In view of his otherwise solid credentials, many have concluded that the Senate's refusal to confirm Rutledge was an act of political retaliation by supporters of the Jay Treaty.[7]

However, a closer inspection of the record indicates that many of those who voted against Rutledge's confirmation may have been concerned not so much with political considerations as with negative reports on Rutledge's health and character. Thus, Rutledge and his speech in opposition to the Jay Treaty were characterized in the press as "crazy" and "shocking." His speech was reported to have contained "gross invectives against both Washington and Jay."[8] The excited manner in which Rutledge delivered the speech may have had something to do with these characterizations. Jacob Read, one of Rutledge's supporters, suggested that Rutledge's speech was viewed by many in the Senate as tantamount to an incitement to riot that "if repeated, could not fail to unhinge all order and destroy our government."[9]

Other widely circulated rumors about Rutledge were that he had a drinking problem and that he repeatedly failed to pay his debts. In addition, Rutledge's mental stability appears to have been questioned. Ralph Izard, a friend of Rutledge, wrote that "[a]fter the death of [Rutledge's] wife, his mind was frequently so much deranged, as to be in a great measure deprived of his senses and I am persuaded he was in that situation when the treaty was under consideration."[10]

No doubt, many of the reports concerning Rutledge were exaggerations or outright fabrications by supporters of the Jay Treaty. Nevertheless, these reports seem to have had a substantial impact on senators who voted against confirmation. In short, those who rely on the Rutledge case as a precedent for Senate rejection of Supreme Court nominees on ideological grounds appear to have misread the historical record. But even if Rutledge were shown to have been rejected because of his speech on the Jay Treaty, his rejection would not support a policy of denying confirmation of judges on the basis of the candidate's *judicial* philosophy.

Alexander Woolcott

The second Supreme Court nominee rejected by the Senate was Alexander Woolcott, who was nominated by James Madison in 1811. Woolcott, a prominent Democratic-Republican leader in Connecticut, was disliked by Federalists because he had vigorously enforced the embargo and nonintercourse laws. But more important, even his supporters viewed him as a mediocre candidate for the Supreme Court. Levi Lincoln, who had declined Madison's nomination for the Supreme Court, said of Woolcott: "Whatever . . . may be his present attainments and legal habits, an industrious application to professional studies and official duties will soon place him on a level at least with his Associates."[11] Damned by such faint praise, Woolcott was rejected by a vote of 24 to 9.

Roger B. Taney

The next Supreme Court nominee to be denied Senate confirmation was Roger B. Taney. He was first nominated in 1835 for the position of associate justice. Daniel Webster and the Whigs, angered by Taney's opposition to the Bank of the United States, were able to block his confirmation by postponing consideration of the nomination indefinitely. However, the Whig victory proved to be short lived when Jackson nominated Taney a year later to be chief justice, and Taney was duly confirmed.

In 1832, Taney had urged President Jackson to veto a bill renewing the charter of the Bank of the United States. Taney also advocated that federal funds be withdrawn from the bank and placed in state institutions. President Jackson gave Taney a recess appointment as secretary of the treasury, and Taney presided over the withdrawal of federal funds from the bank.[12] Taney's conduct so enraged the Whigs, many of whom had received loans and other retainers from the bank, that they voted to reject his appointment as secretary of the treasury in 1834 and, later, to postpone indefinitely the vote on his nomination to be associate justice. But Taney's initial failure to win confirmation was based on political considerations and provides no support for Senate rejection of Supreme Court nominees on the basis of judicial ideology. Indeed, Taney was rejected not only for a judicial position but also for a cabinet post, which few observers believed—at least until the Bork controversy arose—could be legitimately based on ideological grounds.

John C. Spencer

John C. Spencer, a prominent New York attorney nominated by President Tyler, was also denied confirmation for political reasons. Whig leaders had no confidence in Tyler, a former Democrat who had accepted the Whig nomination for vice president and had assumed the presidency on William Harrison's death. Tyler was virtually a president without a party, and Whig leaders were anxious to embarrass him by refusing to confirm many of his nominations, including those for members of his cabinet. The Whigs also harbored some hope that if they defeated Spencer's nomination, the appointment could be deferred until after the 1844 election so that their candidate, Henry Clay, could make the appointment. Spencer's nomination was accordingly rejected, and three other Supreme Court nominees were denied confirmation for similar reasons during Tyler's waning days in office.[13]

George W. Woodward

In December 1845, George W. Woodward, a judge in the Pennsylvania lower court system, was nominated by President Polk to be associate justice of the Supreme Court. The Senate refused to confirm Woodward for a number of reasons, some of which were clearly political. Woodward had given support to the Know-Nothing movement, a movement that had defeated loyal Democrats in the next election. His nomination was also opposed on the basis of senatorial courtesy.[14] Finally, although Woodward was a man of "high talents and sterling ability," there was some question as to his legal qualifications. Thus, one of the leading judges in Pennsylvania stated that "it would shock the bar, the bench and the public, to learn that a judge of an inferior court in the woods without any evidence of great legal condition, has been translated to the Supreme Court of the United States."[15]

Ebenezer Hoar

The Senate's vote against the confirmation of Ebenezer Hoar, a nominee of impeccable legal qualifications, was undoubtedly attributable to political considerations. Hoar, as attorney general, had demanded that newly created judgeships be filled by men of "the highest character and experience." Furthermore, his support of civil service reform and his opposition to President Johnson's impeachment had antagonized many senators. Hoar's brusque personal manner may also have annoyed some senators. Charles F. Adams said of Hoar: "First and last, he snubbed seventy senators—all there were—and they, after their kind, 'got even with him.'"[16]

George H. Williams

On December 1, 1873, President Grant nominated Attorney General George H. Williams to be chief justice. Williams had rather modest judicial experience, and most of the press was critical of his nomination. One newspaper wrote that "[t]he Country cannot afford to have any second-rate man, or anyone whose qualifications are not beyond dispute, placed at the head of the Supreme Court."[17] Perhaps more important was opposition from the bar. For example, the New York Bar Association passed a resolution stating that the nomination "'disappoints the just expectation of the legal profession and does not deserve the approval of the people for the reason that the candidate proposed is wanting in those qualifications of intellect, experience and reputation which are indispensable to uphold the dignity of the highest National Court. . . . '"[18]

In addition, various ethical charges were leveled against Williams. It was claimed that he had spent $1,600 in Justice Department funds for a carriage for his wife and that he had otherwise mingled Justice Department funds with his own. Williams was also charged with having fired a U.S. Attorney who was about to investigate voter fraud in which Williams was implicated. Faced with this record, the Senate declined to act for six weeks, and President Grant withdrew Williams's name at the nominee's request.

Caleb Cushing

Caleb Cushing, who, like George Williams, was a close friend of the president, was Grant's next nominee. Cushing had impeccable legal credentials. He had been attorney general of the United States and judge of the Supreme Judicial Court of Massachusetts. However, Cushing had a checkered political past, having been successively "a Whig, a Tyler man, a Democrat, a Constitutional Conservative in the confidence of Johnson and a Republican."[19] His rather advanced age of seventy-four also drew negative comments. Finally, there was criticism in the Radical Republican press that Cushing had been a "pro-slavery Democrat" and might not interpret the Fourteenth and Fifteenth Amendments in the manner favored by Radical Republicans.

The incident that destroyed Cushing's chance to become chief justice was the discovery of a letter that Cushing had written to Jefferson Davis in March of 1861 "recommending to his attention a young man who was then returning to Texas."[20] Although the letter contained no proof of disloyalty, it provoked an outcry that resulted in Grant's withdrawal of the nomination four days after the nomination was made.

William B. Hornblower and Wheeler H. Peckham

Two of Grover Cleveland's nominees, William B. Hornblower and Wheeler H. Peckham, both men of substantial legal ability, were denied confirmation because of the opposition of Senators Hill and Murphy, who invoked senatorial courtesy to defeat the nominations.[21] Senator Hill opposed Hornblower because Hornblower had exposed election corruption of Hill's political allies. Both Hill and Murphy were annoyed that they had not been consulted by President Cleveland before he nominated residents of their state to fill the vacant Supreme Court seat.

John J. Parker

John J. Parker, nominated by Herbert Hoover in 1930, was rejected by the Senate for both political and ideological reasons. First, his opinion for the court of appeals, enforcing so-called "yellow-dog" contracts in the *Red Jacket* case,[22] caused an outcry by organized labor against his nomination. Second, a racially offensive speech that Parker gave while running for governor of North Carolina in 1920 caused the NAACP to oppose his nomination. Third, the appointment of Parker, a Republican from North Carolina, was thought to promote Republican Party interests in the South, which prompted Democrats to oppose Parker's nomination.

Although opposition to Judge Parker centered largely on ideology, other arguments were also raised against him. Some suggested that as special assistant attorney general, Parker had prosecuted an individual in a case in which he knew there was insufficient evidence. Others criticized Parker's appointment, at age forty-five, on grounds of youth and inexperience. Finally, partisan politics may have had as much bearing on opposition to the Parker nomination as the concern about Parker's judicial ideology. The fact that Hoover was apparently using the nomination to advance the Republican Party's political interests in the South undoubtedly caused some southern Democrats to vote against Parker.[23] But it is also true that many senators voted against Judge Parker because of their disagreement with him on civil rights and labor law issues or because of their fear that anti-Parker lobbyists would take reprisals against those who supported him.

Despite overwhelming support for Parker from the legal community, the Senate rejected Judge Parker's nomination by a vote of 41 to 39. Ironically, Parker came to be viewed as a more liberal jurist than Owen Roberts, who was ultimately chosen to fill the Supreme Court seat for which Parker had been nominated.

Abe Fortas

After Parker's rejection, thirty-eight years elapsed before the Senate denied confirmation to another Supreme Court nominee. In 1968, the Senate was unable to shut off debate on Justice Abe Fortas's nomination to be chief justice, and the nomination was withdrawn. Although Fortas's liberal voting record on the Court influenced some of the senators who opposed him, a variety of factors unrelated to his judicial philosophy contributed more importantly to his defeat.

First, the fact that the Senate was nearing the end of its session, combined with President Johnson's lame-duck status, helped to facilitate Fortas's defeat. Second, Fortas was vulnerable to attack for having accepted a stipend of $15,000, paid by five wealthy businessmen, for delivering a series of lectures at American University. Third, and perhaps most significant, Fortas's extrajudicial activities seem to have crippled his nomination.[24] Fortas was viewed as having violated the principle of separation of powers by advising President Johnson on a wide range of issues, including the Vietnam war, and by drafting legislation for the Johnson administration.[25]

Clement Haynsworth

The next nominee to be denied confirmation was Clement Haynsworth. The American Federation of Labor and Congress of Industrial Organizations (AFL-CIO) and some civil rights groups opposed Haynsworth because of his judicial record in areas of concern to them. Undoubtedly, some senators also opposed Haynsworth in retaliation for the Republican opposition that had blocked Fortas's appointment as chief justice. Finally, much of the opposition to Haynsworth was expressly based on a series of ethical problems.[26]

Haynsworth's ethical problems stemmed largely from two incidents. He had been a shareholder, vice president, and director of Vend-a-Matic, a corporation with substantial vending machine contracts with Deering Milliken, a textile conglomerate.[27] While on the court of appeals, Haynsworth had cast the deciding vote in an important case in favor of Darlington Mills, a Deering subsidiary. Haynsworth also owned shares of stock in another textile manufacturer, J. P. Stevens, whose economic interests were substantially the same as Deering's. In short, Haynsworth was charged with participating in a case while having an undisclosed interest in the outcome.

Haynsworth also participated in a case involving the Brunswick Corporation, despite having a substantial financial interest in the corporation, which warranted his disqualification. Haynsworth had purchased $16,000 worth of Brunswick stock after participating in a preliminary decision in Brunswick's favor and before a final decision was rendered. Moreover, after buying the stock, he had proposed some changes in the final decision in the case.

G. Harrold Carswell

Following the Senate's failure to confirm Judge Haynsworth, President Nixon nominated G. Harrold Carswell, a little-known federal judge from Florida. Carswell had had a lackluster career as a trial judge, having been reversed more often than all but six of the sixty-seven federal trial judges in the South.[28] He had no publications to his credit, and his opinions were rarely cited. Dean Pollack of Yale said Carswell had "more slender credentials than any Supreme Court nomination put forth in this century."[29]

Carswell was also accused of lacking judicial temperament. There was testimony before the Judiciary Committee that Carswell was hostile to litigants who sought to ensure their right to vote under the 1965 Voting Rights Act. He was also criticized for having made a racist speech while running for the Georgia legislature in 1948 and for having been one of those responsible for converting a public golf course, originally built with $35,000 of federal funds, into a private club.[30] The final nail in Carswell's coffin was a statement of support from Senator Roman Hruska of Nebraska, who said that "[e]ven if [Carswell is] mediocre, there are a lot of mediocre judges and people and lawyers. They are entitled to a little representation, aren't they?"[31] With support like this, it is not surprising that Carswell never recovered. His nomination was defeated by a vote of 51 to 45, with several prominent Republicans voting in the negative. Although some senators undoubtedly voted against Carswell for other reasons, his defeat has been widely viewed as attributable to his lack of professional qualifications.

Summary

In sum, most of the Supreme Court nominees voted down by the Senate were rejected because of senatorial courtesy, personal animosity toward the candidate, or antagonism based on political activity. Concern about the nominee's judicial philosophy was rarely the basis for the Senate's action. The reliance on grounds other than ideology clearly reflects that, traditionally, most senators have been unwilling to vote against an otherwise qualified Supreme Court nominee on the basis of ideology alone.

In his July 23rd speech advocating a policy of rejecting Supreme Court nominees on ideological grounds, Senator Biden relied not only on Senate precedents, discussed previously, but also on fragments of the legislative history of the appointments clause of the Constitution. Biden began by noting that early drafts of that clause had conferred the power of appointing Supreme Court justices on the Senate rather than on the president. He said that "it is difficult to imagine that after four attempts to exclude the President from the selection process, the Framers intended anything less than the broadest role for the Senate in choosing the Court and checking the President in every way."[32] Such a broad role was necessary, in Biden's view, to prevent the president from undertaking "to remake the Supreme Court in his own image."[33]

But the early drafts of the appointments clause, which Senator Biden quoted incompletely, extended beyond the Supreme Court. They provided that the Senate would have power "to appoint ambassadors and judges of the Supreme Court." Senator Biden's omission of the reference to ambassadors was not a matter of harmless oversight. His argument was that the attempt to exclude the president from the selection process in early drafts of the Constitution justifies "the broadest role for the Senate in choosing the Court." But since the president was also excluded from the selection of ambassadors, the logic of Biden's argument is that the Constitution requires "the broadest role" for the Senate in choosing ambassadors, a plainly untenable proposition that Biden himself would surely reject. There may, of course, be good reasons to distinguish between ambassadors (who serve in the executive branch at the pleasure of the president) and members of the Supreme Court (who are appointed for life to an independent branch of government). But this merely underscores the oversimplified nature of Biden's suggestion that a commitment of the appointing power to the Senate in early drafts of the Constitution is enough to justify "the broadest role" for the Senate in the confirmation process. The legislative history of the appointments clause simply does not reveal much about what the Framers intended the Senate's role to be, when they shifted the appointments power to the president. Similarly, the ratification debates are not helpful in discerning the intent of the Framers, since the debates seldom focused on the allocation of power over judicial appointments.[34]

Some observers—most notably Professor Charles Black of Yale—have relied on the language of the appointments clause, rather than its legislative history, in urging the rejection of Supreme Court nominees on ideological grounds. In an influential article in the Yale Law Journal, Professor Black argued that the phrase "advise and consent" suggests an expansive role for the Senate. Black asked rhetorically: "Can you conceive of sound 'advice' which is given by an advisor who has deliberately barred himself from considering some of the things that the person he is advising ought to consider, and does consider?"[35]

But, in fact, it is not unusual for advisers to confine their advice to a limited part of what the president himself will consider—with some advisers focusing, for instance, on military matters and others focusing on questions of diplomacy, foreign intelligence, or domestic politics. Furthermore, it seems clear that some of the factors considered by the president in making Supreme Court nominations would be entirely inappropriate for consideration in the confirmation process. Presidents often consider a candidate's "confirmability" before making a nomination, but it surely does not follow that a senator could properly base his or her vote on the nominee's popularity with other members of the Senate. Similarly, if the president chooses a Supreme Court nominee who will help the president win reelection, senators cannot legitimately respond by making their votes on confirmation turn on their own attitude toward the presidential election.[36] Professor Black advocates "the taking of a second opinion on [Supreme Court appointments] from a body just as responsible to the electorate, and just as close to the electorate, as is the President."[37] But Black cannot claim to be interpreting the appointments clause when he takes that position. Although the Framers' intent is ambiguous on some matters, it is quite clear that the appointments clause was adopted at a time when members of the Senate were chosen by the state legislatures and not by the general public. The Framers, therefore, could not have intended that clause to ensure "the taking of a second opinion . . . from a body just as responsible to the electorate, and just as close to the electorate, as is the President."

The central fact about the confirmation power is that neither the language of the appointments clause nor its legislative history tells us whether a Supreme Court nominee may properly be rejected on the basis of ideology. The *Federalist Papers* stated that the need for Senate confirmation "would tend greatly to prevent the appointment of unfit characters from State prejudice, from family connection, from personal attachment or from a view to popularity."[38] But the Constitution is generally silent on the question of what criteria the Senate may use in exercising the power of advice and consent. Apparently the only criterion that was specifically forbidden by the Constitution was the use of any "religious test."[39] Moreover, even the clear prohibition against religious tests for public office can evidently be violated with impunity in confirmation proceedings, since no court could require that a nominee be confirmed or that the Senate disregard his or her religion.[40] The appointments clause, in short, contains no enforceable right to be confirmed, regardless of what criteria—ideological or otherwise—the Senate might use.

Ultimately, the question of whether to impose ideological requirements for appointment to the Supreme Court presents a prudential or political issue, not a legal one. The question is, what effect *should* a responsible senator give to matters of judicial ideology? Unfortunately, almost no one gave careful attention to this question during the Bork proceedings. Even worse, the history of Senate action on Supreme Court nominations—which speaks powerfully to the prudential issue—was seriously misread in Senator Biden's speech; and yet Biden's reading of history went largely unanswered. Since Senator Biden's position on ideological inquiries conformed to popular opinion, as shown in public opinion polls, it quickly became the conventional wisdom. Ironically, Judge Bork's confirmation hearings, which began with an assumption that ideologically based Senate rejections are legitimate, will now be treated as establishing the legitimacy of ideological inquiries. Supported initially by almost no precedent, the Bork case has now itself become an unmistakable precedent for ideologically based rejections of Supreme Court nominees. Nevertheless, the rejection of Supreme Court nominees for ideological reasons has serious implications for judicial independence and for public confidence in the courts, and those issues must ultimately be addressed by the Senate and by the president as well.[41]

PART TWO

COMMITTEE HEARINGS

5
THE JUDICIARY
COMMITTEE

The Senate Judiciary Committee was established in 1868. However, the committee's review of Supreme Court nominees in the nineteenth century was largely *pro forma*. No public hearings were held, and no written reports were issued. Public hearings began in 1916 with the controversial nomination of Louis D. Brandeis, but no nominee testified before the committee until Felix Frankfurter appeared in 1939. In the twentieth century, approval by the Judiciary Committee has been necessary, but not always sufficient, to ensure approval by the full Senate. The only nominee to receive a negative vote in committee before Robert Bork was Judge Parker, who was eventually denied confirmation by the Senate on a vote of thirty-nine to forty-one.

The Judiciary Committee that would conduct hearings on the Bork nomination consisted of eight Democrats and six Republicans. However, no one expected a straight party-line vote, and Bork, of course, could not win a party-line vote. A more useful analysis divided the committee into three groups, each including both Democratic and Republican members. The first group was made up of senior senators who would inevitably play an important role in the hearings. A second group consisted of senators who had either committed themselves on the Bork nomination or whose votes were entirely predictable, even in the absence of specific commitments. The third and perhaps the most important group was made up of uncommitted senators whose votes could not be easily predicted.

THE SENIOR PLAYERS

Committee Chairman Joseph Biden and Senator Edward Kennedy, the senior members on the majority side, were key players in opposition to Judge Bork. On the minority side, ranking Senator Strom Thurmond and his staff played an important part in support of the Bork nomination. However, due to Thurmond's advanced age, Senator Orrin Hatch became a de facto leader of the pro-Bork group.

Chairman Joseph Biden

The Judiciary Committee was to play a crucial role in the Bork confirmation battle, and the 1986 senatorial elections were instrumental in determining the composition of the committee. President Reagan, campaigning against southern Democratic senators, asked his audience whether it would not prefer to have a Republican chairing the Judiciary Committee and overseeing judicial confirmations rather than have Ted Kennedy in charge. Democrats nevertheless succeeded in retaking control of the Senate from Republicans by a margin of fifty-five to forty-five. With control of the Senate, the Democrats were then able to chair committees and to set the schedule and the agenda.

Senator Kennedy had served long and hard on the Judiciary Committee and had been active in opposing conservative judicial nominees. Because of his seniority, Kennedy had the option of chairing either the Judiciary Committee or the Labor and Human Resources Committee.[1] It was an uneasy choice for Kennedy. The Judiciary Committee had scheduled hearings on the enforcement of civil rights laws by the Reagan administration. Kennedy had a long-standing interest in civil rights statutes, as well as in antitrust enforcement, employment discrimination laws, and judicial confirmations, all of which fell within the committee's jurisdiction. On the other hand, Kennedy's crusade for a comprehensive national health care system and his interest in national labor laws tended to prod him toward chairing the Labor Committee.

The impending presidential election of 1988 was also an important factor. If Kennedy chose Labor, Senator Biden, who was considering a run for the presidency, would get an opportunity to chair Judiciary—a somewhat mixed political blessing. Chairing the Judiciary Committee would give Biden the kind of national television exposure he needed. A study by Stephen Hess of the Brookings Institute showed that the Judiciary Committee attracts more national television coverage than any other committee, except Foreign Relations.[2] Indeed, Biden himself had earlier gained national recognition for his part in opposing other Reagan nominees, such as William Bradford Reynolds, nominated to be associate attorney general, and Jefferson B. Sessions and Daniel Manion, nominated to the federal courts of appeals.[3] On the other hand, as chair of the Judiciary Committee, Biden might be forced to lead the fight against a conservative judicial nominee at the same time that he was trying to appear "moderate" to southern Democrats.[4] Biden was also concerned that chairing Judiciary would consume too much of his time, when he needed to be out campaigning.[5]

In the end, after consulting Biden, Senator Kennedy chose to chair the Labor Committee, leaving Biden to chair the Judiciary Committee. In some ways, this arrangement served the needs of both men. Kennedy was able to chair Labor and Human Resources, an area in which he was deeply committed, and he would not have to take a back seat to Senator Metzenbaum, who was next in line to chair Labor. On Judiciary, Kennedy would be able to take a leading role in opposing conservative judicial nominees, and it seemed likely that Biden, a good friend, would be willing to share responsibility with him. By relying on Kennedy to assume some responsibility, Biden could get out on the political hustings, when necessary. He also would be able to appear more moderate than Kennedy, even while opposing conservative judicial nominees.

After some initial uncertainty, Biden indicated in early July that he would lead the fight in opposition to the Bork nomination.[6] That decision left Biden in a somewhat awkward position. First, he had to explain why he would oppose Judge Bork after having stated in 1982 that if President Reagan nominated Bork to the Supreme Court, he would have to support the nomination and "take the heat" from the special interests.[7] Biden also had to explain how he could chair the Judiciary Committee fairly, after having decided to oppose Judge Bork without even hearing Bork's testimony.[8] These problems caused Biden to suggest that he was not firmly opposed to Judge Bork but merely had "grave doubts."[9] Since everyone understood Biden's need to appeal to the civil rights community in order to get the Democratic nomination for President, Biden's "clarification" of his position was not taken very seriously.

Senator Biden tried hard to appear to handle the proceedings fairly. Still, conservatives like Patrick McGuigan and Phyllis Schlafley believed that Biden deliberately scheduled the hearings in such a way as to give prime-time coverage to the witnesses opposing Bork.[10] But Walter Dellinger, a Duke law professor who assisted Biden during the hearings, insisted that the reason the pro-Bork witnesses often testified at night was that Bork's supporters on the committee spent too much time trying to cross-examine anti-Bork witnesses. He said it made no sense for people like Charles Grassley or Gordon Humphrey to try to question Laurence Tribe, William Coleman, or Barbara Jordan.[11]

In fact, both sides could, and did, influence the timing of a witness's appearance, either through the length of their questioning or through the original scheduling. But while both sides sought optimal timing for their best witnesses, the Democrats were in the majority, and they could generally work their will in these matters. Nevertheless, Dellinger is quite right in charging that Republican Senators sometimes engaged in prolonged questioning of articulate anti-Bork witnesses, which was clearly counterproductive to their cause.

Strom Thurmond

Strom Thurmond, at age eighty-four the ranking Republican on the Judiciary Committee, had been through the confirmation wars many times. In 1968, he opposed Lyndon Johnson's nomination of Abe Fortas to be chief justice, principally because of Fortas's liberal voting record but also because of Fortas's extrajudicial activity as an adviser to President Johnson.[12] Thurmond was a principal architect of the strategy that succeeded in delaying, and ultimately defeating, the Fortas nomination. In 1987, as a member of the Senate minority, Thurmond found himself in the position of opposing delay in the confirmation process.

Senator Thurmond, like Biden, had articulated varying views of the appropriate role of the Senate in Supreme Court confirmations. During the Fortas hearings, Thurmond argued that the Senate should closely scrutinize a nominee's judicial philosophy: "[I]t is my contention that the Supreme Court has assumed such a powerful role as a policymaker in the Government that the Senate must necessarily be concerned with the views of the prospective Justices or Chief Justices as they relate to broad issues confronting the American people, and the role of the Court in dealing with these issues."[13] On the other hand, during the hearings on Sandra Day O'Connor and on William H. Rehnquist's nomination to be chief justice, Thurmond argued for a narrow role for the Senate. He said the questions the Senate should examine in deciding whether to confirm a Supreme Court nominee were whether the nominee has integrity and courage, whether he is learned in the law, whether he has compassion, whether he has the necessary judicial temperament, and whether he understands the powers given to the federal government, the states, and the Court.[14]

At the Bork hearings, Thurmond argued for a limited examination of a nominee's judicial philosophy but tried to show that he had been consistent and was acting in a principled way:

> Some have said that philosophy should not be considered at all in the confirmation process. In fact, I have been incorrectly aligned with that position. Others say that philosophy should be the sole criteria. I reject both of these positions. I believe that a candidates's philosophy may properly be considered, but philosophy should not be the sole criteria for rejecting a nominee with one notable exception. The one exception is when the nominee clearly does not support the basic, long-standing consensus principles of our nation.[15]

More than some of his colleagues, Thurmond appeared to take Bork's defeat in stride. Perhaps that is attributable to his having seen it all before. Another possible explanation is that Thurmond, who had favored the nomination of Judge Wilkins of South Carolina, was not particularly enthusiastic about the northern professor in the first place.

Edward M. Kennedy

Even before the Bork hearings, Senator Kennedy had frequently used the Judiciary Committee as a forum for challenging the civil rights record of conservative nominees to the Supreme Court. In 1970, Kennedy had extensively questioned witnesses at the confirmation hearings for Judge G. Harrold Carswell about the judge's civil rights record. Kennedy expressed the view of the minority on the committee that Carswell's "decisions and his courtroom demeanor have been openly hostile to the black, the poor and the unpopular. This record raises serious questions about his judicial temperament and his ability to provide a fair hearing on many of the great issues that will come before the Supreme Court."[16]

The next year, Kennedy vigorously opposed William H. Rehnquist's nomination to be associate justice. In what was to presage the attack on

Judge Bork, Kennedy joined Senators Birch Bayh, Philip Hart, and John Tunney in criticizing Rehnquist for his narrow interpretation of the Bill of Rights and for his expansive view of presidential powers.[17] Kennedy sharply questioned, and later harshly criticized, Rehnquist for his record on civil rights.[18]

Rehnquist's opponents, like Bork's sixteen years later, tried to use the nominee's own words against him. Kennedy quoted a letter, written by Rehnquist in 1967 on the use of bussing to achieve school integration. It read: "[W]e are no more dedicated to an 'integrated' society than to a 'segregated' society."[19] Kennedy and the other three senators concluded with a stinging attack on Rehnquist: "Unrelieved by actions showing an affirmative commitment to social justice, Mr. Rehnquist's record is one of persistent indifference to the evils of discrimination and an almost hostile unwillingness to accept the use of law to overcome racial injustice in America."[20]

The similarities between the Bork hearings and the hearings on Rehnquist's nomination to be chief justice are even more striking. At the start of the hearings on Rehnquist's elevation to chief justice in 1986, Kennedy gave an impassioned speech in opposition to Rehnquist that was strikingly similar to the speech he was later to give about "Robert Bork's America." In 1986, the subject was "Justice Rehnquist's America," but the indictment was no different in tone from Kennedy's indictment of Judge Bork a year later:

> Imagine what America would be like if Rehnquist had been Chief Justice and his cramped, narrow view of the Constitution had prevailed. . . . The schools of America would still be segregated. Millions of citizens would be denied the right to vote under scandalous malapportionment laws. Women would be condemned to second-class status. Courthouses would be closed to individual challenges against police brutality and executive abuse—closed even to the press. The wall of separation between church and state would be in ruins. State and local majorities would tell us what we can read, whether to bear children, how to bring them up, what kinds of people we may become.[21]

During the Rehnquist hearings, Kennedy consistently challenged the nominee's attitude on civil rights. There was a great deal of testimony about Rehnquist's alleged role in harassing and intimidating black voters in Phoenix in the 1960s.[22] This testimony contradicted statements by Rehnquist at both of his confirmation hearings. Kennedy spent much of his allotted time questioning Rehnquist about the accusations of five people who had charged Rehnquist with voter harassment. At one point Kennedy asked, "Are all the witnesses wrong?" Rehnquist replied, "I suppose if they said I did it and I say I didn't, yes they are wrong."[23] Kennedy also pressed the issue of the racially restrictive covenants in the deeds to Rehnquist's home in Phoenix and his summer home in Vermont. Rehnquist denied knowledge of these restrictions and took steps to remove the restrictions after learning about them.[24]

In his separate minority statement after the hearings, Kennedy went into great detail on Rehnquist's insensitivity to racial minorities. Kennedy did not limit himself to Rehnquist's pre-judicial activities but also argued that as a member of the Supreme Court, "Justice Rehnquist has been quick to seize on the slightest pretext to justify the denial of claims for racial justice. . . . " Kennedy added that Rehnquist's "appalling record on race . . . [was] sufficient by itself to deny his confirmation."[25]

Kennedy went on to argue that Rehnquist's judicial philosophy was "outside the mainstream of American jurisprudence in other significant areas. In his 15 years on the Supreme Court, Justice Rehnquist has compiled a record of consistent opposition to individual rights in all areas on minority rights, women's rights, religious liberty, rights of the poor, rights of aliens and rights of children."[26] Kennedy used statistics to bolster his argument about Rehnquist's insensitivity to minorities. In particular, he pointed out that "[i]n 14 race discrimination cases brought by or on behalf of blacks, Justice Rehnquist cast the deciding vote against the civil rights claimant every time."[27] In a striking recitation of arguments he would later use against Judge Bork, Kennedy said that whenever possible, Rehnquist resolved conflicts between the individual and the government against the individual, resolved those between the state and federal governments in favor of the state, and decided questions of federal jurisdiction against the exercise of such jurisdiction.[28]

Kennedy later led an unsuccessful filibuster to block Rehnquist's confirmation.[29] The final vote in favor of Rehnquist was sixty-five to thirty-three. With thirty-three negative votes, Rehnquist exceeded his own previous record of twenty-six for the most negative votes to date of any confirmed nominee.[30] Although he was not successful in blocking Rehnquist's appointment as chief justice, Kennedy was buoyed by the vote totals.

Orrin G. Hatch

Senator Hatch is a Mormon lay minister, and to some degree his political views have been molded by his cultural and religious background.[31] Nevertheless, Hatch is someone who defies easy stereotyping. He has been an ardent opponent of federal funding for abortion, and he remarked a few years ago that the Democratic Party was "a party of homosexuals." However, he later apologized for this remark, admitting that it was "a dumb thing for me to say." He added, "I feel very deeply about people's heartaches and problems, and I don't care what their sexual preferences are."[32] Hatch went on to become a leading advocate for the hate-crimes bill, recently enacted into law, which requires the Justice Department to compile statistics on bias crimes, including those against homosexuals. He also helped defeat Senator Jesse Helms's attempt to attach a crippling amendment to a bill on AIDS education.[33]

Conservative lobbyist Paul Weyrich reportedly charged that Hatch's apparent contradictions are easy to explain. Hatch, according to Weyrich, has a "burning desire" to be on the Supreme Court, and his support for liberal measures is a cynical attempt to quiet the opposition. Hatch said such comments offend him, adding, "I'm not going to let anybody tell me how I must think."[34]

Although Hatch's opposition to certain matters on the conservative agenda earned him the wrath of some on the right, Hatch has been constant as a member of the Judiciary Committee in his support for conservative judicial nominees. Fueling Hatch's support for a more conservative judiciary has been his concern about the way the Supreme Court handled abortion, which he termed a "new form of slavery," and affirmative action.[35] In 1986, Hatch led the fight to confirm William Rehnquist as chief justice. A year later, he was an enthusiastic supporter of Judge Bork, and he played a leading role in lining up witnesses and orchestrating the presentation of the pro-Bork side. Hatch initially argued for a narrow role for the Senate in the confirmation process.[36] After that battle was lost, he used his time at the hearings to persuade his colleagues and the general public that Bork was in the judicial mainstream.

Interestingly, Senator Alan Simpson suggested that if Bork were not confirmed, President Reagan might nominate someone who was just as conservative but more confirmable, such as Orrin Hatch.[37] In fact, Hatch was never on the White House short list, in part because constitutional questions would likely have been raised about whether a senator who is in office at the time a pay raise is approved for the Judiciary can then be confirmed to the Court by that same Senate. The answer to the constitutional question raised by the emoluments clause of the Constitution is not clear, since it is conceivable that a nominee could avoid the constitutional problem by refusing to accept the salary increase. Nevertheless, concern about this issue was one factor that caused Hatch not to be seriously considered by the White House. In addition, there was concern that if Hatch went on the Court, his resignation from the Senate would damage Republican Party interests.

THE PRE-COMMITTED VOTES

A number of senators, not publicly committed on Judge Bork, nevertheless had a firm position on the question of confirmation. Three of the committee members who were opposed to Bork's nomination from the beginning were Howard Metzenbaum, Patrick Leahy, and Paul Simon. Those supporting the nomination from the beginning were Alan Simpson, Gordon Humphrey, and Charles Grassley.

Howard Metzenbaum

As a member of the Judiciary Committee, Senator Metzenbaum had strongly opposed several Reagan nominations, including those of Edwin Meese to be attorney general and of William H. Rehnquist to be chief justice of the United States. Given this record and Metzenbaum's liberal voting pattern, it was widely assumed that Metzenbaum would do everything in his power to block Bork's confirmation. As will be seen later,[38] Metzenbaum did just that.

Patrick Leahy

Pat Leahy, a liberal Democrat from Vermont, was believed from the start to be a firm vote against Bork, despite the fact that he insisted throughout the hearings on calling himself "undecided." Senator Leahy had opposed the nomination of William Rehnquist to be chief justice. Leahy foreshadowed the controversy over Bork when he observed during the Rehnquist hearings that the Senate "has an affirmative obligation to consider a nominee's philosophy. Indeed, we'd be remiss if we did not scrutinize a nominee's views."[39] Leahy had also delivered a speech at Georgetown University, in which he said that the Reagan administration "bears much of the blame" for nominating unqualified judges but that the Senate was also to blame for "not adequately discharging" its responsibility to advise and consent.[40]

Paul Simon

Senator Simon, like Leahy, was perceived rather early as a likely Bork opponent, although he did not officially indicate his opposition until September 29.[41] Simon, whose trademarks are his bow tie and his resonant baritone voice, had announced that he was a candidate for President in May 1987. Unlike many of his opponents in the primaries, he ran as an unabashed New Deal Democrat.[42] Since much of his support, as well as his financial backing, came from liberals who were opposed to everything Bork represented, it was widely assumed that Simon could not vote for Bork and remain in the presidential race.

Alan Simpson

Shortly after President Reagan announced Bork's nomination, Senator Simpson declared himself "pleased" with the selection.[43] Although he differed with Bork on abortion, Simpson liked Bork's overarching view that the Court should not act as a super-legislature.[44] After the battle lines were drawn, Simpson became one of Bork's most vocal defenders. In an effort to forestall a bitter fight over the nomination, Simpson issued a statement on August 28, expressing the hope that members of the committee would avoid the type of "Justice bashing" that took place during the confirmation proceedings on William Rehnquist's nomination to be chief justice.[45] But during the Bork hearings, Simpson became increasingly frustrated with the "lies" and "distorted" statements coming from some of Bork's opponents.[46] Simpson was particularly angered by charges that Bork was a "sterilizer" and a "racist." Simpson criticized unnamed Bork opponents who "raised some legitimate arguments" but made use of a "deft blend of emotion, fear, guilt or racism" to further their cause.[47]

Gordon Humphrey

Throughout his political career, Senator Humphrey has been a fierce opponent of legalized abortion. In his first senatorial election campaign in

1978, Humphrey railed against the Supreme Court's decision in *Roe v. Wade*,[48] and in 1985, Humphrey organized a group of seventy-seven congressmen to sign an amicus brief in an effort to get the Supreme Court to overturn the decision.[49] While calling for a constitutional amendment to protect the unborn, Humphrey compared the "struggle against the cruel evil of abortion" with the battle against "the evil of human bondage."[50]

Abortion was a key issue for Humphrey in deciding whether to support candidates for public offices ranging from tax commissioner to vice president of the United States. Humphrey questioned Lawrence Gibbs, a nominee for tax commissioner, on whether Gibbs would make any change in the policy of granting tax-exempt status to organizations performing or funding abortions.[51] Humphrey later raised similar concerns about President Bush's nomination of Louis Sullivan to be secretary of Health and Human Services, because of contradictory statements by Sullivan on the abortion issue. Humphrey also expressed strong reservations about the possibility that Bush would choose Senator Alan Simpson as his running mate. Simpson, though a conservative, is pro-choice on abortion.[52] Robert Bork's position that the Supreme Court's decision in *Roe v. Wade* was "illegitimate" made Bork and Gordon Humphrey natural allies.

Charles Grassley

Senator Charles Grassley, a conservative Republican from Iowa, was a strong Bork supporter from the beginning. Grassley, a former farmer, has a reputation for being rather distrustful of lawyers.[53] He has been especially critical of the American Bar Association for its role in judicial confirmations. During the Judiciary Committee hearings, Grassley expressed concern that some members of the ABA's Standing Committee on the Judiciary may have voted against Bork for political or ideological reasons.[54]

ROBERT BYRD AND THE SWING VOTES

Senator Robert Byrd was technically a swing vote, but as Senate majority leader, Byrd could be expected to oppose Bork if a majority of his party did so. Reflecting the pressure he was feeling from both sides, Byrd said on August 7 that "[b]etween myself and God, I do not know at this time how I will vote."[55] The other three swing votes—Senators Heflin,

Specter, and DeConcini—were the subject of greater attention than Senator Byrd, since their votes were up for grabs regardless of how the other members of their party voted.

Howell Heflin

Elected to the Senate in 1978, Howell Heflin helped to craft a compromise on the Voting Rights Act of 1982 that was acceptable to southern senators. He cast crucial votes against the nominations of Jefferson Sessions to be federal district court judge in Alabama and of William Bradford Reynolds to be associate attorney general of the United States. Both of these votes helped win him support from Alabama's black community. On the other hand, Heflin can hardly be characterized as a liberal. He believes the Supreme Court's decisions in *Roe v. Wade* and the school prayer cases[56] were wrong, but he also believes the principle of *stare decisis* requires that the decisions be respected, absent a constitutional amendment. Before the start of the hearings, Patrick McGuigan of the Conservative Coalition thought that Heflin's belief in judicial restraint gave Bork a good opportunity to win Heflin's support. However, Estelle Rogers of the liberal Federation of Women Lawyers believed that Heflin's suspicion of activism from either the right or the left gave Bork's opponents the edge with Heflin.[57]

Arlen Specter

Arlen Specter, a moderate Republican from Pennsylvania, was always viewed as a swing vote on the Judiciary Committee. In the past, he had opposed a number of controversial Reagan nominations, including those of William Bradford Reynolds to be associate attorney general and of Daniel A. Manion, Jefferson B. Sessions, and Sidney A. Fitzwater to be federal judges.[58] Although Specter voted against these nominations in committee, he also voted to send the nominations to the floor for a vote by the full Senate.[59] Specter opposed Sessions largely because of the nominee's civil rights record, but he felt "that the whole Senate should consider the nomination."[60] In 1986, Specter opposed Daniel Manion's nomination to the federal court of appeals because Manion, according to Specter, expressed the view that decisions of the United States Supreme Court are not binding on the country. After the nomination went to the Senate floor, Specter became one of only four Republicans to vote against it. Manion was confirmed by a vote of forty-eight to forty-six, when Republican Senator Slade Gorton switched his vote, reportedly because the White House promised that it would nominate Gorton's candidate for a federal judgeship in Seattle.[61] Gorton was defeated in the next election, in part because of his flip-flop on Manion. However, his successor, Senator Brock Adams, proved to be much more of an embarrassment than Gorton and was forced to withdraw from a reelection campaign after numerous charges of sexual harassment were lodged against him. Gorton was then returned to his Senate seat. Shortly after Manion's confirmation, Senator Specter said he was "rethinking" his position on sending nominations to the full Senate after they had lost in committee, because of the politicking that took place over Manion's confirmation.

Despite his opposition to several Reagan nominees, Senator Specter could not be counted on to oppose Judge Bork, especially since Specter had earlier reversed his position in the course of other disagreements with the Reagan administration. For example, Specter opposed the MX missile in 1984; but when the issue came up for a vote, Specter switched sides and supported the MX, after the White House threatened not to help him with fund-raising for his 1986 reelection campaign.[62] According to Congressman Robert Walker of Pennsylvania, Specter had also promised not to oppose any of Reagan's future judicial nominations on the basis of legal philosophy. However, by the end of the Bork hearings, Specter denied making that pledge and said his position was only that a nominee should not be rejected on the basis of his views on a single issue.[63]

Dennis DeConcini

Even before the Bork hearings, Senator DeConcini had a reputation as a swing vote or, as some have suggested less kindly, a "fence-sitter" who keeps his finger to the wind. That reputation would be enhanced by his role in the Bork controversy. Six weeks before the start of the committee hearings, DeConcini's public statements gave the impression that he leaned toward supporting Bork. At the end of July, DeConcini said that he had read many of Bork's opinions and that he had met with Bork and was impressed. He added that while he would take Bork's conservatism into account, he had not decided prior judicial nominations on ideology alone: "Otherwise I could not have voted for all but two of Jimmy Carter's nominees. I think 80-something percent of them I disagreed with."[64] DeConcini was also reported to have said he was upset by the fact that many of his fellow Democrats had made up their minds to oppose Bork without having given him a fair hearing.[65]

By the start of the committee hearings, DeConcini's attitude had changed dramatically. During his opening statement, DeConcini listed several areas about which he was greatly concerned, including Bork's positions on civil rights and equal protection. He also expressed concern about Bork's belief that there is no constitutional right to privacy, although he agreed with Bork that *Roe v. Wade* was wrongly decided.

In sum, it appeared prior to the Bork hearings that there were five solid votes against the nomination (Biden, Kennedy, Metzenbaum, Leahy, and Simon) and five solid votes in favor of the nomination (Thurmond, Hatch, Simpson, Grassley, and Humphrey). That left the four undecided senators (Heflin, DeConcini, Byrd, and Specter) in the eye of the storm.

6
THE ULTIMATE STAKES: CONTROLLING THE DIRECTION OF THE COURT

The struggle over the Bork nomination was intense, in large part, because it came to be viewed as a critical battleground in the cultural and legal war between liberals and conservatives. For years, conservatives had been frustrated by the Supreme Court's role in implementing social policies that had not been approved by elected officials. Mandatory bussing, abortion rights, and the ban on school prayer were among the hot-button social issues that had frustrated conservatives for more than a decade. In 1980, Ronald Reagan promised a social and economic revolution. Because Democrats controlled one or both houses of Congress throughout his tenure, President Reagan had to use his executive powers to implement some parts of his social agenda. One way to bring about significant change was through judicial appointments, and as discussed earlier, Reagan and Ed Meese did all they could to select judges who would uphold the decisions of duly elected representatives.

For Robert Bork, judicial restraint and respect for majoritarian rule were paramount values. Bork believed that these values would be advanced if only judges did not try to enforce their own personal predilections in the guise of determining what was constitutionally obligatory. For him, the only legitimate method of judging was by adhering to original intent—whether that of the drafters of legislation or that of the Framers of the Constitution. In a speech on March 31, 1987, Bork explained:

> [T]he judge is required to seek and apply the intentions of the founders. The reason is that a judge has no legitimate power to set at

naught the decisions made by the elected representatives of the American people unless he or she is required to do so by law. What does it mean to say that the Constitution is law? It means that the words of the document, and their historical meaning, constrain judgment. The words must control judges every bit as much as they control legislators, executives, and citizens.

The various systems of moral philosophy that legal academics propound as guides to constitutional adjudication are not capable of constraining the judge. They are capable, instead, of producing any result the judge, or the professor, wants. They also lack democratic legitimacy because there is no reason why those of us who have our own moral visions should be governed by some judge's personal moral views.[1]

Although Bork sometimes spoke of the need to defer to precedent when expectations had been built up in reliance on earlier Court decisions, he failed to convince many observers, who believed he was quite anxious to overrule precedents that he considered "illegitimate." Indeed, some of his prior comments had seemed to promise that he would do exactly that.[2]

Bork's concept of precedent and his view that unelected judges should defer to majoritarian decision making were matters of deep concern to liberals, who argued that the Bill of Rights was largely designed to protect minorities from the tyranny of the majority. But Bork had not taken issue with Court decisions enforcing the Bill of Rights; his objection was to judicial activism that created constitutional guarantees not found in the Bill of Rights or elsewhere in the Constitution. Nevertheless, liberals thought that Bork had a "cramped" view of judicial power and of individual rights, and they were terrified.

For the most part, neither liberals nor conservatives take a detached view of the proper way to interpret the Constitution. Instead, members of both groups tend to view judicial action from the perspective of how a particular method of decision making would affect the issues that are important to them. For example, liberal groups generally favor an expansive interpretation of the Bill of Rights and the Fourteenth Amendment because broad interpretations have recently produced results they liked—abortion rights, freedom of speech, and civil rights. They tend to overlook the fact that expansive interpretations of the Constitution were earlier used to protect property rights, at the expense of the personal freedoms they hold dear.[3] Similarly, conservatives generally favor a narrower interpretation of the Fourteenth Amendment because they believe that approach will lead to results like prayer in schools and less protection for criminal suspects. Both liberals and conservatives have been quite inconsistent in applying their respective methods of interpretation. Thus liberals generally give a narrow construction to the Second Amendment's right to bear arms, despite their support for an expansive reading of the Bill of Rights, while conservatives usually give a broad interpretation to the Second Amendment, despite their narrower view of the Bill of Rights.

In many respects, Judge Bork was far more principled than either his supporters or his detractors. Bork testified in 1981 against the Human Life Bill, which sought to define "life" as existing from the moment of conception.[4] That bill, if upheld, would have seriously undermined the ruling in *Roe v. Wade*. Although Bork had no sympathy for *Roe*, he believed that constitutional adjudications could not be overturned by legislative enactments and therefore opposed the bill. Bork also refused to take the side of many of his supporters on the question whether any form of gun control would violate the Second Amendment. In response to an inquiry from Senator Metzenbaum, Bork stated that he had had no occasion to study the Second Amendment as a scholar or to rule upon it as a judge, and so he would not articulate a position on the subject.

Bork's adherence to principle has been challenged by some critics for lack of consistency. For example, Bork argues that *Brown v. Board of Education*[5] was correctly decided because the principle of "separate but equal" did not comport with the intent of the Framers of the Fourteenth Amendment. While the Framers may not have intended specifically to require school desegregation, Bork argued that their primary intent to promote racial equality must override any subjective expectation that segregation would be permitted. Although his position may be defensible, it shows that discerning the intent of the Framers is no easy task.

The stakes in the Bork hearings were substantially increased by virtue of the fact that with Justice Powell's retirement, the Supreme Court became quite evenly divided along ideological lines. Four members of the Court—Justices Rehnquist, White, Scalia, and O'Connor—were generally "conservative," and the other four members—Justices Brennan, Marshall, Blackmun, and Stevens—were generally "liberal." Thus, as noted earlier, Justice Powell had provided the decisive vote on many important social issues. If Powell's replacement voted in a consistently conservative way, it could fundamentally alter the balance on the Court. Because Judge Bork's position on major issues was fairly clear, both sides expected that his confirmation would have an important impact on future Court decisions. Moreover, the fact that he was viewed as a brilliant spokesman for his position worried liberals, who were concerned that his presence on the Court might exert a strong influence on some of the other justices. But liberals still believed that if they could block Judge Bork and then secure the election of a Democratic president in 1988, they could gain an ideological majority on the Supreme Court. They ignored the fact that even if they were successful in blocking Bork's confirmation, the person ultimately chosen by President Reagan to replace Justice Powell might be no less conservative than Judge Bork.

7
THE RIGHT OF PRIVACY: CONTRACEPTION, ABORTION, AND STERILIZATION

For many years, Robert Bork was one of the country's foremost critics of judicially created rights of privacy. Bork had strongly attacked Supreme Court decisions creating constitutional rights to use contraceptives or have an abortion, and to a considerable extent, his reputation as a constitutional theorist was based on his analysis of the Court's privacy doctrine. But if Bork's loyal following was built on criticism of privacy decisions, so too was much of the vigorous opposition to Judge Bork. Molly Yard, then president of the National Organization of Women (NOW), called Bork "a Neanderthal," and Faye Wattleton, the president of Planned Parenthood, labeled him a "radical" who would permit government intrusion into the privacy of the bedroom.[1] Others would forego the use of pejorative labels, but they nevertheless stood ready to carry out a ferocious struggle against Bork's confirmation.

Although privacy rights had been discussed in the confirmation proceedings of earlier Supreme Court nominees, there is no doubt that these issues received special attention at the hearings for Judge Bork. In part, this focus on privacy reflected an important tactical decision by Bork's opponents. Polls taken by Harrison Hickman for the National Abortion Rights Action League (NARAL) showed that the public was concerned about privacy issues, and the polling results were used both to determine strategy and to influence popular opinion. Nikki Heidepriem, a consultant to the anti-Bork forces, explained the strategy this way: "[W]e had the idea of labeling him as a rigid ideologue . . . with a stifling interpretation of a written [Constitution]. . . . The key surrogate for that notion was privacy."[2] The right of privacy, therefore, became a centerpiece of the Bork hearings. But privacy concerns would also lead to one of the most vicious attacks made against Judge Bork in the course of the confirmation proceedings.

The debate on privacy issues at the Bork hearings was decidedly selective. Both supporters and opponents of the nominee worried that an emphasis on abortion—still a highly divisive subject—might undermine public support for their position. Accordingly, the privacy debate focused, first, on the long-settled issue of contraception and, later, on the nonissue of compulsory sterilization.

It was easy to attack Bork on contraception, since his criticism of the Supreme Court's decision in *Griswold v. Connecticut*,[3] a decision that struck down a state anti-contraception law, was detailed in an article published by the *Indiana Law Journal*.[4] Although adult access to contraceptives had ceased to be a controversial issue long before Judge Bork's nomination to the Supreme Court, Bork's criticism of *Griswold* became a rallying point for opponents of the nomination. *Griswold* also provided a relatively risk-free avenue of attack for Bork's opponents, since the right to practice contraception was supported by a broad national consensus.

The *Griswold* case had involved two Connecticut statutes that made it unlawful to use contraceptives or to assist another person in using contraceptives. Justice Douglas, writing for the Court's majority, found "zones of privacy" in the First, Third, Fourth, Fifth, and Ninth Amendments of the Constitution. From these zones of privacy and the "penumbras" of constitutional guaranties, Douglas inferred a general right of marital privacy, a right that Connecticut was found to have infringed by prohibiting the use of contraceptives. Thus, while the Constitution mentions neither contraception nor a general right of privacy, the *Griswold* case managed to give protection to both. Justice Goldberg wrote a concurring opinion in which he argued that the right to privacy in marriage was protected by the Ninth Amendment, which provides that "[t]he enumeration in the Constitution, of certain rights, shall not be construed to deny or disparage others retained by the people."

Two members of the Court dissented in *Griswold*. Justice Stewart admitted that this was "an uncommonly silly law," but since the Constitution makes no mention of general privacy rights, he could not agree that the law was unconstitutional. Justice Black took a similar position, stating that "the law is every bit as offensive to me as it is to my Brethren of the majority" but denying that "the evil qualities they see in the law make it unconstitutional." Black recognized that many laws—including, for instance, a wide variety of tax and regulatory provisions—may be unwise but are not unconstitutional. He said that "[t]he Court talks about a constitutional 'right of privacy' as though there is some constitutional provision or provisions forbidding any law ever to be passed which might abridge the 'privacy' of individuals. But there is not."[5] Justice Black, therefore, concluded that the remedy for Connecticut's unwise law rested with democratically elected legislators and not with judges who have been appointed for life. This was essentially the same position that Judge Bork would later advance and that would lead to charges that he was outside the "mainstream" of legal thinking.

Judge Bork, writing in the *Indiana Law Journal* in 1971, when he was a professor at the Yale Law School, had sharply attacked the reasoning in the *Griswold* case. He criticized the opinion for creating a right with no defined limits: "The Court, we may confidently predict, is not going to throw constitutional protection around heroin use or sexual acts with a consenting minor." Since there is nothing in the Constitution that distinguishes between these private activities and the private use of contraceptives,[6] Bork saw no basis for protecting one and not the others. And because the right of privacy was almost wholly undefined, Bork complained that its scope would be determined by the personal preferences of five of the nine justices.

The latter prediction proved to be quite correct. The Court followed the *Griswold* rationale in *Roe v. Wade*, which invalidated state antiabortion laws on privacy grounds. But in *Bowers v. Hardwick*, the Court upheld the constitutionality of a prohibition on homosexual sodomy, even though the acts were conducted in private by consenting adults and the rationale of *Griswold* and *Roe* seemed fully applicable to consensual homosexuality.[7]

At his confirmation hearings, Judge Bork repeated his criticism of a "generalized and undefined right of privacy." He asked rhetorically: "Privacy to do what? [P]rivacy to use cocaine in private? Privacy for businessmen to fix prices in a hotel room? We just do not know what it is."[8] The Judiciary Committee did not challenge Bork's assertion that no standards, other than those dictated by the judges' personal predilections, were available to determine which private acts would be constitutionally protected and which would not. Instead, several members of the committee attacked Bork's rejection of a constitutional right of privacy without considering his arguments against recognizing such a right. Their position, in effect, was that a right of privacy must be recognized, whether or not it could be defined. However incoherent that position might seem to be, it struck a responsive cord with the general public, which likes its privacy and is not constrained by difficult problems of legal definition.

Bork had written that *Griswold* was "an unprincipled decision." He said: "The reason is obvious. Every clash between a minority and a majority claiming power to regulate involves a choice between the gratifications of the two groups. When the Constitution has not spoken, the Court will be able to find no scale, other than its own preferences, upon which to weigh the respective claims to pleasure. Compare the facts in *Griswold* with a hypothetical suit by an electric utility company . . . to void a smoke pollution ordinance as unconstitutional. The cases are identical."[9] Bork explained the analogy between these two cases in a way that lay readers—who were not, after all, the primary audience for the *Indiana Law Journal*—would find hard to understand. In *Griswold*, he said, the issue was whether the gratification a couple receive from sexual activity without risk of pregnancy was to be preferred over the gratification the majority receives when its moral norms are observed. In the case of pollution by a utility company, the question was whether the gratification of the utility company in earning higher profits outweighed the gratification of the majority in having clean air. Bork's position was that the Constitution did not give explicit or implicit protection to any of these gratifications, and hence the Court had no legal basis for interfering with the legislature's resolution of competing claims.

But the analogy to a utility company was used by critics to show Bork's insensitivity to human needs. Senator Biden aggressively questioned Judge Bork on whether his views about *Griswold* had changed. Bork's responses made it clear that he would not repudiate those views, although he implied that the *Griswold* result might be reached by some alternative rationale. Bork said: "It may be possible to derive an objection to an anti-contraception statute in some other way. I do not know."[10] When pressed on whether he had found another way of providing constitutional protection to a married couple's use of contraceptives, Bork replied that he had never engaged in "that exercise." Asked whether the Constitution protected a generalized right of privacy as announced in *Griswold*, Bork said: "Not one derived in *that* fashion. There may be other arguments and I do not want to pass on those."[11] These carefully crafted remarks, distinguishing sharply between the rationale and the results in *Griswold*, could not satisfy Bork's critics on the committee, who were understandably skeptical about the possibility that Bork would find an alternative rationale for protecting the privacy rights that he had attacked for so many years.

Conservative senators tried to lead Judge Bork into responses that would pacify the opposition, but they had little success. In reply to a question from Senator Hatch, Bork said he thought the Connecticut law was an outrage and that "it would have been more of an outrage if they ever enforced it against an individual."[12] The latter remark was apparently intended to create the impression that the *Griswold* statute had little practical effect. But as other witnesses reminded the committee, the threat of prosecution had had the effect of closing Planned Parenthood clinics in Connecticut for a quarter of a century. Thus, while married couples were not prosecuted under the statute, the effect of the ban on contraception was more than academic.

Senator Grassley tried to get Judge Bork to say that he was not irreversibly opposed to recognizing a constitutional right of privacy. Grassley asked whether Bork could see himself accepting the majority view on the right of privacy, as one of the *Griswold* dissenters had done when *Roe v. Wade* came before the Court. No doubt, the senator was trying to give Judge Bork an opportunity to reassure the public that he was not locked into the views he had expressed as a professor sixteen years earlier. Judge Bork either missed the point or had little reassurance to give. He replied, "Well, I suppose I could if I became convinced . . . that I was wrong the first time."[13]

Although contraception was the privacy issue most discussed at the confirmation hearings, the issue of greatest concern to the public was abortion. In *Roe v. Wade*, the Supreme Court had held that it was unconstitutional to prohibit abortion in the first trimester and that only regulations designed to protect maternal health would be constitutionally permissible during most of the second trimester. Judge Bork had taken the position that *Roe v. Wade* "was itself an unconstitutional decision, a serious and wholly unjustifiable usurpation of state legislative authority." It was, he said, "in the running for perhaps the worst example of constitutional reasoning I have ever read."[14]

A number of women's groups were worried that Judge Bork, if confirmed, would vote to overrule the *Roe* decision. Planned Parenthood spent $200,000 on a newspaper ad that stated: "Robert Bork's Position on Reproductive Rights, You Don't Have Any." Other groups, like Voters Pro Choice, urged political contributors to lobby senators for Bork's defeat. And NARAL, not given to understatement, warned that Bork might "wipe out every advance women have made in the 20th century."[15]

Prior to the hearings, Lloyd Cutler, one-time counsel to President Carter and now a supporter of Judge Bork, cautioned Bork that he had "managed to arouse the united opposition of all labor groups, all women's groups, and all civil rights groups. It's an extraordinary historical alliance. . . . "[16] Cutler felt that Judge Bork needed to separate himself from the "Meese-Reynolds school of jurisprudence." But Bork's repeated criticism of *Roe v. Wade* made it difficult for him to modify his stance, and in any event, he did not believe in some of the positions that Cutler urged him to take.

Accordingly, when abortion was discussed at the confirmation hearings, Judge Bork offered little reassurance to those who were fearful that he might vote to overrule *Roe v. Wade*. He said that while the reasoning in the *Griswold* case was "utterly inadequate,"[17] the opinion in *Roe v. Wade* "contains almost no legal reasoning."[18] He testified that if faced with the question of overruling *Roe*, he would have to consider whether a constitutional basis for a generalized right of privacy could be found and, if not, "whether the value of preserving an earlier decision was overcome by other factors."[19] He also appeared to dismiss efforts to enlist the Ninth Amendment in support of privacy claims, analogizing the vague language of that amendment to an ink blot that prevented a portion of the constitutional text from being read and must therefore be disregarded.

Despite the limited treatment of abortion at the hearings, the issue clouded the confirmation process from the beginning. Since *Roe v. Wade* was based on the right of privacy established in the *Griswold* case, senators were able to raise the specter of overruling *Roe* by focusing on Bork's criticism of *Griswold*. A few were more direct. Robert Packwood, a liberal senator who sought unsuccessfully to get assurances from Bork that he would protect abortion rights, became the first Republican to announce that he would vote against confirmation. Packwood said, "I am convinced that Judge Bork feels so strongly opposed to the right of privacy that he will do everything possible to cut and trim, and eliminate if possible, the liberties that the right to privacy protects."[20] This assessment—shared no doubt by other members of the Senate—was damaging to Bork's prospects for confirmation, but in light of Bork's public record, it was an entirely fair observation. The same cannot be said of comments made at the hearings about Bork's position on compulsory sterilization.

Perhaps no other subject led to a more striking misrepresentation of Judge Bork's legal views than questions relating to forced sterilization. The public-relations value of this line of questioning is easy to understand. Compulsory sterilization has no more popular support than anti-contraception laws. If Bork could be portrayed as one who was tolerant, or even supportive, of mandatory sterilization, the public would almost certainly believe that he was outside the mainstream of American jurists and scholars. For some, the temptation to reshape Bork's record on sterilization turned out to be irresistible.

Two sterilization cases were used as vehicles for defining the image of Robert Bork as a legal "extremist." The first was *Skinner v. Oklahoma*,[21] in which the Supreme Court invalidated a criminal statute that authorized compulsory sterilization for persons repeatedly convicted of larceny but not for those repeatedly convicted of embezzlement. Although the state could lawfully distinguish between larceny and embezzlement for some purposes, the use of that distinction was found to be unconstitutional in *Skinner* because it intruded upon the freedom of procreation, which the Court said was "fundamental to the very existence and survival of the race."[22] The *Skinner* case was later viewed as a forerunner to the establishment of a constitutional right of privacy.

In his article in the *Indiana Law Journal*, Judge Bork had argued that *Skinner* was as "improper and intellectually empty as *Griswold v. Connecticut*."[23] At the confirmation hearings, Bork said that he disagreed with the reasoning in *Skinner* but not with the result. He thought the *Skinner* statute could properly be struck down on the ground that it lacked a rational basis or possibly because it was rooted in racial discrimination. These remarks seemed to quiet the committee's concerns about *Skinner*, but opponents of confirmation soon found an even more effective weapon in an opinion authored by Judge Bork for the court of appeals in *Oil, Chemical and Atomic Workers v. American Cyanamid*.[24]

The *American Cyanamid* case arose out of an employer's exposure of its employees to ambient lead levels that would be harmful to a fetus. Because federal law required the employer to protect its employees from injury to a fetus, the company barred women of childbearing years from any department in which lead levels were excessively high. But rather than simply dismiss or transfer these women, the company informed them that if they underwent sterilization, they could keep their jobs in the department. A $10,000 fine was levied against the company on the ground that informing the women of the option of sterilization created a "hazard" in the workplace in violation of a statutory provision requiring employers to furnish employees with "a place of employment free from recognized hazards that are likely to cause death or serious physical harm. . . . "[25] Judge Bork, writing for a unanimous Court, ruled that while the company's offer of sterilization might violate other federal laws, it was not a "hazard" within the meaning of this provision.

Senator Metzenbaum challenged Bork to justify the opinion at the confirmation hearings. Metzenbaum said, "I must tell you that it is such a shocking decision, and I cannot understand how you as a jurist could put women to the choice of work or be sterilized. . . . "[26] Judge Bork, of course, had not put women to that choice. He had not even decided that it was permissible for an employer to put women to that choice; he had decided only that the employer's offer of this choice did not violate the particular statute under which a fine had been imposed. Bork attempted to explain this to the committee, stating that the statute was "concerned with physical conditions of the workplace, not with policies offering women a choice."[27] Senator Metzenbaum was not mollified. He charged that Bork "wrote an opinion which said it was okay for a company to achieve safety at the expense of women by preventing its female employees from ever having children. . . . I think it is unfair. I think it is inhumane, and maybe it somehow explains the concerns that women of this country have and have evidenced about your appointment."[28]

Of course, Bork's opinion had not said that the company's policy "was okay" or that the employer could achieve safety at the expense of women. But no response that Bork could give was as effective as the charges that Senator Metzenbaum had lodged against him. And Judge Bork, who at first had difficulty recalling the case, may have aggravated the problem by being unprepared to answer these charges, even though questions about *American Cyanamid* should have been anticipated since they had appeared in opposition literature before the hearings began. Bork said at one point that "[s]ome of [the women], I guess, did not want to have children" and that "the 5 women who . . . chose sterilization, I suppose . . . were glad to have the choice—they apparently were—that the company gave them."[29] These remarks reinforced the widely circulated charge that Judge Bork was insensitive to the plight of women and minorities.

The anti-Bork forces, sensing an opportunity to take advantage of Bork's comments, contacted Joan Bertin, an American Civil Liberties Union (ACLU) attorney who had represented Betty Riggs, one of the women who had been sterilized. At Bertin's urging, Ms. Riggs sent a letter expressing her outrage to Senator Biden and followed this with a telegram that Bertin helped her write, addressed to Senator Metzenbaum. The telegram, which Metzenbaum read at the hearings, said: "I cannot believe that Judge Bork thinks we were glad to have the choice of getting sterilized or getting fired. Only a judge who knows nothing about women who need to work could say that. . . . This was the most awful thing that happened to me."[30]

It is easy to criticize Judge Bork for his testimony about *American Cyanamid*. As Kate Michelman put it, "He came across as someone who was all head and no heart."[31] It was a mistake that future nominees would be careful not to make. They would profit from Bork's experience and learn to turn the committee's fondness for anecdotal testimony to their own advantage.[32]

But it is one thing to criticize Bork for his testimony on *American Cyanamid* and something else to justify his opponents' line of attack. The characterization of Judge Bork's position in *American Cyanamid* was one of the most disgraceful misrepresentations of his legal views in the entire confirmation proceeding. The obvious purpose of raising questions about that case was to suggest that Bork had a tolerant attitude toward forced sterilization. But no fair-minded reader of the opinion could draw any such inference from it. *American Cyanamid* decided only that the employer did not violate the statute under which a fine had been levied. The opinion explicitly left open the question whether the employer's policy might have violated other statutory provisions. It can hardly have been the position of Bork's critics that the employer's policy must violate *every* statute that addresses employer-employee relations. The appropriate question for the Judiciary Committee concerned the quality of Bork's judgment in *American Cyanamid*; in the end, he was vulnerable to attack, not for the quality of his judgment but only for the quality of his testimony about the judgment.

8

CIVIL RIGHTS

In dealing with issues of civil rights, Judge Bork found himself on the defensive from the very beginning. Shortly after the nomination was announced, Ralph Neas said that Bork would "turn back the clock on civil rights."[1] And Senator Kennedy told the Judiciary Committee that "in Robert Bork's America, there is no room at the inn for blacks and no place in the Constitution for women; and in our America, there should be no seat on the Supreme Court for Robert Bork."[2] Although Kennedy's remarks merely caricatured Judge Bork's views, they forced Bork to defend his previous opposition to civil rights laws and to a number of Supreme Court decisions on racial and gender discrimination.

RACIAL DISCRIMINATION AND VOTING

Senator Kennedy questioned Judge Bork aggressively about Bork's earlier opposition to the public accommodations provisions of the 1964 Civil Rights Act. Bork had said that Congress lacked any principled basis for protecting the freedom of blacks to patronize restaurants and hotels rather than the freedom of business owners to serve whomever they pleased. In an article published in 1963, Bork wrote:

> Of the ugliness of racial discrimination there need be no argument.
> . . . But it is one thing when stubborn people express their racial antipathies in laws which prevent individuals, whether white or Negro, from dealing with those who are willing to deal with them, and quite another to tell them that even as individuals they may not act on their racial preferences in particular areas of life. The principle of such legislation is that if I find your behavior ugly by my standards, moral or aesthetic, and if you prove stubborn about

adopting my view of the situation, I am justified in having the state coerce you into more righteous paths. That is itself a principle of unsurpassed ugliness.[3]

Bork told the Judiciary Committee that this article was written in his "libertarian days" and he later came to realize that "we never legislate on a general principle, so there is no danger that this kind of thing would expand into other areas of coercion."[4] The real question was whether the legislation would do more good than harm, and on that basis he had changed his mind about the soundness of the public accommodation provisions.

But Bork's explanation of his original position, and of his reasons for changing that position, could not match the emotional impact of testimony by John Hope Franklin and other black witnesses, who described their personal experiences with racial segregation and used those experiences to castigate Bork. Franklin told of being made to ride in the baggage section of a railway car, while white prisoners of war from Germany were allowed to sit in the coach section. He said that he was deprived of the opportunity to study for his doctorate degree at the University of Oklahoma and was denied library privileges at the University of North Carolina, solely because of his race. He also described earlier times in which he was unable to buy a hot meal in the District of Columbia because the only restaurants that served African-Americans were closed on weekends. Franklin then stated, "Nothing in Judge Bork's record suggests to me that, had he been on the Supreme Court at an earlier date, he would have had the vision and the courage to strike down a statute requiring the eviction of a black family from a train for sitting in the so-called white coach, or the rejection of a black student at a so-called white State university, or the refusal of a white restaurant owner to serve a black patron."[5]

Judge Bork's opponents also forced Bork to defend his criticism of Supreme Court decisions affecting minority rights. Senator Biden said in his opening statement at the confirmation hearings that he was concerned about Bork's criticism of the Court's opinion in *Shelley v. Kraemer*.[6] The *Shelley* case held that a state court could not legally enforce a restrictive covenant in which a homeowner had agreed not to sell his property to racial minorities. Judge Bork had criticized the opinion on the ground that it effectively converted the Fourteenth Amendment's prohibition of *governmental* discrimination into a general prohibition of *private* discrimination. Bork said that under the principle in *Shelley*, if the host of a dinner party got into a political argument with a guest and had the guest removed by the police, a court would be obliged to find "governmental action" and possibly a violation of the guest's First Amendment rights. Many constitutional scholars agreed with Bork's criticism, and in more than forty years since the *Shelley* case was decided, the Supreme Court has conspicuously avoided any use of the rationale of *Shelley v. Kraemer*. Nevertheless, by raising questions about Bork's criticism of the opinion, Senator Biden made it appear that Bork was in favor of restrictive covenants or, at least, in favor of permitting them to be judicially enforced.

Judge Bork was also asked to explain his criticism of *Harper v. Virginia State Board of Elections*,[7] which held that the right to vote could not be conditioned upon the payment of a state poll tax. The Supreme Court found that disenfranchisement for failure to pay the poll tax would deprive some voters, especially the poor, of equal protection of the laws. Bork had criticized the decision on the ground that the equal protection clause was meant to outlaw racial discrimination, not economic discrimination, and no evidence was presented in the *Harper* case to show that the poll tax was enforced in a racially discriminatory way. Nevertheless, it was awkward for Bork to argue that he was defending only a wealth classification rather than a racial classification, even though lawyers understand that wealth classifications are commonplace and are generally upheld if they rest on some reasonable basis.[8]

Reynolds v. Sims[9] was another voting rights decision criticized by Judge Bork. That case established the "one man, one vote" rule, which required state legislative districts to be equal in population so that each voter would have an equal voice in electing a representative. In a 1968 article published by *Fortune* magazine, Bork said that "on no reputable theory of constitutional adjudication was there an excuse for the doctrine [*Reynolds*] imposed." He believed that if the legislature had a rational basis for its apportionment decisions and there was no systematic frustration of majority will, those decisions should be upheld.[10] *Reynolds v. Sims* has also been criticized on the ground that the legislative power to redraw district lines gives public officials as much freedom to dilute the voting strength of a particular group as they had during the years of numerical malapportionment. Often, district lines are now drawn in a way that makes it difficult for the majority party to lose seats in the next election. Thus, the facial equality required by *Reynolds* typically leads to another type of discrimination, based largely on political or ethnic affiliations.

Reynolds v. Sims, like the *Harper* case, involved no racially discriminatory purpose. However, former Congresswoman Barbara Jordan testified to the practical impact of reapportionment on her political career. She told the Judiciary Committee that when she ran for the Texas legislature in 1964, she lost by sixty-four thousand votes. But two years later, after the Texas legislature was required to be reapportioned, she ran again and was elected. Her testimony suggested that legislative malapportionment may have discriminatory effects, even when it lacks a racially discriminatory purpose. Although Bork could give reasoned explanations for his criticism of *Reynolds* and of other Supreme Court decisions, the cumulative impact of the discussion of those cases was to create a strong impression that Bork was insensitive—or, worse yet, simply indifferent—to legitimate concerns of racial minorities and the poor.

GENDER DISCRIMINATION

Senator Dennis DeConcini questioned Bork at length on issues of gender discrimination. He asked whether Bork believed the equal protection clause applies to women. Bork replied that "everybody is covered—men, women, everybody."[11] The equal protection clause, he said, "means what the words say—all persons are protected against unreasonable legislative classifications." Bork explained that even though the original purpose of the equal protection clause was to provide equality for blacks, the clause is not by its terms limited to racial discrimination, and he would not confine it to matters of race.[12] This represented quite a change from Bork's earlier assertion that the Supreme Court had no legitimate basis for expanding the equal protection clause beyond its original purpose.

In his 1971 article in the *Indiana Law Journal*, Bork had written that the equal protection clause requires "that government not discriminate along racial lines. But much more than that cannot properly be read into the clause. . . . "[13] And just three months before the confirmation hearings, Bork said that the equal protection clause should have been "kept to things like race or ethnicity."[14]

In his testimony before the Judiciary Committee, Bork said he differed with the Supreme Court on what the proper test is for measuring claims to equal protection. He then suggested for the first time that a "reasonable basis" test be applied to all equal protection cases.

Traditionally, the Supreme Court has applied a reasonableness standard to most "nonsuspect" classifications.[15] However, the Court gives strict scrutiny to racial classifications, typically requiring that they be shown to have been necessary to some compelling state interest.[16] And gender classifications are subjected to intermediate scrutiny, meaning that they must be substantially related to an important governmental interest.[17] Bork proposed that instead of using this "three-tier" system, all state classifications should be tested under a reasonableness standard.

Bork said his approach was similar to that advanced by Justice Stevens, one of the more "liberal" members of the Supreme Court. He also stated that the legal results under a reasonableness standard would be comparable to the results produced by the Court's three-tier system. Bork explained that under his approach very few racial classifications could be shown to be reasonable,[18] and perhaps not many more gender classifications would be found reasonable.[19]

But even if Bork adopted the same test as Justice Stevens, he would not necessarily apply that test the same way. For example, in *Craig v. Boren*,[20] Justice Stevens voted to invalidate an Oklahoma statute that prohibited the sale of "nonintoxicating 3.2% beer" to males under the age of twenty-one or to females under the age of eighteen. Justice Stevens acknowledged certain empirical evidence that suggested that 2 percent of males between the ages of eighteen and twenty were arrested for driving under the influence of alcohol, while only .18 percent of the females in that age group were arrested for the same offense. But Stevens thought it unlikely that the Oklahoma statute would "have a significant deterrent effect on either the 2% or the law-abiding 98%," and he said that the misconduct of a small number of young men could not justify a gender-based ban on the other 98 percent.[21]

Judge Bork, on the other hand, believed that *Craig v. Boren* had trivialized the federal Constitution. He told the Judiciary Committee: "You would have thought it was the Steel Seizure Case the way they went at it. And I thought, as a matter of fact, the differential drinking age probably is justified because they . . . had evidence that there was a problem with young men drinking more than there was with young women drinking."[22] Ultimately, the difference in the conclusions reached by Stevens and Bork was not a product of methodology. Instead, it was a difference in result caused by the fact that Bork was willing to give more deference to legislative judgments using gender classifications than Justice Stevens was.

Bork's supporters worked hard to find Fourteenth Amendment cases in which Bork had argued for gender equality. Gary Born cited a case in which Bork had submitted a brief as solicitor general, arguing that "the Equal Protection Clause prohibits the assignment of [male and female] students to separate high schools, where the schools do not provide substantially equal educational facilities and professional opportunities" for boys and girls.[23] Bork's brief noted that the boys' high school in that case had a better library, superior science facilities, a more prominent body of graduates, a greater endowment, and a better overall reputation. The brief urged that the case be remanded for a determination as to whether the girls were injured professionally by receiving an inferior education.[24]

Born also cited a case in which Bork had concurred in a ruling that male prisoners should be allowed to show that their petitions for parole were judged under a more stringent standard than the petitions of female prisoners.[25] Born argued that if Judge Bork was receptive to a claim of discrimination by male prisoners, he surely would be receptive to claims of gender discrimination by women. However, Professor Sylvia Law noted that Bork's opinion had focused on statutory questions and had devoted less than one page to the sex discrimination claim. Law pointed out that Bork's opinion said nothing about the constitutional standard that he would apply to laws discriminating on the basis of sex.

One might well think that if Bork's views on the statutory rights of male prisoners revealed little about how Bork would treat constitutional claims of gender discrimination, the same would be said of his views on the statutory right to be free from sexual harassment. Yet critics like Professor Barbara Babcock of Stanford insisted that Bork's opinion in *Vinson v. Taylor*,[26] a case that involved questions about the statutory meaning of sex harassment, had demonstrated a lack of commitment to women's rights.[27] In *Vinson*, a female employee filed a sex harassment charge under Title VII of the 1964 Civil Rights Act, stating that she had a sexual relationship with a supervisor at her place of employment because of fear that she might lose her job if she refused. The trial court rejected her claim on the ground that the sexual relationship was voluntary. The court of appeals reversed that decision because the trial judge had not considered whether the supervisor's conduct might have created a hostile work environment, even if the sexual relationship was "voluntary." The defendant then sought a rehearing, which the court of appeals denied, and Judges Bork, Scalia, and Starr dissented. Bork thought that in some cases, voluntariness should be a defense to a charge of sex harassment because otherwise "sexual dalliance, however voluntarily engaged in, becomes harassment whenever an employee sees fit, after the fact, so to characterize it."[28]

Upon review of the *Vinson* case, the Supreme Court ruled that voluntariness was not a defense to a sex harassment charge but said a showing that the conduct of the alleged harasser was *welcome* would be a defense.[29] Judge Bork might well assert that a showing of voluntariness could have a significant bearing on whether a sexual relationship was welcome. In any event, it is quite a reach to suggest that his opinion demonstrates that he opposes or is indifferent to women's rights. Indeed, the Supreme Court in *Vinson* agreed with much of Judge Bork's opinion. Bork had said that evidence of the woman's behavior and dress should have been admitted because it was relevant to the issue of whether the sexual advances were solicited. The Supreme Court subsequently ruled that Bork was basically correct on this point; the employee's dress was relevant to the issue of whether the advances were welcome. Bork had also argued that an employer should not automatically be liable for the hostile work environment created by an employee, especially if the employer was unaware of the employee's conduct. The Supreme Court agreed that an employer should not automatically be liable, although it held that lack of notice would not necessarily insulate an employer from liability.[30]

THE SOUTHERN STRATEGY

The civil rights debate about Judge Bork was an important part of what his opponents called their "southern strategy." Basically, the strategy was designed to appeal to the fear of southern voters that Bork's appointment to the Court would result in refighting the civil rights battles of the 1960s. Since neither blacks nor whites in the south wanted to see old wounds reopened, the appeal was highly successful.

One factor contributing to the effectiveness of this strategy was the influence of black voters in the South. Blacks had a major impact on the 1986 election that turned the Republican's fifty-three to forty-seven majority in the Senate into a forty-five to fifty-five minority. Several of the newly elected Democratic senators achieved narrow victories only because of the solid support of black voters. For example, Senator Terry Sanford of North Carolina received just 42 percent of the white vote but 88 percent of the black vote. Senator John Breaux received 39 percent of the white vote in Louisiana and 85 percent of the black vote. Similarly, Senator Wyche Fowler of Georgia received 39 percent of the white vote and 82 percent of the black vote, while Senator Richard Shelby of Alabama received 38 percent of the white vote and 88 percent of the black vote. Finally, Senator Howell Heflin had been reelected in 1984 with 46 percent of the white vote and 81 percent of the black vote.

Claims that Bork would "turn back the clock on civil rights" produced a firestorm of black opposition to his confirmation. The resulting pressure was simply too strong for southern Democratic senators to resist. As Senator Breaux said: "If you vote against Bork, those in favor of him will be mad at you for a week. But if you vote for him, those who don't like him will be mad at you for the rest of their lives."

Bork's opponents were quite successful in convincing the public in general, and southern blacks in particular, that Bork's confirmation would be a setback for civil rights. Bork's own speeches and articles were used against him with dramatic effect. In some cases, his views were oversimplified or caricatured, but it seems clear that Bork would construe the equal protection clause more narrowly than many other federal judges. Bork's opponents also succeeded in putting a human face on civil rights issues by having witnesses testify about what it would have meant to them personally for Bork to have been on the Supreme Court when various legal questions were decided. In the end, southern Democratic senators, who had been elected with a minority of the white vote and an overwhelming majority of the black vote, simply could not afford to alienate a vital base of political support by voting for Bork's confirmation.

9
THE REVEREND
AND THE RABBI:
CHURCH-STATE ISSUES

Both the Democratic majority of the Judiciary Committee and their Republican counterparts took pains to find witnesses who would support their positions on whether Judge Bork's confirmation would pose a threat to the separation of church and state. A Democratic staff member called the Brookings Institution and spoke with James Dunn, who served as executive director for the Joint Baptist Committee of Public Affairs. Dunn volunteered that Judge Bork had had a heated exchange with Reverend Ken Dean during a seminar at Brookings in 1985. Reverend Dean, a pastor of the First Baptist Church of Rochester, had also authored a brief article that excoriated Bork for creating "a verbal brawl about the role of religion in American society" during an appearance at the Brookings seminar. Dean wrote that Judge Bork "is to the law and the Supreme Court what Lt. Col. Ollie North was to the White House and the National Security Council."[1] Arrangements were made by majority staff members for the committee to hear Reverend Dean's testimony. Dean then prepared an eleven-page statement and loaded his Volkswagen van for a trip to Washington with his teenage daughter and her girlfriend.

At about this same time, the minority staff of the Judiciary Committee was arranging to call its own witnesses on church-state issues. The staff had received a letter from the Union of Orthodox Rabbis of the United States and Canada; and a decision was made to schedule Rabbi William Handler, a member of that organization, to testify before the committee. The staff had not debriefed Rabbi Handler, but it was known that his testimony would be favorable to Judge Bork. What was not known was that Handler's appearance, like that of Reverend Dean, would be accompanied by some of the most serious charges yet leveled against the committee and its confirmation processes. Together, the reverend and the rabbi would set off a series of unexpected explosions at a time when the committee looked forward to bringing its hearings to a quiet conclusion. But while fireworks of this sort were not typical of the Bork hearings, the committee's treatment of church-state issues was entirely in keeping with its approach to other sensitive constitutional problems.

On Monday, September 28, Reverend Dean met with Mike Epstein and Ron LeGrande, who worked for Democratic members of the committee. A reporter for the *Rochester Democrat and Chronicle*, who was also present during the meeting, noticed a "Biden for President" sticker on the outside of the office.[2] The purpose of the meeting was to debrief Dean before his formal testimony, as was customary for witnesses called by the majority. The committee minority, with its smaller staff and budget, followed a different practice and sometimes accused the majority of "orchestrating" its witnesses. Some minority staffers even believed that certain witnesses called by the majority were allowed to prepare questions to be asked of them by Democratic senators.[3]

Reverend Dean spent an hour talking with Epstein and LeGrande about the testimony that he planned to give before the committee.[4] He was first asked what he would say about Judge Bork being an agnostic. Dean replied that Bork had characterized himself as an agnostic at the Brookings seminar but had quickly retracted that characterization. Dean was not sure that this was something his interviewers wanted to hear, but he was determined to call the shots as he saw them. He also hoped that his candor on this point would add to his overall credibility. Reverend Dean was then asked about the article he had written on Judge Bork's speech at the Brookings Institute. He responded by giving Epstein and LeGrande copies of his prepared testimony. Both men were quite impressed. One said, "This is powerful stuff," and neither saw any problem with the testimony. They told Dean that his statement was important and that "we're glad you are going to say it." Dean then went out to lunch, since he was not due to testify until later in the day. He decided on a bland meal because he did not want to get heartburn. As matters turned out, he was in for more than a little heartburn.

After returning from lunch, Dean was again taken aside by Ron

LeGrande. To his astonishment, Dean was told, "They do not want you to testify." It seemed that three or four people had wanted to testify on the church-state issue, and the committee majority had decided not to get into the issue. Other prospective witnesses had agreed to withdraw their testimony, and Dean was asked to do the same.[5]

Reverend Dean became angry, though he was able to keep his composure. Dean, a former executive director of the Mississippi Council on Human Relations, had been involved with liberal causes in illiberal times and places. He was not accustomed to walking away from a fight on a matter of principle and believed he was testifying as a representative of Americans United for Church and State and of the Joint Baptist Committee of Public Affairs. He told LeGrande in no uncertain terms that the staff had gotten him involved, had looked over his testimony, and now were saying they did not want him. Dean then played his trump card: "Tell Senator Biden we have a problem. If he blocks me from testifying, I will walk into the Rotunda Room and read my testimony and give a press conference."[6]

LeGrande went into the Judiciary Committee staff office, where a number of senators, including Senator Biden, had gone earlier. While LeGrande was gone, Dean told the Rochester reporter that "[i]f they don't want to hear my testimony, they are weak people." LeGrande came out shortly thereafter and spoke with Dean. In that conversation, he indicated that it looked as though things had been worked out, and Dean would be permitted to testify. This was confirmed soon after LeGrande finished talking with Dean. Senator Biden walked into the hallway, and Dean approached him, saying, "I'm Ken Dean. I have a problem." In a hushed tone, Biden replied: "I know we have a problem. You are going to testify. . . . Just don't screw us up too bad."[7]

Reverend Dean testified later that day. His testimony focused on Judge Bork's appearance at the Brookings Institution in 1985. Dean characterized Bork's presentation as a "call for a new weighting between church and state,"[8] a call that had produced heated and emotional debate. Dean urged the committee to look carefully at Bork's speeches and not be "too anxious and too sensitive about the issue of religion." Reverend Dean proceeded to give a detailed description of his own encounter with Judge Bork during the question and answer period at Brookings. Dean testified that he had related to Judge Bork an experience he had as a junior high school teacher in Florida in 1961. Dean had described to Bork the school's practice of "home room devotions," in which each student was expected to take a turn at reading the Bible aloud, sometimes leading with the Lord's Prayer and always saluting the American flag. The students were chosen to lead the classroom devotions in alphabetical order.

One morning a thirteen-year-old boy was waiting for Dean before the beginning of class. It was his turn to lead the group. The boy explained that he was Jewish and that his parents did not want him to lead the class in devotion. Dean told the boy that he could read from the Old Testament rather than the New Testament, but the boy replied that his parents did not want him to participate at all. They believed that religious instruction should be given at home and in the synagogue.

Dean recounted that the boy asked him if he had to do the reading, and Dean told him that he did not. The boy asked what Dean wanted him to do. Dean inferred that the boy wanted to know if he should absent himself from the class and stand in the hall, as was the custom for those who did not want to participate. Dean, sensing the boy's dilemma in not wanting to distance himself socially from his peers, told him that he could remain in his seat while someone else led the devotion.

Dean then asked Judge Bork if he thought that a thirteen-year-old should have to submit to this kind of conflict, hurt and embarrassment, in order to participate in public education. It was an incisive question that went to the heart of the Supreme Court decisions banning officially prescribed prayer in public schools. Dean's clear recollection, which is supported by others who attended the meeting, was that Bork "in a terse voice and with a stern look on his face" replied, "Well, I suppose he got over it, didn't he?" According to Dean, this remark stunned participants at the seminar, who did not know how to respond to such a display of insensitivity.[9] Dean felt he "touched something in Bork that caused a disclosure of his true feelings, which reflected a repressed facet of his personality." After an awkward silence, Bork added that when he was a young boy he had been exposed to a variety of religious beliefs and that it didn't seem to do him any harm.

Reverend Dean's testimony was not well received. As one newspaper reported, "[It] wasn't what Republicans or Democrats wanted to hear," and Dean faced "shabby treatment" from both sides.[10] Senator Humphrey, a conservative from New Hampshire and a strong Bork supporter, was especially upset by Dean's remarks. Many of Bork's supporters were outraged that Bork had already been painted as a "racist" and a "sterilizer," and they were not going to countenance any suggestion of anti-Semitism. Humphrey stated, "I don't know whose idea it was to call Reverend Dean, but if the idea was to create the impression of anti-semitism, it's rubbish."[11] Humphrey pointed out that as a young attorney, Bork had been instrumental in reversing the decision of Kirkland & Ellis, a prestigious law firm in Chicago, to deny a partnership to an attorney in the firm simply because he was Jewish. Humphrey also noted that Bork's first wife, who died of cancer, had been Jewish and that two individuals who had strong influence on Bork's professional life, Professors Alexander Bickel and Aaron Director, were also Jewish. Humphrey added: "[If] the idea is to create the impression that, in private, or in the Brookings Institution, Robert Bork called for some kind of state-sponsored religion, that too is rubbish. I find this whole episode of this last half-hour easily the most distasteful of this entire two weeks of hearings. Again, I don't know who recommended or who is responsible for calling this witness, but it stinks."

Put on the defensive, Senator Biden responded that no one had accused Judge Bork of anti-Semitism. He read into the record Bork's earlier testimony that "I'm certain that I did not say a thing like that about 'a Jewish boy will get over it' . . . I do not know what I said but if I said anything—it must have been in front of a group."[12] Unfortunately for Bork, the group, or at least those who remembered the exchange, supported Dean's version of the event. Reverend Dean agreed that Judge Bork is not anti-Semitic but said Bork "espouses a philosophical understanding of government . . . which leaves open the door for others to be anti-semitic and for others to be racist."[13]

Senator Biden also mentioned that Judge Bork had introduced two letters from participants at the Brookings seminar, including one from Rabbi Joshua O. Haberman of the Washington Hebrew Congregation. Haberman wrote to the *Washington Post*: "As a Rabbi, with a strong commitment to the separation of church and state, I would have been greatly alarmed if Judge Bork had expressed any tendency to move away from our Constitutional guarantee of religious freedom and equality. I heard nothing of the sort."[14]

One participant at the Brookings seminar was rather surprised by Rabbi Haberman's letter in light of remarks that the rabbi himself had made at the seminar.[15] During the question and answer session following Bork's speech, Rabbi Haberman had said to Bork, "You have held up to us the European model [of the relationship between church and state]." Haberman, speaking in a thick Austrian brogue, then asked pointedly, "Why do you think we came here?" Bork was taken aback by

Haberman's remark and did not know how to respond.[16] Some have speculated that Rabbi Haberman, who maintains close contacts with conservative think tanks like the American Enterprise Institute and the Heritage Foundation, had written to the *Washington Post* with that constituency in mind.

Reverend Dean was clearly right on one substantive point: Judge Bork's views on church-state issues deserved far more careful treatment than they received at the hands of the Judiciary Committee. Bork had delivered at least two significant speeches on church-state matters. The first was given at the University of Chicago in November 1984;[17] the second, which was substantially similar in content, was the presentation at the Brookings Institution that became the subject of Reverend Dean's testimony.[18] In these talks, Judge Bork described the three-part test used by the Supreme Court to determine whether government action violates the constitutional prohibition against laws "respecting an establishment of religion." The three-part test provides essentially that government action (1) must have a secular purpose, (2) must have a primary effect that neither advances nor inhibits religion, and (3) must cause no excessive entanglement between religion and government. Judge Bork said that the test was "not useful in enforcing the values underlying the establishment clause," and he proceeded to criticize each aspect of the Court's test.

The first part of the test, prohibiting governmental action animated by a religious purpose, could not be squared in Bork's view with government activity that is known to be constitutionally valid. He gave as examples presidential proclamations that were explicitly religious and legislative appropriations for the payment of salaries to military and other chaplains. The second part of the test, calling upon judges to distinguish between primary and secondary religious effects, he found too difficult to administer and, like the first part, contrary to the weight of historical evidence. Finally, the third part, which prohibits excessive entanglement of government and religion, he said, "is impossible to satisfy," since the "government is inevitably entangled with religion." Judge Bork made no mention of the fact that this rule bars "excessive" entanglements rather than all interconnections between church and state. Perhaps he finds the line between excessive and nonexcessive entanglements unduly tenuous; but it is difficult to avoid some such line if "government is inevitably entangled with religion," unless one is willing to dispense entirely with the "wall of separation" between church and state.

After criticizing the existing rules, Judge Bork predicted that "we may see a major recasting of doctrine" in establishment clause cases not because the attitude of the Court will change but because "present doctrine is so unsatisfactory." He added that "a relaxation of current rigidly secularist doctrine would . . . permit some sensible things to be done" and that "the greatest perceived change would be in the reintroduction of some religion into public schools and some greater religious symbolism in our public life."

Although Bork conceded that the failure to maintain strict separation between church and state can lead to political divisiveness, he asserted that such separation may have similar divisive effects. He noted that religious people may be as upset by attempts to remove religion from public life as others are by attempts to maintain or restore it. Accordingly, Judge Bork urged that more deference be paid in this area to the desires of the political majority, a position consistent with his general philosophy that legislation adopted by elected representatives should not be overturned without a clear constitutional mandate. Bork also urged the Court to resist the trend toward a privatization of morality, whether in religious spheres or in nonreligious areas like obscenity or human sexuality.

Judge Bork emphasized in his speeches that the current law under the establishment clause is "designed to erase all traces of religion in governmental action, to produce, as Richard John Neuhaus put it, a 'public square naked of religious symbol and substance.'" He argued that "if religion is officially removed from public celebration, other transcendent principles, some of them very ugly indeed, may replace them." He concluded by again quoting Neuhaus with approval: "'There is nothing in store but a continuing and deepening crisis of legitimacy if courts persist in systematically ruling out of order the moral traditions in which Western law has developed and which bear, for the overwhelming majority of the American people, a living sense of right and wrong. The result, quite literally, is the outlawing of the basis of law.'"

Judge Bork's references to Richard John Neuhaus were not lost on members of the Brookings audience, many of whom were familiar with Neuhaus's work and were quite critical of it. When the floor was opened to questions, a vigorous debate ensued. Nearly all of the questioners challenged Bork's presentation in one way or another, although only three or four expressed strong opposition. Judge Bork, an experienced and skillful academician, appeared to enjoy the exchange, but at the end of the evening he allowed that "I now know better than to quote Neuhaus before you religious types."[19]

Despite a rich source of available information, there was virtually no discussion of Bork's views on church-state issues at the confirmation hearings. The only witness to testify on those issues besides Reverend Dean, and for a few moments Judge Bork himself, was Rabbi William Handler. The rabbi testified on Wednesday, September 30, just two days after Reverend Dean. Rabbi Handler began his testimony with a startling accusation in which he claimed that Diana Huffman, chief investigator for the majority staff, had tried to manipulate him into not testifying.[20] Rabbi Handler stated that he had received two telephone calls from Melissa Nolan, an investigative clerk on the minority staff of the Judiciary Committee. In the first call, Ms. Nolan asked him his name and the organization he represented. She called him back half an hour later to tell him that he would be testifying on the fourth panel and to explain when and where he should appear.

Rabbi Handler testified that about an hour later he received a call from Rabbi Hirsch Ginzburg, the executive director of Handler's organization. Rabbi Ginzburg told Handler that Ginzburg had received a call from Diana Huffman. She told him that due to a change in procedure, Rabbi Handler was not to appear and that there would be no outside witnesses on the day he had been scheduled to testify. Diana Huffman allegedly told Rabbi Ginzburg that Handler should submit a written memorandum and that the Committee would publicize it at a later date.

Rabbi Handler termed this conduct a "shabby trick to be played on a reputable Jewish organization, to try to censor our views by telling us, falsely . . . that I am not to appear because of policy considerations." He believed this was an unfair attempt to manipulate the process and that it was "shameful." Handler added that he thought Ms. Huffman should be fired for this conduct. Senator Biden, visibly embarrassed, said: "We will look into it. . . . You are welcome. Now, please testify. Within five minutes."[21] Given an opportunity to comment later, Ms. Huffman said that Rabbi Handler was "100% in error," but when asked for specifics, she refused to elaborate.[22]

On substantive issues, Rabbi Handler testified that he supported the confirmation of Judge Bork because Bork favors the Framers' views of the Constitution. Rabbi Handler argued that the Framers "believed that there would be a multi-denominational establishment of church in this country, and that there would be freedom of religion, not freedom from religion." He added that "decent moral parents . . . find it very difficult to raise children in this inhospitable super-secular atmosphere that has been created as a result of the Supreme Court's extreme separation of church and state which was never intended."[23] Rabbi Handler said that Judge Bork "has the old traditional viewpoints. He is not that kind of liberal whose mind is so open that his brain falls out."[24]

The senators did not know quite how to handle Rabbi Handler. Senator Leahy, a Bork opponent, suggested that Rabbi Handler might find Judge Bork's view on parochial schools troubling because Bork disagreed with the reasoning in two cases holding that states could not require children to attend public schools nor forbid schools from teaching foreign languages. Senator Leahy argued that "both these precedents would seem really essential to protect the Jewish parochial school,"[25] a suggestion that rested on the dubious assumption that the states would reenact the two prohibitions if given the chance. Rabbi Handler countered that perhaps Senator Leahy misunderstood Judge Bork. As Senator Humphrey later pointed out, Judge Bork in fact agreed with the results in the two cases, although Bork had suggested that the grounds for decision should have been different.

The committee's treatment of church-state issues left much to be desired. The problems were both substantive and procedural. First, there is the matter of Rabbi Handler's charge that the committee staff attempted to manipulate the process to prevent his testimony. That charge has never been convincingly rebutted. Although Senator Biden promised that "we will look into it,"[26] no evidence has been found that the committee ever investigated the matter. Diana Huffman, who was accused by Rabbi Handler of making the deceptive phone call, says the rabbi was "100% in error" but offers no evidence to support her denial. Ms. Huffman claims that anyone who wished was given an opportunity to speak at the hearings.[27] Yet it is clear that other prospective witnesses were asked by Democratic staffers not to testify. There is no doubt that this was Reverend Dean's experience, and he was told by staff members that three or four others had agreed to withdraw their testimony. At least one of the others, Reverend Dean Kelley of the National Council of Churches, has confirmed that after speaking with Diana Huffman about whether the church-state issue should be pursued, he decided not to testify.[28] Given this state of the record, Rabbi Handler's charge of manipulation leaves a serious cloud hanging over the issue of fairness of the confirmation hearings. If the rabbi's charge of unfairness stood alone, it might be dismissed as the product of a misunderstanding. Unfortunately, that charge, as will be seen in later chapters, does not stand alone.

Second, the committee's attention to substantive issues of church and state was woefully inadequate. Although it is sometimes suggested that the committee labored under an insufficient record of Judge Bork's views on these matters, there was in fact ample evidence of Bork's positions on church-state issues. Bork had called for "a relaxation of current, rigidly secularist doctrine," which he found "so unsatisfactory," and had attacked each aspect of the Supreme Court's three-part test of constitutionality. Such a relaxation, he believed, would lead to "the reintroduction of some religion into public schools and some greater religious symbolism in our public life." His criticism of the establishment clause cases was no less strident than his criticism of other Supreme Court decisions to which the committee devoted great attention. But a number of the establishment clause rulings, including the school prayer cases,[29] were quite unpopular with the general public. It was, therefore, politically hazardous to attack Bork's views on the establishment clause. Just as the committee resisted the opportunity to criticize Bork's position on the abortion cases and concentrated instead on his criticism of politically more popular decisions protecting the right to use contraceptives, so too it resisted Reverend Dean's invitation to scrutinize Bork's views on church-state issues. Yet by concentrating on the politically popular opinions that Bork had attacked, the committee appeared to legitimize the criticism of those who said the entire confirmation process had been politicized. The fact that the decision to restrict the inquiry into church-state questions was made near the end of the hearings, when Bork's nomination was faltering, seemed to reflect an attitude of leaving "well enough alone" and thereby gave added support to the charge of politicization.

But if the committee's treatment of church-state issues was inadequate, it is no less true that Judge Bork's own performance at the confirmation hearings was sadly wanting on those issues. Bork told the committee that his criticism of the Court's establishment clause cases was only "on the margin." Yet there was substantial evidence of deep dissatisfaction on his part with those cases. Although Bork testified that he had criticized just two Supreme Court decisions in this area, the more important fact is that he severely attacked the Court's underlying test of constitutionality and thereby raised the prospect of undermining a number of other establishment clause cases as well. In the church-state area, as in other areas, Judge Bork appeared to moderate his views before the committee and to create the impression that he, like retiring Justice Lewis Powell, was essentially a centrist. The result was a charge of "confirmation conversion" from which Bork would never be able to extricate himself. Judge Bork thus found himself in a difficult, perhaps impossible, position. If he adhered to his earlier positions, he ran the risk of being viewed as an extremist. But if he attempted to depart from those positions, he was accused of posturing for the purpose of securing Senate confirmation.

10
FREE SPEECH

While it may have been politically hazardous to attack Judge Bork's position on the establishment clause, issues of free speech provided an inviting target for Bork's opponents. Bork's views on freedom of speech were well documented. Moreover, some members of the Judiciary Committee thought those views were out of step both with Supreme Court rulings and with the sentiments of the general public.

In his article in the *Indiana Law Journal*,[1] Bork had taken the position that only speech that is explicitly political should be given constitutional protection. Other forms of expression, whether "scientific, literary . . . or pornographic," he believed, provided no basis for protection under the First Amendment. Furthermore, even political speech would be unprotected if it advocated forcible overthrow of the government. The latter view was in direct conflict with the Supreme Court's decision in *Brandenburg v. Ohio*[2] and was the subject of much discussion at the confirmation hearings. As Bork himself would concede, his theory of free speech might well "strike a chill into the hearts of some civil libertarians."[3]

An initial premise of Bork's article was that the history of the adoption of the First Amendment provided little help in developing principles of free speech. According to Bork, the Framers had no coherent theory of free speech and were not greatly interested in the subject. The amendment was hastily drafted, and because its history offered little assistance, the construction of a free speech theory was left to later development. Bork agreed that the very existence of the First Amendment indicated that "there is something special about speech." But at this point he committed what he described at the hearings as a "logical fallacy."[4]

Bork had stated in his article that freedom for political speech would have to be protected, even if the First Amendment did not exist. The fact that the Constitution creates a system of representative democracy would require protection for political speech because that form of government would be "meaningless without freedom to discuss government and its politics." During questioning by Senator Leahy, Judge Bork discussed his logical fallacy: "If political speech would have to be protected anyway, then why did they put the [first] amendment in? And why did they speak of freedom of the press, which is not restricted to political speech?"[5] His conclusion was that the category of protected speech must be broader than he had previously believed. Significantly, this change in thinking made an attack on Bork's position more difficult for his opponents to mount.

The modern law of free speech, as Bork acknowledged in his article, grew out of several World War I decisions by the Supreme Court. Ironically, the law was based on a series of dissenting and concurring opinions rather than on any majority opinion. More precisely, it was the minority opinions of Justices Holmes and Brandeis that had such a profound influence on First Amendment case law.[6] As Bork noted, Justice Brandeis had described four basic functions or benefits of free speech: (1) the development of the faculties of the individual, (2) the happiness derived from engaging in the activity, (3) the provision of a safety valve for society, and (4) the discovery and dissemination of political truth. From these basic functions, it was possible to determine what kind of speech should be protected.

The first two functions listed by Brandeis did not distinguish speech from any other form of human activity. An individual could develop his or her faculties and derive happiness in any number of ways. As Bork saw it, "speech with only the first two benefits can be preferred to other activities only by ranking forms of personal gratification." Because these functions were indistinguishable from those of other human activities, Bork believed that a principled judge could not "on neutral grounds, choose to protect speech that has only these functions more than he protects any other claimed freedom."[7]

The third benefit of speech—the so-called "safety valve" function—relates not simply to the gratification of the individual but to the welfare of society as a whole. However, this safety valve function, Bork thought, could raise only issues of expediency or prudence, which should be determined by the executive and legislative branches of government. The bottom line was that decisions involving "judgments of expediency are for the political branches and not for the judiciary." Thus, as Bork viewed it, only the fourth function of speech—discovery of political truth—is different from any other form of human activity, and even that difference existed only with respect to "expressly and predominantly political speech." "All other forms of speech," Bork wrote, merely raise "issues of human gratification and their protection against legislative regulation involves the judge in making decisions of the sort made in *Griswold v. Connecticut.*"[8]

But even before his nomination to the Supreme Court, Judge Bork had concluded that no workable test could be devised for determining what constitutes "political speech." In part, this change in Bork's thinking resulted from a change in political realities. In testimony at his confirmation hearings, Bork noted that because of "the spread of government throughout life . . . the area of what is political or what affects politics has expanded enormously. . . . " Limiting constitutional protection to explicitly political speech became, in Bork's words, "just silly, and the more I thought about it, the sillier it became."[9]

At the hearings, it was Senator Leahy and Senator Specter who raised most of the questions about free speech. Senator Leahy began by quoting the segment of Bork's article that described the boundaries of protected speech. The stated purpose of Leahy's questions was to discover the evolution, "if there is one," in Bork's views on free speech. Leahy wasted no time in getting to the heart of the matter. He asked how far Bork's views had moved since publication of the article in the *Indiana Law Journal.* Judge Bork's surprising answer was brief and to the point. On First Amendment law, he said he was now "about . . . where the Supreme Court currently is."[10] Senator Specter was to note later in the confirmation hearings that if this was so, the hearings could be very brief. However, further questioning did little to resolve the matter. In fact, the free speech waters seemed to get muddier as time went on.

After eliciting the statement that Bork was now "about where the Supreme Court currently is," Senator Leahy tried to find out just what the word "about" might mean. Judge Bork stated that political speech is at the core of the First Amendment but that no bright-line test is available to determine when speech is political in nature. Asked by Leahy whether there are First Amendment rights outside the political core, Bork replied, "Certainly." When asked what kind of expression might not be protected, Judge Bork simply said, "Pornography."[11] It seemed that the Robert Bork who testified before the Judiciary Committee held very different views from the First Amendment scholar who had written the *Indiana Law Journal* article. However, skeptics still remained.

In a complicated exchange later in the hearings, Senator Specter attempted to define the scope of the exception created for speech that is pornographic.[12] Specter apparently thought that Bork would permit speech to be restricted whenever a state court determined that the speech was pornographic. To support this interpretation, Specter quoted a statement in Bork's article asserting that "there is no basis for judicial intervention to protect that variety of expression we call obscene or pornographic." Specter took this statement to mean that if a state court found a speech to be obscene, the Supreme Court could not even consider whether the finding of obscenity was legally justified. Judge Bork's testimony to the contrary did not seem to satisfy Senator Specter. In trying to state his position succinctly, Bork said: "The [Supreme] Court must protect speech that the first amendment covers. It must not protect speech that the first amendment does not cover and which a community wishes to outlaw. A community's definition or characterization of a particular magazine or book or movie as 'pornographic' cannot be taken as final."[13] Indeed, if a community's characterization were final, a state could effectively censor speech by simply calling it "pornographic." After Judge Bork stated that the Supreme Court must rely on its own definition of obscenity, Senator Specter asked, "Isn't it exactly the same, that the Supreme Court must make a determination as to what is equal protection of the law, and . . . as to what is due process of law?" When Bork answered in the affirmative, Specter responded that the main thrust of Bork's writing was that the Court should not make such interpretations without a specific constitutional provision. But as Bork noted, the First Amendment guarantee of free speech is just such a specific provision. No question of judicial legitimacy arises in First Amendment cases because that guarantee constitutes a specific mandate for judicial intervention. Senator Specter nevertheless insisted that "it all depends on whether the Court, legitimately, may apply the first amendment to pornography cases, and you have said that they should not."[14] But Judge Bork, of course, was speaking of cases found by the United States Supreme Court to involve obscenity. That is an entirely different matter from rejecting judicial intervention whenever a state *believes* that obscenity is involved.

In a later round of questioning, Senator Leahy returned to this issue after referring to Senator Specter's inquiry. A statement made by Judge Bork in a speech at the University of Michigan became cannon fodder for another series of questions. Bork had made this comment in the speech: "The Court tends to assume that there is not a problem if willing adults indulge a taste for pornography in a theater whose outside advertising does not offend the squeamish. The assumption is wrong. . . . The attitudes, taste and moral values inculcated do not stay behind in the theater. A change in moral environment—in social attitudes toward sex, marriage, duties toward children and the like—may as surely be felt as harm as the possibility of physical violence."[15] Leahy then noted that Bork had told Senator Specter that the Supreme Court must decide for itself when material is obscene and should prevent nonobscene material from being banned. This response seemed to Leahy to be incompatible with the Michigan speech. Taken through a series of questions, Bork repeated his position on the role of the Court.

Judge Bork's responses on this issue were consistent throughout the hearings. The fact that he believed, as he told his Michigan audience, that the Supreme Court should consider nonphysical harms of obscenity does not suggest that someone other than the Court should determine what is obscene. It is hard to believe that Senator Leahy and Senator Specter, both of whom are lawyers, did not understand the straightforward point that Judge Bork was making. But if they did understand it, they knew that Bork's position on this issue was entirely noncontroversial and must simply have decided to get as much mileage as possible out of statements that the public might not fully comprehend.

Senator Leahy and Senator Specter also raised questions about speech advocating the forcible overthrow of government. Judge Bork had addressed this issue in some detail in his writings and had specifically rejected the Supreme Court's decision in *Brandenburg v. Ohio*, which was the Court's most recent and most important opinion on this subject. Of all the speech issues that Bork had discussed, he seemed most vulnerable on this one.

In his *Indiana Law Journal* article, Bork had expressly excluded from the area of constitutional protection any speech "advocating forcible overthrow of the government or violation of law."[16] He wrote that "[the] process of the 'discovery and spread of political truth' is damaged or destroyed if the outcome is defeated by a minority that makes law enforcement, and hence the putting of political truth into practice, impossible or less effective."[17] This position was clearly at odds with *Brandenburg v. Ohio*, which held that speech advocating violation of law could not be prohibited "except where such advocacy is directed to inciting or producing *imminent* lawless action and is likely to incite or produce such action."[18] The *Brandenburg* holding was designed to maximize free speech by protecting advocacy except where it was likely to produce imminent lawlessness. Recognizing the conflict between this holding and the position that he had outlined, Judge Bork explicitly rejected *Brandenburg* in a speech at the University of Michigan, calling the decision a "fundamentally wrong interpretation of the first amendment."[19]

When Judge Bork initially addressed the *Brandenburg* case at the confirmation hearings, he described the Court's position as "okay; [it] is a good position."[20] When later asked by Senator Leahy whether he agreed with the *Brandenburg* case, Judge Bork said, "Yes, I do."[21] It certainly appeared at this point that Bork's position had taken a dramatic turn since he delivered his speech at Michigan. He reinforced the belief that his original view had changed when he said of the *Brandenburg* decision, "It is right."[22] Senator Leahy closed out his round of questions by remarking, "You felt *Brandenburg* was fundamentally wrong but today you feel it is right?" Bork again stated that he did and went on to explain the reason for his change of mind. Bork had previously believed that *Brandenburg* did not take sufficiently into account the danger posed when many speakers advocate violence or overthrow of the government. Later he came to believe that American society was not susceptible to such a threat, and he now felt that the First Amendment says, "We will take that chance." Nevertheless, his apparent endorsement of *Brandenburg* soon became less than ringing.

When Senator Leahy returned to *Brandenburg* in a later round of questioning, Judge Bork backed away from the comments that suggested his agreement with the decision. Bork admitted that if he were again to argue the case theoretically, he might still criticize it. What had appeared to be agreement with the reasoning of the Court now looked only like a willingness to abide by the decision. In response to a question from Senator Specter, he said: "I accept *Brandenburg* as a judge, and I have no desire to overturn it. I am not changing my criticism of the case. I just accept it as settled law."[23] Bork later remarked that "as a judge facing it for the first time, I might not vote for *Brandenburg*."[24] If committee members thought that Bork's position had traveled a long way since 1971, it now appeared to have made a return trip overnight.

No doubt, Judge Bork's recitation of views on *Brandenburg* could have been delivered more effectively. Rather than give unqualified support for the Court's decision and then back away, as he appeared to do, Bork would have done better simply to state, as he eventually did, that he would abide by the decision, even though he did not necessarily agree with it. Instead, Judge Bork tried first to give reassuring answers to questions about *Brandenburg*, only to find charges of "confirmation conversion" quickly surfacing in the *Washington Post*. Within twenty-four hours, Bork then reaffirmed his original position on *Brandenburg* but agreed to abide by the decision.

Clearly, Judge Bork was in a difficult position. If he adhered to his original criticism of *Brandenburg*, he would alienate moderate senators whose support he badly needed. But any changes in his position were likely to be interpreted as self-serving efforts to win confirmation. Bork recognized the dilemma and later vented his frustration, stating, "I've been getting criticism because I never change my mind and now because I [have] changed my mind."[25]

11
ETHICAL QUESTIONS: WATERGATE REVISITED

Judge Bork's nomination came to the Senate amid widely published reports of the nominee's reputation for integrity and intellectual honesty. The only known blemish on Bork's record at the time of the nomination involved the dismissal of Archibald Cox as special prosecutor during the investigation of Watergate offenses. Despite repeated efforts by Bork to explain his decision to fire Cox, critics like Senator Kennedy continued to charge that "the man who fired Archibald Cox" was unfit to serve on the Supreme Court.[1] Although another charge of misconduct would surface briefly during the confirmation process,[2] Watergate remained the focus of attention for ethical questions throughout the hearings.

Allegations of ethical misconduct have provided fertile ground for derailing Supreme Court nominees in recent years. The nomination of Judge Clement Haynsworth offers a good example. Judge Haynsworth was defeated by Senate Democrats in 1969, at least in part, because of charges of ethical improprieties. Haynsworth had been a shareholder and officer of Vend-a-Matic, a corporation that had substantial contracts for its vending machines with a textile conglomerate called Deering Milliken. While serving on the federal court of appeals, Judge Haynsworth had cast the deciding vote in a case involving Darlington Mills, a Deering subsidiary, and much was made of this indiscretion by Haynsworth's opponents in the Senate.[3]

But there is substantial evidence that ideology, not ethics, was at the root of Democratic opposition to Haynsworth. Shortly after the Haynsworth and Carswell nominations were defeated, President Nixon nominated Judge Harry Blackmun to the vacant seat on the Supreme

Court. Blackmun's nomination was quickly confirmed, despite some rather serious ethical charges against him. Judge Blackmun was known to have participated in four cases involving a corporate party in which Blackmun had a direct financial interest.[4] This was a more serious infraction than that of Judge Haynsworth, which had involved only ownership in a company that had contracted with the parent corporation of a party to the suit rather than ownership in the very company that was bringing suit or was being sued. However, there was not strong opposition to Blackmun from labor and civil rights groups, as there had been to Haynsworth. The vote in favor of Blackmun was 94 to 0, and critics charged that he received "kid gloves" treatment from Democrats who had opposed Haynsworth.

However, the use of ethical charges as a cover for ideological opposition has not been confined to one political party. In 1968, it was Senate Republicans who took advantage of ethical charges against Justice Abe Fortas to defeat his nomination to be chief justice.[5] Although there was much opposition to Fortas's liberal voting record on the Court, particularly in the areas of criminal procedure and obscenity, Fortas's adversaries did not appear to lean heavily on ideology. Instead, they relied primarily on various allegations of ethical improprieties. Fortas was portrayed as having violated the principle of separation of powers by drafting legislation and advising President Johnson on a wide range of issues while he sat on the Supreme Court. Fortas was also charged with violating ethical standards by accepting a $15,000 stipend, paid from the contributions of five wealthy businessmen, for delivering a series of lectures at American University. These issues, combined with President Johnson's lame-duck status, helped ensure the effectiveness of a Republican filibuster against Justice Fortas.

Given this history of recent success in the use of ethical charges against Supreme Court nominees, it is hardly surprising that Democrats on the Senate Judiciary Committee, who were opposed to Judge Bork for ideological reasons, would attempt to scuttle the nomination by questioning his role in the Watergate controversy. The major ethical charges against Bork were that he violated the law when he fired Special Prosecutor Archibald Cox and, more generally, that his conduct at this time threatened to impede a proper investigation of Watergate. Some critics also accused Bork of shading his testimony about Watergate and of attempting to "rewrite history."[6]

The record of events leading to the dismissal of Archibald Cox is fairly clear.[7] Cox had demanded White House tape recordings that might resolve the conflict between President Nixon's claims of innocence and the testimony of former White House counsel John Dean, which implicated the President in the Watergate cover-up. Nixon invoked executive privilege and refused to produce the tapes. Cox then obtained a court order, later upheld by the court of appeals, which directed Nixon to produce the tapes. The President had until Friday, October 19, to seek review of the order in the Supreme Court.

During the week of October 19, Attorney General Elliot Richardson, at Nixon's urging, proposed that Cox accept a White House "summary" of the tapes which would be verified by Senator John Stennis. Stennis was a seventy-two-year-old conservative Democrat from Mississippi, who was highly respected but was in poor health and hard of hearing. Cox rejected the offer, largely because summaries of the tapes would be inadmissible at trial and because the proposal did not provide for access to additional tapes and White House documents.[8]

Nixon then had his attorney, Professor Charles Alan Wright of the University of Texas Law School, deliver a letter to Cox informing him that Nixon's proposal was reasonable and that Cox's objections were "unacceptable." The letter added that if Cox did not reconsider, "we shall have to follow the course of action that we think in the best interest of the country." At 9:00 P.M. on October 19, the White House released a statement announcing that because of "overriding national interest," Nixon would not seek Supreme Court review of the order to produce the tapes. Archibald Cox could accept Nixon's compromise offer or run the risk of being fired and getting nothing.

Cox did not blink. On Saturday morning, October 20, he held a press conference at which he stated that he could not accept Nixon's offer and remain true to his promise to conduct a thorough investigation. Later that day, White House Chief of Staff Alexander Haig telephoned Attorney General Richardson and instructed him to fire Cox. Richardson said he could not do this because he had made an agreement during his Senate confirmation hearings that the special prosecutor would not be removed except for "extraordinary improprieties."[9] Richardson would therefore go to the White House to deliver his letter of resignation. But first he had a long meeting with Bork, then the solicitor general, and William Ruckelshaus, the deputy attorney general. After discussing the crisis that was swirling around them, Richardson said he could not fire Cox.[10] He turned to William Ruckelshaus and asked, "Can you, Bill?" Ruckelshaus, who considered himself bound by assurances he had given the Senate at his confirmation hearings, as well as by his having come to the Justice Department as Richardson's aide, said no. Richardson then asked Bork, "Can you do it, Bob?" Neither Richardson nor Ruckelshaus viewed Bork as being bound by Richardson's commitment to remove Cox only for extraordinary improprieties. Richardson told Bork that he might have to decide whether he was going to carry out Nixon's order to fire Cox.

Bork asked for time to think. As Richardson and Ruckelshaus continued to talk, Bork paced around the room, realizing the high stakes of the game he was about to play. Bork seemed to be torn.[11] On the one hand, he believed the President had authority to discharge any employee of the executive branch and felt some obligation to comply with a presidential order even if he disagreed with it. On the other hand, he was concerned about how it would look if he fired Cox and how it might affect his own career.[12]

Bork finally said, "Yes, I can do it, but I will resign immediately afterwards."[13] The others asked why he would resign. Bork replied, "Because I do not want to be regarded as an apparatchik"[14]—an organization man who keeps his job by doing what he is told. Both Richardson and Ruckelshaus encouraged Bork not to resign if he fired Cox.[15] They said the Department of Justice would be facing tremendous pressure and would need strong leadership in order to forestall additional resignations and give policy-level direction to the department. Richardson made it clear to Bork that Nixon was determined to fire Cox at any price. Delay or refusal by Bork to fire Cox would not thwart the president's determination in this matter.

Later that afternoon, Richardson went to the White House to submit his resignation. Nixon attempted to persuade him that for national security reasons, he should delay his resignation and fire Cox. Richardson again refused. While Richardson was gone, Bork discussed with Ruckelshaus what the outcome might be. At one point, Bork asked him, "Don't you think my moral position is different from yours?"[16] Ruckelshaus agreed that it was. Bork also turned to his wife and to his Yale colleague, Alexander Bickel, for advice. Bickel could not be reached, and Bork's wife said simply that she would support whatever decision he made.[17]

Soon, Alexander Haig called Ruckelshaus and told him to fire Cox. Ruckelshaus refused and tendered his resignation.[18] In the course of the conversation, Ruckelshaus told Haig, "Bork's your man." The White House, ignoring Ruckelshaus's resignation, later announced that Ruckelshaus had been fired for failing to follow orders.[19]

After determining that Bork was next in the chain of command at the Justice Department, Haig called Bork, who came to the White House. When Haig began to cajole him, Bork interrupted to say that he had already decided to fire Cox.[20] The White House released a statement at 8:24 on Saturday night, announcing that Cox and Ruckelshaus had been fired and that the resignation of Elliot Richardson had been accepted.[21] White House press secretary Ron Ziegler also announced that the office of special prosecutor was abolished as of 8:00 P.M. and that its duties were transferred to the Justice Department, where they would be carried out "with thoroughness and vigor."[22]

Bork immediately placed Henry Peterson, a respected assistant attorney general, in charge of the Watergate case; but Bork retained the entire staff assembled by Archibald Cox to conduct the day-to-day investigation. The next week Bork held a news conference, at which he promised to take steps to obtain any evidence from the White House that was vital to a criminal prosecution. He said, "If the law entitles us to any item of evidence, I will go after it."[23] He added that he would not be the person "who in any way compromised the investigation."[24] He said Nixon had told him to carry out the investigation and prosecute fully. Bork believed that on the basis of this statement, he was free to conduct the Watergate investigation in the way he thought it ought to be done.[25]

On November 1, under heavy pressure from Congress, Bork announced the appointment of Leon Jaworski as the new special prosecutor. Bork said that Jaworski would have the same independence as Cox—an assurance which Jaworski had made a condition for accepting the job—and that President Nixon would not exercise his constitutional prerogative to fire him without the concurrence of a substantial majority of eight congressional leaders.[26] Bork added that Jaworski would have the full cooperation of the Justice Department and that if a disagreement arose over the release of presidential materials, there would "be no restrictions placed on his freedom of action."[27] In response to a question about the status of the staff of the special prosecutor, Bork said he had told Jaworski that the staff was "indispensable to the rapid investigation and prosecution of these cases, and Mr. Jaworski fully agrees."[28]

At the hearings on Judge Bork's nomination to the Supreme Court, Senator Kennedy and Senator Metzenbaum charged that Bork had violated the law by firing Archibald Cox while a Justice Department regulation was in effect, which forbade the firing of Cox except for "extraordinary improprieties."[29] Both senators relied on a decision by Judge Gerhard Gesell. Judge Gesell had ruled in a suit against Bork that the firing of Archibald Cox was illegal for two reasons: (1) because the agreement protecting the independence of the special prosecutor was embodied in a federal regulation, it had the force of law and could not be violated so long as the regulation remained in effect; and (2) although the regulation was rescinded three days after Cox's dismissal, the rescission was merely a "ruse" to get rid of Cox since virtually the same regulation was put into effect a few weeks later, when Leon Jaworski became the new special prosecutor.[30]

Judge Bork argued that his action in firing Cox was, in effect, an informal rescission of the federal regulation. He also said that Judge Gesell was wrong in ruling that there had been some kind of ruse because there was no plan to name another special prosecutor at the time Cox was fired. It was only some days later, after a firestorm of protest, that a decision was made to name a new special prosecutor. Finally, Bork noted that the court of appeals, finding Judge Gesell's decision to be moot, had vacated the judgment, thereby making it a nullity.[31]

Judge Bork was not alone in challenging Gesell's view of the case. Former Attorney General Elliot Richardson also took issue with the "excessively legalistic" nature of Judge Gesell's decision. Richardson insisted that his agreement to retain Cox was not binding on future attorneys general and said that this "was precisely what I wanted to resist" by negotiating an agreement which avoided "the creation of some external mechanism beyond my [own] accountability as Attorney General."[32] And even Archibald Cox, the intended beneficiary of the agreement, admitted that the failure to rescind the federal regulation until three days after his dismissal was only a "technical defect."[33]

Judge Bork was also accused of having mislead the American Bar Association by claiming that after firing Cox, he had acted "immediately" to find a new special prosecutor.[34] It seems clear that within a few days of dismissing Cox, Bork began to consider the possibility that a new independent prosecutor would have to be appointed.[35] At least two prominent law professors had conversations with Bork within three days of the discharge and were asked to recommend a special prosecutor. The names of Lewis Powell, who had recently been appointed to the Supreme Court, and Leon Jaworski surfaced quickly. Nevertheless, it is apparent from Bork's own testimony that only after the firestorm of protest following the Saturday night massacre was a decision made to appoint a new special prosecutor. Bork testified, "We did not initially contemplate a new special prosecutor until we saw that it was necessary because the American people would not be mollified without one."[36] This, in fact, is the very point that Bork used to rebut Judge Gesell's assertion that the rescission of the regulation protecting the independent prosecutor had been a ruse for getting rid of Cox.

Ironically, the fact that a new special prosecutor was initially not contemplated also suggests that Bork was looking for a new prosecutor at the same time that he was revoking the regulation that protected the independence of Archibald Cox. If the latter events coincided, as appears to be the case from Bork's own testimony,[37] it becomes more difficult to dismiss Judge Gesell's claim that revocation of the regulation was a ruse for firing Cox. Perhaps Bork contemplated a special prosecutor who would not have as much protection as Cox, but it is easy to understand why Bork did not mention that possibility at his confirmation hearings. Of course, Bork could rely instead on his argument that the regulation was informally revoked by Nixon's order to fire Cox—at a time when no new special prosecutor was contemplated—and the action was merely formalized a few days later, albeit at a time when a new prosecutor was contemplated.

Whether there was a "technical defect" in the dismissal of Archibald Cox or a delay in appointing Leon Jaworski is much less important, however, than the question of Bork's commitment to a full and impartial investigation of Watergate. Before the Saturday night massacre, President Nixon had told Elliot Richardson that he intended "to get the Watergate Special Prosecution Force disbanded," an objective that went far beyond the removal of Archibald Cox. The president's letter instructing Bork to fire Cox plainly reflected this broader objective. The letter said, "In your capacity as Acting Attorney General, I direct you to discharge Mr. Cox immediately and to take all steps necessary to return to the Department of Justice the functions now being performed by the Watergate Special Prosecution Force."[38]

But Bork did not disband the Watergate staff. Instead, he deliberately gave a narrow interpretation to the president's instructions and worked actively to persuade members of the staff to continue their investigation under the supervision of Henry Peterson. Bork also approved a plan to seek a protective order from the Court to safeguard evidence that had already been gathered, and he told friends the day after Cox's dismissal that he would "go after" presidential tapes "if they are relevant to the criminal investigation."[39] In the end, the decision to keep Cox's hand-picked staff intact—a decision later ratified by Leon Jaworski—was perhaps the most important judgment Bork made during his brief encounter with Watergate. Since any large-scale investigation necessarily relies on staff rather than on the prosecutor alone, the removal of Watergate staff members could have caused, as one of them said, "substantial and perhaps irreparable obstruction of the ongoing criminal investigations."[40] On the other hand, the dismissal of Archibald Cox, which has drawn more attention, would almost certainly have been accomplished regardless of what Bork decided to do. Elliot Richardson, who was in regular contact with the White House during the week of Cox's dismissal, said that the president was determined to remove Cox at all costs, and it is obvious that he could have accomplished this by simply naming an acting attorney general from outside the Justice Department, if necessary.[41]

Henry Ruth and George Frampton, two members of the Watergate staff, testified that Bork was "irrelevant" because "the show was being run by the White House."[42] They characterized Bork's role in the weeks after the Saturday night massacre as basically like "a leaf floating on an ocean during a hurricane."[43] They also raised questions about why Bork had tried to keep the Watergate staff intact. Ruth testified that the "White House wanted us to stay together to offset the independent special prosecutor bill introduced into the Congress, which Mr. Bork thought was unconstitutional."[44]

But Bork's decision to give a narrow interpretation to the president's instructions and to retain the Watergate staff was made *before* the firestorm of protest had threatened to breed legislation for the appointment of a new special prosecutor. Bork had revealed his intentions toward the staff to Philip Lacovara, then counsel to the special prosecutor, within hours of the dismissal of Cox.[45] And while it may be true that "the show was being run by the White House," that fact could have no bearing on a reasoned assessment of Bork's ethical standards or of his qualifications for the Supreme Court. If Bork was "irrelevant," this would suggest that he had relatively little power as acting attorney general. However, the important question is not how much authority Bork had but how he exercised that authority. In short, the assessment of Bork's commitment to a thorough investigation of Watergate must be based on what he did or attempted to do, not on whether he had the power to overcome White House resistance. Significantly, Henry Ruth eventually admitted to the Senate Judiciary Committee that he did not regard Bork's actions in Watergate to be "a matter of ethics."[46]

But if Bork's actions in Watergate can be defended, the same cannot always be said of his characterization of those actions. In testifying before the Senate Judiciary Committee on his nomination to the court of appeals in 1982, Bork said that "there was never any possibility" that his dismissal of Archibald Cox "would in any way hamper the [Watergate] investigation" and that he had acted to prevent massive resignations from the Department of Justice. Bork then concluded: "That was my choice, Senator. On the one hand there was no threat to the investigations from the discharge and no threat to the process of justice. On the other hand, I preserved an ongoing and effective Department of Justice. The only thing that weighed against doing what I did was personal fear of the consequences, and I could not let that, I think, control my decision."[47]

This testimony contained serious, though of course not necessarily deliberate, distortions. It is certainly an exaggeration to say that "there was never any possibility" that Cox's dismissal would impede the investigation. The dismissal was intended by President Nixon to do exactly that. And while Bork did not share the president's intent, he surely could not foreclose the possibility that the dismissal "would in any way hamper the investigation." As members of the Watergate staff later pointed out, Bork simply did not have control over all of the events that were exploding around him. It also seems somewhat self-serving for Bork to assert that the "only thing that weighed against doing what I did was personal fear of the consequences."[48] His dismissal of Cox required considerable courage, whatever might be said of the underlying judgment, but it surely carried risks for the administration of justice as well as for Bork's own career.

In 1987, when Bork testified on his nomination to the Supreme Court, his statements about Watergate were more circumspect than they had been five years earlier. He reiterated his basic position—expressed to Philip Lacovara immediately after the Saturday night massacre—that the president had the right to fire Cox in any event and that Bork's own action was designed to prevent further deterioration in personnel and morale at the Department of Justice.[49] But by 1987, Bork had already given credence to the claim that his version of the Watergate events had changed in the retelling.

Of course, Bork's actions in Watergate could not have a decisive role in the confirmation hearings. Those actions were well known when the Senate confirmed his nomination to the court of appeals five years earlier, and his opponents could hardly suggest that the ethical standards for service on the federal bench should vary from court to court. But Bork's opponents knew that he would be tarred by the events of Watergate and that his nomination might be damaged in the process. Senate Democrats correctly sensed that Bork appeared to be on the wrong side of history in the Watergate drama. His two major decisions during the Saturday night massacre were to fire Archibald Cox and not to fire other members of the staff. It was almost inevitable that Bork would be remembered for what he did about Cox rather than for what he refused to do about the others, even though the latter decision may have been more important than the former. Bork's actions in Watergate could not defeat his nomination to the Supreme Court, but they branded him in the eyes of many as the "apparatchik" he wished not to be, and they helped critics to portray him as an unyielding champion of executive power and executive privilege.

12

THE ABA

The first witnesses to testify after Judge Bork were the representatives of the American Bar Association (ABA). Traditionally, the ABA has tried to exert substantial influence over the selection of federal judges. Since 1952, the ABA has had a formal role in the process of screening judicial candidates. But even before that, the organization was active in scrutinizing various applicants for the federal bench. Recently, the ABA's participation in the screening process has been rather controversial, and its role in the Bork proceedings seemed to peak that controversy.

In September 1987, the ABA's Standing Committee on the Judiciary formally gave Judge Bork an endorsement of sorts, but four of its fifteen members said Bork was unqualified for the Supreme Court. To the general public, this may not have been particularly noteworthy. To insiders, however, the ABA seemed to have fired a shot that would resound long after the Bork hearings were concluded.

As early as September 4, rumors were circulating that the ABA's Standing Committee had not been unanimous in support of Judge Bork. The story was confirmed on September 10: After exhaustive interviews and lengthy discussion, Bork had been recommended by the Standing Committee on essentially a two-thirds vote. Ten members of the committee found Bork to be "well qualified," the highest ranking available for Supreme Court nominees. Four members voted "not qualified," and one member voted "not opposed."[1] Although there had been divided votes on nominees for lower federal courts, much would be made of the fact that the committee had been unanimous on all Supreme Court nominations for nearly twenty years.[2]

White House and Justice Department officials responded quickly to the news, noting that Bork had been evaluated by the same committee when nominated for the court of appeals in 1981 and had been found "exceptionally well qualified." Critics of the ABA said that the new vote reflected the committee's political bias rather than a careful assessment of Bork's judicial qualifications and should be given little weight. The announcement also invited Senate and media criticism. On the day of the announcement, Senator Orrin Hatch held a news conference to chastise committee members for being "willing to play politics" with Supreme Court nominations.[3] Other conservative members of the Judiciary Committee complained that the ABA had abandoned its role as neutral evaluator. *New York Times* columnist William Safire wrote a scathing essay on the ABA vote, calling the dissent "dishonest" and referring to the dissenters as "the gang of four."[4] Safire said that the four dissenters "cloaked their disagreement with Judge Bork's philosophy in an objection to his temperament."[5] Further, he claimed that they operated from their own "pure left" preferences and had "joined a witch hunt directed at damaging the reputation of a member of the profession . . . whose philosophy differed from theirs."[6]

The ABA vote also provoked a particularly bitter response from conservative legal and lobbying groups like the Washington Legal Foundation (WLF). Already convinced of the liberal leanings of the Standing Committee and frustrated by the special status afforded the committee, conservatives looked on the vote as another disturbing episode in an increasingly contentious relationship.

The liberal coalition, on the other hand, was able to capitalize on the split vote, claiming that it showed the nation's lawyers—ostensibly Bork's colleagues and peers—were deeply divided over his fitness for service on the Supreme Court. The widely publicized vote seemed to lend credibility to the liberal campaign and was a useful tool in convincing wavering senators and the general public. Estelle Rogers, who at the time of the Bork hearings was executive director of the Federation of Women Lawyers, confirmed that the ABA vote was one of the ingredients legitimizing the opposition to Bork.[7]

The vote focused both camps on the role of the ABA's Standing Committee on the Judiciary. But this debate was hardly a new one. Over the course of the committee's history, discussion had frequently been spirited, following a number of recurring themes. Committee chairman Ralph Lancaster noted that his files revealed that the issues "were exactly the same in the 50's as they were in the late 80's."[8] To understand the ABA's role and function, it will be useful to review its controversial history.

BACKGROUND

The ABA has historically sought to influence decisions of the president and the Senate on appointments to the federal courts. As pointed out by Joel Grossman, the ABA's initial purpose, in large part, was to protect its organizational interests and conservative ideology from liberal encroachment.[9] The bar sought to influence judicial selections in order to preserve entrepreneurial prerogative and to maintain the judiciary as a bulwark against progressive state legislation on economic matters.[10] It should be remembered that this effort was begun in an era when the Court was busy striking down social and economic legislation, such as minimum wage laws and restrictions on working hours, on the ground that the statutes violated either the contract clause or the due process clause of the federal Constitution.[11] By promoting conservative candidates and securing a bench sensitive to traditional ideology, the ABA could help to preserve the status quo.

A 1908 report from the ABA Committee on Professional Ethics asserted that "it is the duty of the Bar to endeavor to prevent political considerations from outweighing judicial fitness in the selection of judges."[12] However, when the nominee's ideology differed from that of people in positions of power in the ABA, political considerations became paramount.[13] In 1916, for example, six former presidents of the ABA and the incumbent president, Elihu Root, sent a strong letter to the Senate Judiciary Committee opposing the confirmation of Louis Brandeis: "The undersigned feel under the painful duty to say to you that in their opinion, taking into view the reputation, character and professional career of Mr. Louis D. Brandeis, he is not a fit person to be a member of the Supreme Court of the United States."[14] Signing the anti-Brandeis letter were some of the pillars of the organized bar: William Howard Taft, Simeon E. Baldwin, Joseph H. Choate, Francis Rawle, Elihu Root, and Moorfield Storey. Peter Meldrim filed a separate letter of the same general nature with the Senate Judiciary Committee.[15] The letters from these distinguished attorneys, like the ABA's vote on Judge Bork, lent some credibility to opponents of confirmation and helped to cast doubt on the notion that the opposition was motivated by bias or other extraneous considerations.[16] It should be noted that in 1916 the ABA had no formal mechanism for giving its input to the president and the Senate, except by letter or petition. It was not until 1948 that the Senate Judiciary Committee requested a formal opinion from the Standing Committee.[17]

In the years that followed the Brandeis hearings, the ABA tried to formalize its role in judicial selection, stating that "it is both the right and the duty of the bar to act in this selection process."[18] In 1932, encouraged by friendly signals from the Hoover administration, the ABA established a special committee to advise the Senate Judiciary Committee on judicial nominations. Two years later the ABA disbanded the special committee, which had not achieved the kind of influence its organizers had expected, but the ABA did not abandon its efforts to guide judicial selection. In fact, the organization was by then engaged in a battle with President Roosevelt and was publicly criticizing his plan to pack the Supreme Court.

In 1946, the ABA established a Special Committee on the Judiciary to consider and recommend a course of action to the ABA House of Delegates.[19] Later named the Standing Committee on the Judiciary, it was this group that came to occupy a privileged and controversial position as adviser to the White House, the attorney general, and the Senate.

At its inception, the committee's function was not well defined. In its first report to the ABA House of Delegates, the Special Committee on the Judiciary recommended important changes in the way that nominees for the federal courts were selected. In addition to suggesting that the ABA lobby to require certain minimum years of experience for judicial positions, the committee asked for a charter change that would allow it actively to promote candidates for the bench. After some debate, the Special Committee won on both counts, its new charge being "to promote the nomination of competent persons and to oppose the nomination of unfit persons."[20]

During the early years of the Truman administration, the Standing Committee submitted evaluations of nominees to the Senate and frequently offered suggestions on potential nominees to the Justice Department. The committee received strong support from Senate Judiciary Chairman Alexander Wiley, himself a former ABA member and a staunch Republican. When the Senate came under Democratic control in 1949, Pat McCarran assumed leadership of the Judiciary Committee and was reluctant to afford the ABA any power in the selection process. McCarran said, "[T]he bar associations shall not choose the judiciary of this country."[21]

Although the ABA made great strides in influencing judicial selection during the Truman administration, it was in the Eisenhower years that the ABA reached the zenith of its influence. Deputy Attorney General Ross Malone, who had served on the ABA's Board of Governors and in its House of Delegates, believed strongly in the value of an independent consulting body. Malone first proposed a formal structure in which the ABA Committee would submit names for federal court nominations. However, this idea never took hold in the Eisenhower administration. As an alternative, the ABA agreed to evaluate the qualifications of possible nominees when names were submitted by the attorney general. President Eisenhower agreed to provide the names of nominees and gave the ABA a major boost when, in 1956, he expanded their role to include nominations to the Supreme Court.[22] The ABA's prestige was heightened by Eisenhower's statement that "we must never appoint a man who doesn't have the recognition of the American Bar Association."[23]

The decision to give the ABA an important role in judicial selection may have benefited President Eisenhower as much as it helped the ABA. There had been much criticism by members of Congress about the increasingly activist decisions of the Warren Court. The ABA's involvement gave added credibility to the selection process and may have insulated Eisenhower from charges that he was responsible for the Court's liberal leanings.

In 1958, under an agreement forged by Attorney General William Rogers and Bernard Segal, the chairman of the ABA's Standing Committee, the committee became even more influential. Typically, several names were given to the committee for evaluation, even before lower court nominations had been made. The ABA Committee then rated the candidates and provided its ratings to the White House. By using this rating process, the ABA could wield great influence over the administration's choice and could promote its own favored candidates.

The ABA's role declined somewhat after the election of John Kennedy in 1960. Kennedy continued the practice of submitting names in advance of formal nomination. For example, Attorney General Robert Kennedy asked committee chairman Bernard Segal how the committee would react to the nomination of his deputy, Byron White, to the Supreme Court. Kennedy was told that several committee members would heartily approve of the nomination. Kennedy was relieved because he and the president had feared an adverse public reaction, since White was known to be a close friend of the Kennedys.[24] Nevertheless, President Kennedy did not always heed the committee's evaluations, and on at least one occasion he bypassed the committee completely. In two years, Kennedy named eight judges to the lower federal courts that the ABA had rated "unqualified." Responding to criticism from committee members, Deputy Attorney General Nicholas Katzenbach replied that "the responsibility is the President's and the Senate's, and this Association does not have and would not wish to have a veto over the appointments to be made."[25]

In 1965, President Johnson nominated Francis X. Morrissey to the federal district court in Boston because Morrissey, an old family friend of the Kennedys, had been given a commitment of a judgeship shortly before President Kennedy was assassinated. The ABA gave Morrissey a rating of "unqualified"; and extensive hearings revealed that he had graduated from a Georgia "diploma mill," had failed several courses there, and had barely passed the Georgia bar exam on the third try. Although Senator Edward Kennedy championed his cause, Morrissey was barely approved by the Judiciary Committee on a vote of 6 to 3, with seven members not voting. Later, Morrissey's nomination was withdrawn when it encountered growing opposition in the Senate. Whether Johnson actually wanted Morrissey to be confirmed—or wanted only to bring embarrassment to the Kennedys—is open to question, but Johnson was fairly scrupulous thereafter in sending forward only nominees who had passed muster with the ABA.[26]

At its inception, the Nixon administration gave the ABA even more influence, tantamount almost to a veto power. With cooperation from Attorney General Richard Kleindienst, ABA recommendations had a great deal of influence in the selection of nominees.[27] However, when the ABA started to flex its muscle, relations between the ABA and the Nixon administration became badly strained. Initially, the Standing Committee unanimously approved the selection of Judge Clement Haynsworth for the Supreme Court, with a rating of "highly qualified." After revelations concerning some stock purchases by Haynsworth, they reconsidered and approved his nomination by a vote of 8 to 4.[28] Later, the committee unanimously concluded that Judge Carswell was "qualified" for appointment to the Supreme Court.[29] However, after the Senate voted down the Carswell nomination, the committee was much less sympathetic to President Nixon's next two potential nominees, Mildred L. Lillie and

Herschel H. Friday. The committee voted unanimously that Lillie was not qualified and deadlocked 6 to 6 on Friday, with six voting "not qualified" and six voting "not opposed." The committee's vote on Herschel Friday was particularly surprising since he had been a member of the ABA House of Delegates and the Board of Governors over the previous twenty years and was quite popular with members of the bar.[30]

Attorney General John Mitchell reacted angrily to the ABA Committee votes, declaring that the White House would abandon its practice of submitting the names of Supreme Court candidates to the ABA for their advice. Instead, the attorney general would submit his recommendations directly to the president.[31] Nevertheless, after President Nixon announced the nominations of Lewis F. Powell and William H. Rehnquist, the Standing Committee, under the chairmanship of Lawrence Walsh—more recently independent prosecutor in the Iran-Contra matter—did its normal background investigation and submitted its findings to Judiciary Committee Chairman James Eastland. During the Ford administration, with the appointment of Judge John Paul Stevens, the ABA returned to its more traditional position.[32]

As part of a campaign commitment to diversity in government appointments, President Carter instituted a system for judicial selection that relied heavily on local community recruitment and screening. Yet, in practice, Attorney General Griffin Bell and the Carter White House often selected nominees without regard to any local or state input. Bell and his staff worked with the ABA but did not afford the committee a great deal of influence. In fact, several lower court nominations were made despite the committee's adverse recommendation.[33]

Professor Abraham has written that the ABA Committee has had to "bend" its own standards in order to stay on solid footing with recent administrations.[34] Former Attorney General Edward Levi describes this fluid role as negative in nature—preventing the nomination of problematic candidates rather than promoting the most qualified individuals to judgeships.[35] Nevertheless, by the time Ronald Reagan assumed the presidency, the ABA had gained a special status in the selection of federal judges.

THE ABA IN THE REAGAN YEARS

The Reagan administration was much less willing than previous Republican administrations to defer to the ABA. At times, there was even outright hostility to the role played by the ABA. Bruce Fein, a former Justice Department attorney who was active in the judicial selection process, remarked, "We didn't think one second about ABA ratings."[36] More important, the judicial selection process in the Reagan years was structured in a way that served to minimize the role of the ABA. The initial screening and interviews were conducted by the Office of Legal Policy of the Justice Department. After hearing the candidates' views and discussing the matter informally with various White House officials and department heads, Attorney General Meese then recommended a single candidate to the president's Federal Judicial Selection Committee, which Meese chaired. It was only at that point, after a decision had been made to proceed with a candidate, that the name of the individual was forwarded to the FBI and the ABA to allow them to do background checks.[37] This procedure reduced the ability of the ABA to play an active role in the prenomination stage, as it had during the Eisenhower, Nixon, and Ford years.[38]

But contrary to the implication of Bruce Fein's remark, the Reagan administration and its chief point man on judicial selection, Edwin Meese, could not afford to ignore the ABA. Meese has said that the Standing Committee was a valuable resource, especially with respect to lower court appointees, who might not be well known. A nominee's peers might be willing to speak more candidly to an ABA representative than to an FBI agent conducting a background check.[39] Meese, however, was keenly aware of the problems surrounding the ABA's role, problems that would set the stage for new battles during and after the summer of 1987.

THE BORK NOMINATION

The controversy over the ABA's action on the Bork nomination would lead to a close examination of the evaluation process. Critics attacked the process on several fronts. However, most of the criticism was focused on (1) the composition of the Standing Committee, (2) the guarantee of confidentiality, and (3) the committee's consideration of Judge Bork's judicial philosophy.

The Composition of the Standing Committee

Although there have been some procedural changes over the years, the committee structure remains substantially the same as it was when first constituted in 1946. The Standing Committee on the Judiciary consists of fifteen members appointed by the president of the ABA to represent particular regions, defined by the jurisdictional lines of the federal courts of appeals. Committee members serve three-year terms, with a two-term limit, and many have previously served on other ABA committees or in positions of leadership. To avoid obvious conflicts, members may not seek or accept an appointment to the federal bench while serving on the committee or for a year thereafter. Apart from these simple provisions, there are no formal rules limiting the legal or political activities in which members may be involved.[40]

When the Standing Committee's vote on the Bork nomination was announced, critics suggested that the members' political affiliations presented conflicts of interest. Since the names of those voting against Bork were not divulged, there was great speculation about who had cast the negative votes. Senator Hatch and Senator Grassley would later denounce both the confidentiality of the vote and the composition of the committee, which, they contended, was weighted too heavily on the liberal side.

Bork, apparently agreeing with the senators, charged in his book[41] that the committee had been "balanced for political considerations." Former ABA committee chairman Harold Tyler disputed this assertion: "[F]rom everything I know, I doubt the existence of a policy or practice to pick people for the committee to add political balance. On the other hand, I do know that in times past, the committee and the ABA have been criticized for not having a wide variety of people on this particular committee. As I understand that criticism, it has been focused to urge that better representation of women and minorities be achieved."[42] He made no mention of the possibility that this change in representation would itself affect the political balance, whether or not designed for that purpose.

Ralph Lancaster, who was a member of the Standing Committee at the time of the Bork nomination, made an even stronger denial. Lancaster stated that as far as he knew, there was nothing political about how people were appointed. Lancaster added that in all the years he served, he never saw any evidence of political bias; he would have frequently been wrong, he said, if he had predicted voting results on the basis of the members' backgrounds and political affiliations. "I could not track it. There was no pattern." Lancaster lauded the dedication of committee members and stated that while each member had individual biases, everyone he knew tried to put them aside when faced with the serious process of judicial evaluation.[43] Nevertheless, as noted by Professor Sheldon Goldman, it appears that in recent years members of the committee have been more willing to vote their ideological biases, which may explain the greater number of divided votes of the Standing Committee during the Carter and Reagan administrations.[44]

The Guarantee of Confidentiality

Another frequent criticism of the ABA was that the committee was not accountable for its actions because it was allowed to operate in secrecy. Complete confidentiality for all discussions and votes had been considered essential to its mission. Practicing attorneys needed the independence provided by anonymity when voting on judges before whom they might later appear. And a nominee's colleagues usually needed the promise of confidentiality in order to give candid information about the nominee.

The confidentiality issue reached a boiling point in 1985, when it was discovered that the Standing Committee had given the names of nominees to liberal lobby groups. Organizations like the Federation of Women Lawyers and the Alliance for Justice provided informal input to the ABA Committee and, presumably, received a head start on their own lobbying activities. Conservative groups complained loudly when they asked for the same advance notice and were turned down. They took their complaints to Attorney General Meese, who spoke to committee chairman, Robert Fiske, and was assured by him that the practice would be stopped immediately.[45]

For the Washington Legal Foundation, (WLF), a conservative think tank, the sharing of information with groups like the Federation of Women Lawyers and the Alliance for Justice was further evidence of the committee's liberal ideological bias. They were not persuaded by Harold Tyler's claim that unsolicited information was submitted from a wide variety of special interest groups, who had equal access to the process, and that the information had no real effect on the process.[46]

Frustrated by unequal access to information and upset by the ABA's role in the Bork hearings, WLF filed a suit against the ABA Committee, claiming that its confidential meetings and records violated the Federal Advisory Committee Act (FACA). WLF Director Paul Kamenar said that the committee held secret, "Star Chamber-like proceeding[s]" and leaked confidential information to "certain liberal activist groups such as the Alliance for Justice."[47] Unmistakably, the WLF's purpose was to topple the ABA's exalted position in the judicial selection process. Referring to the lawsuit, Patrick McGuigan said: "I hope it ends up with the ABA being thrown out on its ear. It is unrepresentative of the American people and unaccountable. The U.S. Senate may not be perfect, but it is both."[48] WLF was joined in the suit by an unlikely ally: Ralph Nader's liberal Public Citizen Litigation Group. Public Citizen had also asked the committee for names of nominees and had been refused. Commenting on the unusual pairing, Public Citizen's Eric Glitzenstein chuckled, "It's obviously a weird case of alignment."[49] Nevertheless, participation by Public Citizen brought new credibility to the WLF lawsuit, suggesting that it involved an issue of good government and not simply an ideological catfight.

Both WLF and Public Citizen wanted the ABA Committee to be governed by FACA's sunshine provisions. Passed in 1972, FACA represented an attempt to standardize the operations of the more than three thousand committees advising the federal government. Under its provisions, advisory groups had to meet in public, establish a politically balanced membership, and maintain public records.

According to its literal terms, FACA would have controlled the ABA Committee. In fact, until 1974 the Justice Department believed that FACA did apply, and Attorney General Saxbe raised the issue with the ABA.[50] At that time, the committee stated that it would terminate its evaluations if FACA applied, because committee confidentiality was critical to its ability to operate effectively. Asked to advise the Department of Justice, then Assistant Attorney General Antonin Scalia wrote an opinion saying that application of the sunshine provisions of FACA to the ABA Committee would raise constitutional problems under the doctrine of separation of powers.[51] Saxbe then decided that the Justice Department would not seek to enforce FACA's provisions against the ABA "in accord with the principle that legislation should be interpreted to avoid serious constitutional questions." From 1974 until 1987, there was little mention of the committee's right to operate confidentially.

However, the divided vote on Judge Bork generated a great deal of controversy. WLF leaders thought Saxbe's analysis avoided the real problem of political influence, so it brought suit demanding that the ABA Committee comply with FACA if it was to continue to advise the Justice Department on judicial nominations.[52] The Supreme Court, affirming the decision of the lower court, held that the committee did not constitute an advisory committee for purposes of FACA, and therefore the statute did not apply.[53] The Court ruled that the application of the act would violate the separation of powers doctrine, which authorizes the president alone to nominate judges. The act would restrict the president's freedom to seek and evaluate advice during the nomination process. Although the Court's decision disposed of FACA, the underlying problems of confidentiality were left untouched. These problems would surface again at the Bork confirmation hearings.

During the Bork controversy, the media distributed speculative and sketchy information on the ABA, but the senators could not challenge the committee's vote because of an almost impenetrable barrier of confidentiality. They felt justified in their anger: Not only had the ABA's vote provided liberal lobbyists with powerful ammunition, but the senators' only source of information about the ABA was the daily newspaper. News reports characterized the committee's debate as intense and divisive, but almost no other information about the meetings was divulged.

Consideration of Bork's Judicial Philosophy

The ABA's confidentiality rule exacerbated the concern among conservatives that dissenting members of the Standing Committee had impermissibly considered Judge Bork's judicial philosophy in reaching the conclusion that he was not qualified for the Supreme Court. The committee's official guidelines provided that integrity, competence, and judicial temperament were the factors that should be considered in deciding whether a nominee was qualified and that judicial philosophy generally should not be considered. However, the guidelines left considerable wiggle room because they created an exception of undefined scope. Specifically, the guidelines provided that "[p]olitical or ideological philosophy are not considered, except to the extent that extreme views on such matters may bear upon judicial temperament or integrity."[54]

Ralph Lancaster, chairman of the Standing Committee, offered an example of how the rule might operate. Lancaster stated that a very bright, hardworking, and honest individual who is convinced that blacks are inferior to whites and who believes that blacks are not as credible as whites would be unqualified to sit on the Supreme Court. He added that if someone is closed minded and his approach to issues is preordained, that also is proper for the committee to consider.[55] Obviously, it is a highly subjective matter whether a nominee's views bear on his judicial temperament. Moreover, because of the confidentiality of the process, it is difficult to determine whether committee members have based their decisions on ideology. In response to a question whether the people who voted against Bork might improperly have considered his legal philosophy, Lancaster stated that this question would put him on a "slippery slope" and that he could not answer it. He added: "[W]e promised confidentiality as part of the process and we really can't defend ourselves. We have to bite our tongue when we are criticized. . . . "[56]

It was widely rumored that the committee members who gave Bork a rating of "not qualified" were Samuel Williams of the Los Angeles law firm of Hufstedler, Miller, Carlson & Beardsley; Joan Hall, a partner with the large Chicago firm of Jenner & Block; John Lane of the Washington, D.C., firm of Wilkes, Artis, Hedrick & Lane; and Jerome Shestack of the Philadelphia law firm of Schnader, Harrison, Segal & Lewis.[57] All four of these individuals have strong Democratic and liberal credentials.

Williams, a prominent black lawyer in Los Angeles, is a close friend and adviser of former Mayor Tom Bradley.[58] Hall, a former official of the Legal Assistance Foundation of Chicago, is a member of the board of directors of the liberal Chicago chapter of the Lawyers Committee for Civil Rights Under Law.[59] It was later rumored that Hall cast one of the two "unqualified" votes on the Clarence Thomas nomination.[60] Lane, a prominent Democrat, was denied reappointment to the committee after he angered conservatives by aggressively questioning several of Reagan's judicial nominees.[61] Shestack was a member of the National Committee of Lawyers, which supported Senator Biden in his bid for the presidency. He also made financial contributions to the Biden campaign.[62] Like Joan Hall, Shestack is active with the Lawyers Committee for Civil Rights Under Law. He was formerly United States representative to the United Nations Human Rights Commission and became president of the International League of Human Rights and chairman of the Lawyers Committee on International Human Rights.

James Hewitt, a committee member from Nebraska, felt that the dissenting votes were substantive as well as political. "No one thought there was any question concerning [Bork's] technical competency. [The opposition] was all on the basis of an agenda he would bring to the Supreme Court and his feelings on precedent." Hewitt did not think it impermissible to consider Bork's judicial philosophy, stating that "if somebody were an appellate judge and had a particular point of view that *stare decisis* had no value at all—no matter how brilliant he was—it would seem to me that he could have some problems."[63] One unnamed committee member was quoted as saying that the panel members debated whether Bork's views were "so far out of the mainstream that they threaten the constitutional process."[64]

By the time Fiske and Tyler, the outgoing and the newly elected chairmen, appeared at the Bork hearings to present the Standing Committee's report on Judge Bork, the battle lines had already been drawn. Senator Thurmond got right to the point, asking Tyler what prevented a committee member "from using ideological issues under the guise of evaluating [judicial] temperament."[65] Tyler responded that members should not do so unless there is a pattern of "such extreme ideology . . . as to then make an impact on appropriate judicial temperament."[66] Thurmond questioned how well the members abided by that statement, claiming that "almost without fail, every criticism indicated by your letter is really based on ideology."[67]

Senator Hatch, upset that the committee vote had been leaked in "an enormous breach of confidentiality," wondered aloud if the person who leaked the information, once found, would be allowed to stay on the committee.[68] Hatch also brought up the issue of conflicts of interest, pointing to member Jerome Shestack, who had publicly criticized the caliber of Reagan nominees.[69] Hatch asked Tyler if he thought antipathy toward the administration presented a conflict for committee members.[70] Tyler answered that there was no rule prohibiting members from being involved in political activities and that it was "up to the sound good sense and decency of each member to put aside this kind of activity in his committee work."[71]

Hatch was unpersuaded. Since the ACLU, the Lawyers Committee for Civil Rights Under Law, and other liberal groups had publicly opposed Bork, Hatch felt that members who affiliated with these groups had compromised the committee. Tyler, himself a former cochair of the Lawyers Committee for Civil Rights, came under fire as Hatch told him, "I think others like you should not be affiliated with committees that may be questionable with regard to their high fidelity to doing this job."[72]

Senator Alan Simpson questioned the ABA panel in his own inimitable fashion, freely admitting that "[w]hen our people do not get confirmed, we raise a lot of hack about you, and when our people do, we think you are the most noble people in America."[73] But Simpson also expressed real concern over the ABA report. He saw references to ideology and political views that belied the panel's assurance that Bork was fairly evaluated. How was it, Simpson wondered, that Bork could receive an "exceptionally well qualified" rating a mere five years before when Bork was nominated to the court of appeals? What had changed?[74] Tyler responded that the committee membership had changed in the intervening years.[75] Although he had previously discussed the committee's tendency to do a more searching investigation with Supreme Court nominees,[76] senators were left to make their own judgment as to whether the ABA's evaluation of a nominee's qualifications should depend on the composition of the Standing Committee.

The question of member bias and conflict arose with almost every conversational exchange. Under questioning by Senator Grassley, Tyler refused to divulge information on whether any committee member who personally interviewed Bork had voted against him. "I am sorry," Tyler said, "but to answer that would start us down the road as to who voted how, which I am trying my best to avoid."[77]

Clearly, the ABA's divided vote had damaged the Bork nomination. But in part the damage was caused by the reaction of Bork's own supporters, who made the crucial mistake of treating the ABA vote as a defeat and thereby helped turn it into a virtual disaster. It certainly was not obvious that a 10 to 4 vote, finding Bork to be "well qualified," should be viewed as a negative reaction from the bar. Four years later, the Bush administration, having learned from the Bork episode, treated a divided vote on Clarence Thomas as highly favorable, and thus helped to make it so, even though the vote on Thomas was much less favorable than the one on Bork. In any event, by the time Bork's nomination reached the Senate floor, the ABA vote had been identified as a significant factor in his downfall.

Aftermath: Pressure on the ABA

On the heels of the contentious Bork hearings came another difficult episode for the ABA. A member of the Standing Committee was quoted anonymously in the media as stating that Douglas Ginsburg, the new nominee for the Supreme Court, was a "Borklet." To many, the statement typified the bias and prejudgment manifested in the Bork vote. It also demonstrated the insularity of the committee, because members could make damaging, offhand remarks without fear of being identified. Finally, the news report provided yet another illustration of the committee's inability to control leaks. Although the "Borklet" statement was soon overshadowed by revelations about Ginsburg and the subsequent withdrawal of his nomination, the statement was not forgotten when ABA witnesses next appeared before the Senate Judiciary Committee.

Conservative animosity towards the ABA created tense moments during the final morning of confirmation hearings for Anthony Kennedy, the president's third candidate for Justice Powell's seat on the Supreme Court. Members of the Judiciary Committee took ABA witnesses to task for both the Bork and Ginsburg episodes. Committee members wanted to make sure that their points hit home with the ABA representatives.

Senator Hatch stated: "I am not raising [the confidentiality issue] to make your job uncomfortable here today. I just want to make sure that in the future, that type of breach really does not occur, because to me, it is highly unethical. . . . " Hatch asked Tyler whether the committee had considered "removing the cloak of anonymity" from ABA proceedings. In Hatch's opinion, the Standing Committee should release information on the credentials of its members, provide a list of the individuals interviewed by the committee, and state the reasons for each committee member's vote.[78] Tyler disagreed, noting that the fifteen members served not as private individuals but as part of a committee. "To say that we have to have sunshine laws apply to us, or that we have to individually account, would really turn the whole process, and the work of your committee, on its head, sir." Hatch was not satisfied with Tyler's response, and countered, "If we see another repeat of what happened to Judge Bork, this Senator is going to do everything in his power to make sure that there will be explanations given in full, fair and open hearings."[79]

Senator Charles Grassley was angered by news reports that a member of the committee had anonymously told reporters, even before the committee began reviewing Ginsburg's records, that Ginsburg would not win unanimous approval because he was too much like Bork. Grassley raised with Tyler the propriety of the committee's consideration of Ginsburg's judicial philosophy.[80]

When Patrick Leahy took his turn, he tried to rebut the charges against the ABA. "There seems to be some kind of feeling," he said, "that the ABA sunk the Bork nomination, or that the pressure groups sunk the Bork nomination. That is not so." Leahy continued: "Judge Bork is the one witness that really counted on the Bork nomination and it was his testimony . . . that determined that he was not going to go on the Supreme Court. It was not the testimony of the ABA or anyone else."[81]

The underlying anger about Bork was revealed throughout the morning. Senator Simpson believed the Senate had "elevated the ABA Committee to a position of omnipotence." Simpson also criticized the committee's ability to maintain secrecy in light of the divided vote on Judge Bork:

> ABA rejects Bork. That is what it said, all over the United States. Then you read it and find out that they had not rejected Bork, it was ten to four. But, that is the way it came out. The four were unknown to us and still remain so, while we have to trot out all our work here right under these lights. That is the way it ought to be for the ABA next time. I am going to help assure that it is, because I think it is wrong to give anonymity to some guy who has got a political idea about a nominee and is trying to shroud himself in a bunch of stuff.[82]

Chairman Biden, anxious to minimize the conflict, deflected some of the controversy by agreeing to hold subsequent hearings on the ABA's role in judicial selection. The Republican senators readily agreed, no doubt anticipating an opportunity to make real changes outside the glare of a pending nomination.

After Kennedy's confirmation and in response to the uproar generated by the remark that Ginsburg was a "Borklet," the ABA reinforced its long-standing rule prohibiting any committee member other than the chairman from making comments to the press. It was specifically provided that a violation of this rule could lead to dismissal of an offending committee member.[83]

Hearings on the Role of the ABA

In June 1989, Senator Biden chaired a hearing of the Judiciary Committee on the ABA's role in the judicial selection process. Biden set the tone in his opening statement: "Regardless of how these issues are resolved, I strongly believe that the [Judiciary] Committee must consider the ABA rating in light of the many other comments and recommendations the committee receives from outside groups. The views of the ABA are not and should not be given exclusive weight when we look at a nominee."[84]

Senator Thurmond wasted no time in spelling out the changes he wanted. He called for disclosure of the factors used in selecting members of the Standing Committee, a list of those consulted in evaluating judicial nominees, the votes of individual committee members together with their reasons for voting as they did, and a statement of the weight accorded to academic and scholarly performance. Thurmond also wanted the ABA to discipline members who violated its rules by leaking information to the press or the public. Finally, he proposed that the ABA make recommendations only when specifically requested to do so and that it determine only whether a nominee was "qualified" or "not qualified." Although he made no reference to Bork, Thurmond's shopping list neatly restated the controversies surrounding the Bork nomination.

Senator Hatch also took a strong stand: "I do want to say that I've been a member of the American Bar Association for almost 27, 28, 30 years—somewhere around that area—I'm proud of membership and so I bear no ill will. . . . But I personally believe that it's time to pull the plug on the American Bar Association."[85] Hatch thought that the ABA's recommendation should be given the same weight as the recommendation of any other organization. If the administration persisted in giving it special deference, the Senate should not. Hatch claimed that senators were giving up a great deal of their advise and consent authority by placing too much reliance on the ABA.[86]

Senator Howard Metzenbaum disputed these assertions and alluded to the historic criticism that the ABA was too conservative. Metzenbaum found it hard to believe that "so many people would be here and the lights would be on because the ABA has gotten too liberal and we better keep them out of the process with respect to choosing judges."[87] In his view, the controversy was more a matter of politics than of principle.

Attorney General Richard Thornburgh appeared at the oversight hearings at Biden's invitation to talk about the problems the Justice Department had with the ABA Committee. Senators Kennedy and Metzenbaum took the opportunity to quiz the attorney general on the administration's use of litmus tests for judges and on the input received from conservative lobby groups. Kennedy also focused on the administration's attitude toward judicial nominees who belonged to social clubs that discriminate against women and minorities.[88]

Senator Grassley pressed for changes in ABA screening practices. He said: "[T]here is much to clean up [and] I hope the Attorney General has brought his broom today. The Standing Committee operated in complete secrecy, assuredly to protect the confidential nature of the review. Yet the routine disclosure of information to the general public and to select groups by committee members when it suits them belies this concern."[89]

Biden's goal, more than anything else, was to give the senators a chance to discuss their long-standing problems with the ABA. Although the Judiciary Committee itself did not announce any change in the ABA's role, some significant changes were soon made. In the wake of the hearings on the ABA, the Standing Committee's guidelines were amended to make clear that a nominee's judicial philosophy was not to be considered. The language allowing the committee to consider the nominee's views, if they were extreme, was deleted. This effectively eliminated the only ground on which the committee's four-member minority could have defended its conclusion that Bork was unqualified for the Supreme Court. Thus, the strong reaction to the ABA vote on Judge Bork helped to change the rules governing ABA review but only after that review had helped to sink the Bork nomination.

Still, the controversy over the ABA's role would not die. In 1989, Robert L. Fiske Jr., former chairman of the Standing Committee, was denied the opportunity of serving as associate attorney general under Richard Thornburgh because of protests from conservatives over the committee's conduct during his years as chairman. It was during Fiske's tenure that notable conservatives like William Harvey and Lino Graglia were treated badly by the Select Committee, apparently because of their conservative legal views. It was also during Fiske's watch that liberal interest groups had received advance warning of conservative nominees.[90] Reaction to Fiske's nomination among conservatives was fierce. Patrick McGuigan and other activists lobbied against him.[91] And Senator Strom Thurmond, together with thirteen other Republican senators, sent a letter to Attorney General Richard Thornburgh opposing the nomination.[92] Finally, in July 1989, Thornburgh yielded to conservative pressure and abandoned the Fiske nomination.[93]

Abortion and the ABA

Conservatives found added support for their case against the ABA when, at a mid-year meeting in 1990, the ABA's Board of Governors passed a resolution of support for abortion rights. Even though the resolution was not directly related to the ABA's role in judicial selection, critics argued that the resolution showed the ABA's partisan posture.

The Justice Department reacted quickly and publicly. Attorney General Thornburgh, who had seriously considered suspending the Standing Committee's access to the names of potential nominees, was concerned that the ABA's pro-choice position could trigger an abortion litmus test for judicial candidates. Stanley Chauvin, then president of the ABA, announced that the abortion issue would not influence judicial ratings. Standing Committee chairman Ralph Lancaster declared that the committee did not and would not question candidates about their views on abortion. "That's a political area," Lancaster said, "that's for the Senate and the Administration to take up."[94]

Supporters of the abortion resolution believed the Justice Department was searching for a reason to discredit the Standing Committee. They pointed out that hundreds of existing ABA policies and resolutions—some highly controversial—had had no effect on judicial ratings. Nevertheless, the ABA's Board of Governors rescinded the abortion resolution, partly in response to protests from ABA members, more than fifteen hundred of whom had resigned in protest over the resolution. But some conservatives continued to express anger over the ABA's role in judicial selection because they objected to the organization's political positions.[95]

The Souter Nomination

The steady pounding of the ABA by conservatives appeared to take its toll on the Standing Committee. In April 1990, Kenneth Ryskamp, an extremely conservative judicial nominee, was found by the committee to be qualified for the federal court of appeals. The nomination of David Souter to the Supreme Court produced a similarly muted response from the ABA Committee. Under Lancaster's cautious leadership, the committee avoided conservative criticism for its evaluation of David Souter. Although Lancaster has denied that the committee was intimidated, staff members of the Senate Judiciary Committee told the *New York Times* that the committee had become more accommodating since being threatened with removal from the process.[96] Professor Sheldon Goldman concluded in *Judicature* magazine that the ABA Committee had been more accommodating to President Bush's lower court appointments than it was to Reagan's appointments.[97]

Lancaster prevailed upon the deans of the Northwestern and Stanford law schools to create independent reading committees to review Souter's opinions and to submit a written report advising the Standing Committee of the "nominee's analytical ability and writing skills in the context of his professional competence." Rex Lee, former solicitor general and president of Brigham Young University, headed up a third reading group. These three groups replaced the teams of practicing lawyers who were previously used to evaluate nominee writings.[98] In addition, committee members themselves reviewed Souter's opinions as attorney general, trial judge, and member of the New Hampshire Supreme Court. In short order, the committee determined that Souter was "well qualified" for the Supreme Court.

Nonetheless, during the Judiciary Committee hearings, ABA panelists were questioned on the issues that had created so much controversy during the Bork proceedings. Senator Grassley came right to the point, stating that "the ABA is at best an irrelevancy." Referring not to the Souter nomination but to the Bork vote, Grassley asked rhetorically, "When you smuggle illicit considerations into your process, why do we need the ABA?" Grassley concluded by saying, "I honestly think the time has come to give the ABA a gold watch and retire them from what they've been doing."[99]

Senator Specter correctly observed that a mere "irrelevancy couldn't have inspired Senator Grassley's comments." Specter praised the ABA's efforts in assisting the Senate. In his view, any irrelevant factors in the ABA's evaluation were ultimately the Senate's problem: "If you do exceed the bounds of relevancy, we'll figure that out."[100]

As the panelists concluded their brief testimony before the Judiciary Committee, both strong support and veiled hostility resounded throughout the room. In the three years since the Bork nomination, animosities had faded, but they still colored the hearings. Senator Biden drew a laugh on closing, when he told the panelists, "You must be doing something right because everyone's been mad at you."[101]

The Thomas Nomination

Continued discrediting of the ABA was exactly what conservatives had in mind when President Bush nominated Clarence Thomas to replace retiring Justice Thurgood Marshall. A senior White House official, who called the ABA "politicized," said the White House intended to "inoculate Thomas" against a low ABA rating by showing that the panel is comprised of corporate lawyers who do not value government service of the kind given by Thomas. The official was not deterred by the fact that a similar panel had given high ratings to Judge Souter.[102]

Senator Hatch was even more strident in his criticism of the ABA. He stated that if the ABA gave Thomas less than the "qualified" rating given him when he was nominated to the court of appeals, it could result in the ABA's removal from the process. Senator Grassley added, "If they [the ABA] go beyond their charter . . . I will help pull the plug."[103]

In the end, the ABA gave Thomas a rating of "qualified," although two committee members rated Thomas "unqualified" for the Supreme Court, and one member abstained. Both Thomas's opponents and his supporters hailed the committee's action as helpful to their cause. Arthur Kropp of People for the American Way said the committee's conclusion "is a direct contradiction of President Bush's assertion that Clarence Thomas is the best man for the job."[104] Judith Lichtman of the Women's Legal Defense Fund remarked that "the ABA's lukewarm endorsement, coupled with a minority finding of 'unqualified,' indicates that Judge Thomas is the wrong man for the job."[105]

On the other hand, Thomas's chief supporter in the Senate, John Danforth, said the committee's rating was "a further step toward his confirmation." He added that it was "consistent with the many positive impressions he has made among senators."[106] White House press spokesman Marlin Fitzwater issued a statement saying, "[W]e are very pleased that the ABA's Standing Committee . . . has found Judge Thomas qualified to be an associate justice of the United States Supreme Court."[107] In contrast to the reaction over the ABA's vote on Judge Bork, little attention was paid to the minority who found Thomas to be unqualified. Conservatives simply dismissed the minority as "liberal ideologues."

According to Ron Olson, chairman of the Standing Committee, the dissenters voted against Thomas on the basis of professional competence. They focused particularly on Thomas's law review articles and found them to be "shallow." In their judgment, Thomas's articles "were not well documented and supported and he failed to confront and deal with strong arguments on the opposite side of the issue."[108] In the end, the ABA's vote on Thomas had little impact on his nomination.

13
OTHER WITNESSES

An unprecedented number of witnesses testified at the Bork hearings. Bork's own testimony had taken thirty hours over a five-day period. The testimony of other witnesses consumed fifty-seven hours over an eight-day period. In all, 112 witnesses testified. There were an equal number of witness panels supporting and opposing Bork's confirmation. But even this appearance of parity worked against Bork. In a typical confirmation hearing, most of the testimony is favorable to the nominee. The very fact that half of the panels testified in opposition to Bork suggested that this nomination was highly controversial and that it was somehow different from nearly all the ones preceding it.

The selection of witnesses was also revealing. The procedure was for the Democratic majority to select its witnesses and for the Republican minority to do the same. Both sides chose speakers who were thought to be good advocates and who would not be identified as representatives of "special interests." Accordingly, a large number of the witnesses selected to testify were law professors or other members of the legal profession. Noticeably absent were representatives of groups like NOW, the NAACP, and organized labor. This chapter sets forth some of the highlights of the testimony of those witnesses.

VOICES FROM THE MINORITY COMMUNITY

The first witness to testify after Judge Bork and the ABA representatives was William T. Coleman, former secretary of transportation for President Ford and now a prominent Los Angeles attorney, who testified against Bork's confirmation. The fact that Coleman, a black Republican and a Reagan supporter, would testify against Bork was significant because it showed that opposition to Bork was not confined to partisan Democrats. Coleman's testimony was also significant because he had been a member of the ABA panel that earlier found Bork to be "exceptionally well qualified" to serve on the federal court of appeals, and he could therefore address the question of whether that finding could be reconciled with a rejection of Judge Bork for the Supreme Court.

Coleman explained that the standard which the ABA applied to Supreme Court nominees was different from the standard applied to nominees for the court of appeals.[1] But while Coleman was correct that the ABA held Supreme Court nominees to a higher standard of professional competence and ability, that standard still did not provide a basis for giving a low rating to a nominee simply because of disagreement with his or her judicial philosophy. However, Coleman argued that whether or not the ABA could consider judicial philosophy in rating Supreme Court nominees, the Senate had a wider responsibility and a range of inquiry which extended beyond the issue of a nominee's professional qualifications—competence, judicial temperament, and integrity. As will be seen later, this was an argument that played well to public opinion.[2]

Coleman then proceeded to make his case against Judge Bork on the merits. He focused on three principal issues: the right to privacy, civil rights, and Bork's view of precedent. Coleman argued that Bork gave too narrow a reading to the liberty clause of the Fourteenth Amendment.[3] In his opinion, if Bork's view had prevailed, there would be no constitutional right to travel, no constitutionally protected right to marry, and no constitutional right to use contraceptives. But neither the right to travel nor the right to use contraceptives had been based on the liberty clause, and the right to marry would clearly be protected through the political processes and through the equal protection clause, no matter how the liberty clause was interpreted.

Coleman made a somewhat stronger case on the other two issues. He said that Bork had been on the wrong side of every major civil rights case except *Brown v. Board of Education*.[4] In support of that assessment, Coleman observed that Bork had once argued that the equal protection clause should be applied only to racial discrimination and not to discrimination based on gender or illegitimacy. Although Bork had testified that the Fourteenth Amendment applies to all people, Coleman remained skeptical.

Coleman's final point was that Bork believed a judge has no duty to adhere to a prior case that cannot be reconciled with the intent of the Framers. Coleman thought this made it too easy for Bork to vote to overturn any Supreme Court decision with which he disagreed. In his testimony, Bork had expressed a greater willingness to defer to precedent, indicating that he would do so where settled expectations had grown up around prior Court decisions; but Coleman simply noted other instances in which Bork had expressed less compunction about adhering to precedent.[5]

Although Bork's supporters could readily muster legal arguments in response to Coleman, the important aspect of the testimony was not what Coleman said about specific issues but the very fact that he had testified against Bork's confirmation. As a moderate Republican, Coleman helped to legitimize opposition to Bork from moderates and independents. Bork's opponents realized quite early that the confirmation process involved not an intellectual or legal battle but a political one. By controlling the symbols of the debate, they were able to prevail in the forum that mattered most—the forum of public opinion.

Former Congresswoman Barbara Jordan testified immediately after William Coleman. Jordan related her own experience in twice losing elections in Texas because of political gerrymandering that diluted the voting strength of blacks. It was not until after the Supreme Court handed down the reapportionment decision in *Baker v. Carr*[6] that she won election to the Texas House of Representatives. Jordan said that if the Supreme Court had subscribed to Judge Bork's views, she would never have been elected. In slow and measured speech, Jordan scoffed at Judge Bork's notion that there is no "theoretical basis" for the one-man, one-vote principle, stating: "Maybe there is no theoretical basis for [it], but I will tell you this much. There is a common sense, natural rational basis for all votes counting equally."[7]

Jordan was not entirely accurate in her characterization of Bork's views on apportionment. Judge Bork thought that *Baker v. Carr* was correctly decided because the legislature in that case was so malapportioned that a majority of voters had no real opportunity to enact a new apportionment plan. Jordan was correct, however, in observing that Bork believed the principle of one-man, one-vote was "too much of a straightjacket" and was not required by the Fourteenth Amendment. Bork said the legislature could adopt the one-man, one-vote rule if it wished, but he found nothing in American constitutional history that dictated such a result. Bork argued that legislative districting, the executive veto, and the legislative committee system are all inconsistent with a constitutional requirement of one-man, one-vote.

Jordan also criticized Judge Bork's view on the constitutionality of the poll tax. Bork had testified that there was no evidence that the poll tax, which the Supreme Court invalidated, had been applied in a racially discriminatory fashion.[8] Jordan again drew on her personal experience to relate the effect that the poll tax had in Texas: "That poll tax was used to keep people from voting. The Supreme Court said it was wrong [and] outlawed it."[9]

The next witness against Bork was the eminent historian John Hope Franklin. Franklin told about an incident in 1922 when he and his mother boarded a train in Oklahoma. After they had seated themselves in the nearest seats, the conductor ordered them to go to the Negro coach, half of which was used for baggage. When his mother refused to move, the conductor stopped the train and put them off in the woods. Franklin also testified that he had been barred from studying for his doctorate degree at the University of Oklahoma and that while teaching at Howard University, he was obliged to bring his lunch with him on weekends because no restaurant in Washington would serve him. Franklin went on to praise the Supreme Court for decisions that opened restaurants to blacks. He pointed out that the Civil Rights Act of 1964, which Bork had opposed, was instrumental in establishing the right of blacks to gain access to places of public accommodation.

Echoing the theme of Senator Kennedy, Franklin argued that the country would have been quite different if Bork had been on the Court and his views had prevailed. Franklin said, "Nothing in Judge Bork's record suggests to me that, had he been on the Supreme Court at an earlier date, he would have had the vision and the courage to strike down a statute requiring the eviction of a black family from a train for sitting in the so-called white coach, or the rejection of a black student at a so-called white state university, or the refusal of a white restaurant owner to serve a black patron."[10]

Coleman, Jordan, and Franklin were powerful symbols of minority opposition to Judge Bork. Jordan and Franklin were extremely effective in portraying the evils of racial discrimination. At the same time, Coleman, Jordan, and Franklin were able to raise the concerns of the civil rights community without being identified as part of any "special interest." They were not speaking as representatives of the NAACP or of any other organization. It was difficult, therefore, to characterize their opposition to Bork as merely a product of special-interest politics.

VIEWS FROM THE ACADEMY

The role of law professors in the Bork proceedings was quite different from the role played by academics in previous hearings for Supreme Court nominees. Law professors had been rather inactive in confirmation battles until Justice Rehnquist's nomination to be chief justice in 1986. Nan Aron of the Alliance for Justice, one of the members of the coalition trying to block Bork's confirmation, remarked that law professors "like to write books and wax eloquent in writing but . . . I've always felt they were more derelict when it came to taking a stand."[11]

However, dereliction was not the only cause for the passivity of law professors in previous confirmation struggles for Supreme Court nominees. Because prior confirmation hearings had generally not focused on the nominee's judicial philosophy, the testimony and assistance of law professors would have been much less useful than they seemed to be in the Bork case. For example, Judge Haynsworth was opposed explicitly on grounds of conflict of interest, although some liberal senators may have been motivated by ideological considerations in deciding to raise these ethical questions. Not surprisingly, only three law professors— Charles Alan Wright of Texas, William Van Alstyne of Duke, and G. W. Foster, Jr., of the University of Wisconsin Law School—made submissions, and all of them supported Haynsworth's nomination.[12]

Similarly, only five law professors testified at the hearings on Judge G. Harrold Carswell, who was nominated after Judge Haynsworth's confirmation vote had failed.[13] Since Carswell was defeated largely because of charges of mediocrity and of injudicious temperament,[14] it might seem that the testimony of law professors would have been fairly useful. But, in fact, almost no one had tried to rebut the charge of mediocrity. Instead, one of Carswell's supporters in the Senate argued that mediocre lawyers should be entitled to some representation on the Supreme Court.[15] With the issue thus drawn not on the question whether Carswell was mediocre but on whether mediocrity should be a qualifying or disqualifying factor, the outcome was a foregone conclusion, and there was no need to spend much time listening to law professors. Only Professor James Moore of Yale, who delivered a five-minute statement, testified on behalf of Carswell. Professor William Van Alstyne of Duke, who had testified in favor of Judge Haynsworth, appeared in opposition to Carswell. Van Alstyne, as John Frank has pointed out, was a strong witness for Haynsworth and an equally strong one against Carswell.[16] No purpose would have been served by calling many more academics to testify to Carswell's shortcomings.

Law professors played a larger role in the nomination of Justice Rehnquist to be chief justice. Professor Arthur Berney of Boston College drafted a letter opposing the Rehnquist nomination. The letter, which was distributed by Senator Metzenbaum on the eve of the Senate debate on confirmation, was signed by seventy-six law professors. Another thirty professors called Senator Metzenbaum's office to ask that their names be added to it. The letter criticized Rehnquist for insensitivity on certain ethical and moral issues. It charged that evidence relating to voter harassment by Rehnquist, restrictive covenants on his property, and a prosegregation memorandum revealed a high degree of "moral obtuseness." The letter also criticized Rehnquist for failing to disqualify himself in an army surveillance case, after having participated in defending the army's surveillance policy as head of the Attorney General's Office of Legal Counsel.[17]

The participation of law professors in the Bork hearings contrasted sharply with their participation in previous confirmation proceedings. First, the sheer number of law professors opposing Bork was staggering. There were three important letters from the academic community opposing Bork's confirmation. One of the letters was signed by 1,925 law professors, fully 40 percent of the faculty members in ABA-accredited law schools.[18] Other letters, signed by law school deans and constitutional law professors, were also submitted in opposition to confirmation.[19]

The chief organizers of the academic opposition were William Taylor, a civil rights lawyer and an officer of the Leadership Conference on Civil Rights; John Haber, a legislative aide with People for the American Way; and law professors Herman Schwartz of American University, Walter Dellinger of Duke, Laurence Tribe of Harvard, and Philip Kurland of the University of Chicago. Taylor was asked by Senator Kennedy if he would coordinate the law school deans' opposition to Bork. Taylor also helped coordinate the opposition among constitutional law professors.[20] He sent letters to all constitutional law teachers who had been teaching the subject for more than five years, except those who were known to be supporting Bork. Taylor said, "It wasn't that scientific an effort." He generated a list of law professors simply by looking in the annual *Directory of Law Teachers*, published by the American Association of Law Schools.[21]

John Haber, with the assistance of Herman Schwartz and William Taylor, drafted a letter to be sent to law professors, asking that they sign their names to indicate their opposition to Bork. Haber apparently "tried to identify a contact person at each law school and to find out if that contact person would get other people who would take a position."[22] In many cases, the contact person was essentially self-selected. The professors who called or wrote to People for the American Way offering to help were the ones who collected signatures from their colleagues to add to the form letter.[23]

The forces favoring Judge Bork's nomination were able to generate some support from law professors but not nearly as much as the anti-Bork side had generated. The list of "Selected Law Professors" signing the pro-Bork letter numbered only 107, although it is clear that other law professors also supported Bork's nomination.[24] While the two sides were more evenly matched in their formal testimony before the Judiciary Committee, the difference between 107 supporters and 1,925 opponents was a stark reminder of the controversial nature of this nomination.

In all, forty law professors and deans testified at the Bork hearings, compared with the previous record of five, who had testified at the hearings on Judge Carswell. Professor Laurence Tribe of Harvard Law School was given the most time—two and a half hours—to explain his reasons for opposing Bork's confirmation. Tribe argued that because of Bork's potential influence on the Court and because of Bork's legal views—which, Tribe believed, would pose serious risks to the traditional role of the Court as a defender of civil liberties—those favoring confirmation should bear the burden of proof. Tribe criticized Bork's views on the right to privacy, equal protection, free speech, and executive power. The prospect of Bork's appointment was especially worrisome to Tribe because he thought that Bork would be less respectful of precedent as a member of the Supreme Court than he had been as a member of the court of appeals. In short, Tribe believed that Bork had an agenda to overrule prior cases which were not consistent with his own view of the Constitution and with the intent of the Framers.

Tribe also argued that the Senate should not be persuaded by Bork's "confirmation conversions." In his written statement, Tribe said that

Bork's earlier record on free speech, constructed over a period of two decades, was a better indicator of how he might rule in future cases than Bork's grudging acceptance of *Brandenburg* as "settled law."[25] Tribe added that there was a considerable risk that as the law unfolds over the next decade or two, Bork's more restrictive views would shrink the scope of First Amendment protection.

Professor Walter Dellinger of Duke who, like Tribe, had been one of Senator Biden's consultants, testified that Judge Bork's narrow view of the liberty clause of the Fourteenth Amendment, particularly his refusal to recognize a right to privacy, "is inconsistent with the text, the original intention, and the history leading up to that clause."[26] Similarly, Professor Sylvia Law of New York University criticized Bork for his "cramped" view of the equal protection clause. She argued that until recently, Bork's view of equal protection prohibited certain forms of racial discrimination and little else. Law also maintained that Bork's position on federal civil rights statutes "does not reflect empathetic concern for women's aspirations for equality and liberty."[27]

Finally, Bork's Yale colleague, Burke Marshall, who served as assistant attorney general for civil rights in the Kennedy and Johnson administrations, was also sharply critical of Bork. In his written statement, Marshall said that he opposed Bork's confirmation not because of his views on any particular case but because of the general tenor and substance of Bork's judicial philosophy. According to Marshall, Bork showed "no awareness, no understanding of the enormity and the scope of the system of racial injustice that was implemented by law in this country. And that insensitivity has to do importantly with what is wrong, both historically and in terms of constitutional purpose, with Judge Bork's ungenerous concept of the role of the federal judiciary, and especially the Supreme Court, under the equal protection clause and the other provisions of the Civil War Amendments."[28] But Professor Marshall had not registered this objection against Antonin Scalia, whose views were similar to those of Judge Bork; nor would he later register it against Clarence Thomas, who was more conversant with racial injustice than Professor Marshall but nevertheless was generally in agreement with Bork and Scalia.

In Bork's defense, several law professors echoed the theme advanced by Lloyd Cutler that Bork was "well within the mainstream" of legal scholars. Professor Michael McConnell of the University of Chicago Law School argued that Bork's philosophy of judicial restraint is a well respected one and is central to democratic government in this country. He stated that as a civil libertarian, he shared Bork's view that Supreme Court justices should defend values found in the Constitution and should not be "expositors of their own social and economic opinions."[29] McConnell said that Bork's record as a judge—unanimous decisions in 86 percent of his cases, dissents in relatively few, and not a single reversal by the Supreme Court—demonstrated that Bork "is plainly in the mainstream of American law."[30]

Professor George Priest of Yale argued that Bork's academic writings were not indicative of how he would act as a Supreme Court justice. Priest said that Bork's work as solicitor general and as a federal judge were in sharp contrast to his performance as an academician. In his public-service work, there was no slashing disregard of previous opinion, no single-mindedness, and no "extreme fidelity to the purity of an idea." Priest argued that with few exceptions, Bork's opinions as a federal judge were supported by his colleagues because they were reasonable, moderate, and respectful of prior opinion.[31]

But in the end, the best that Bork's academic supporters could achieve against opposing witnesses was a draw, and even that assessment gives them the benefit of the doubt. Yet, a standoff was not nearly enough, because Bork's writings and his own testimony, together with the media campaign against confirmation,[32] had seriously damaged Bork with members of the committee and with other senators as well.

AN OBJECTION FROM THE BENCH

After Bork's nomination to the Supreme Court was announced, Judge James F. Gordon sent a letter to the Judiciary Committee in which he complained vigorously about Bork's conduct in *Vander Jagt v. O'Neill*,[33] a decision of the federal court of appeals in which Bork and Gordon had participated, along with Judge Roger Robb. Gordon charged that Bork had written an opinion which changed the agreed-upon basis for decision and that Bork had basically tried to sneak the change past Gordon and Robb. Judge Gordon concluded his letter to the committee by stating, "I do not believe one who would resort to the actions toward his own colleagues and the majesty of the law as did Judge Bork, in this instance, possesses those qualities of character, forthrightness and truthfulness necessary for those who would grace our highest Court."[34] Although Gordon did not testify at the Bork hearings, his accusations were aired and were fully considered by the Judiciary Committee.

The *Vander Jagt* case arose out of a complaint by several Republican congressmen, charging that they were underrepresented on various House committees, which thereby diluted their political influence and that of their constituents. The case presented a significant question as to whether the congressmen had standing to sue. However, Judge Gordon wrote in his letter to the committee that he and Robb and Judge Bork had agreed on March 19, 1982, to sustain the district court's dismissal of the lawsuit not on the basis of standing but on the basis of the court's "remedial discretion."[35]

On September 17, 1982, Bork sent a copy of his draft opinion to Judge Gordon, but Bork failed to mention in his cover letter that he had changed the basis for the court's decision to one of "no standing."[36] A week later, Bork wrote to Gordon, "It occurs to me too late that I should have notified you in advance that I had changed the rationale in the *Vander Jagt* case to one of lack of standing."[37] At his confirmation hearings, Bork told Senator DeConcini that he could not recall whether he had heard of Judge Gordon's concerns before writing to him a second time.[38] In any event, Gordon continued to believe that Bork's failure to point out the change to him was intentional and was designed by Bork to cause his own minority views on standing to become the prevailing law.

In his testimony and in a lengthy letter submitted to the committee, Bork contradicted the basic thrust of Gordon's charges. Bork conceded that his cover letter to Judge Gordon did not call attention to the change in the basis for decision. Bork argued, however, that it was not his intention to deceive anyone. On the contrary, he said that he spoke to Judge Robb and that Robb concurred with him at the time, although Robb could not recall that conversation later in the year.[39]

Some support for Bork's account is provided by Paul Larkin, a law clerk who worked on the case with Judge Bork. Larkin says that he definitely remembers talking to Bork after Bork had spoken with Robb. Larkin recalls Bork telling him at the time that Robb agreed with Bork on the "standing" rationale.[40] In addition, Robb's former secretary, Ruth Luff, remembered seeing Bork go into Judge Robb's chambers to speak with him about the case. She stated in an affidavit submitted to the committee that because of Robb's ill health, she was not surprised that Robb could not recall his meeting with Bork.[41]

Joseph Lee, Robb's law clerk when *Vander Jagt* was decided, disputes Ms. Luff's characterization of Judge Robb's memory at that time. In an affidavit submitted to the Judiciary Committee, Lee stated that Robb had consistently impressed him as an intelligent and thoughtful individual and that he was unaware of any significant memory lapses by Robb prior to Robb's stroke in November 1982. Lee thought it unlikely that if Robb had agreed to a change in the *Vander Jagt* rationale some time after March, he would have completely forgotten this by October. In his affidavit, Lee also said that after reading Bork's draft opinion, he called Judge Robb, who was then hospitalized with a broken hip, and expressed surprise that Bork's draft had disposed of the case on grounds of standing to sue. Judge Robb asked whether Bork or his clerks had said anything about the change. Lee replied that they had not. Lee says that Robb was both surprised and angered.[42] He apparently did not expect the case to be decided on grounds of standing.

Shortly thereafter, Robb sent a memorandum to Bork, expressing his surprise that Bork's opinion was based on standing. Bork then tried once more to mend his fences by writing a memorandum to Robb and Gordon in which he again apologized for his previous failure to communicate with Judge Gordon. He also mentioned that he had spoken earlier with Judge Robb about the change but that "Robb does not remember my conversation with him, does not doubt it took place, but is sure he must have misunderstood what I proposed."[43]

Bork apparently thought he had succeeded in placating Judge Gordon since he received a letter from Gordon, dated December 17, 1982, in which Gordon expressed his pleasure at sitting on the case with Judge Bork and wished him a "joyous Yuletide Season."[44] Bork was obviously surprised at Gordon's strenuous objection to his nomination to the Supreme Court. Although Bork may have hoped to discredit Gordon by referring to the friendly Yuletide greeting that Gordon had sent him, most observers would take Gordon's remarks as only a courteous gesture, which is what Gordon says they were. Gordon also said that he wanted to protect himself because he was afraid that he might have to sit with Judge Bork again.[45]

An interview with Judge Gordon revealed why he sincerely believed that Bork engaged in deliberate deception. As Gordon tells it, Judge Robb asked Bork to draft the opinion in *Vander Jagt* after the three judges decided to affirm the trial court's dismissal of the case for reasons other than standing. Before they left the conference room, Judge Bork restated a position he had taken earlier in the conference that perhaps the case should be decided on the basis of lack of standing. Gordon stated that both he and Robb took "vigorous exception" to that position and reiterated their view that the case should be decided on the basis of "remedial discretion."[46]

Gordon heard nothing more about the matter until he received Bork's draft opinion in September. Gordon's law clerk, David Tachau, read the opinion and was intrigued by the "no standing" rationale. Tachau, who was then a recent graduate of the University of Michigan Law School, had written a law review note on standing to sue, so he was quite familiar with the issues presented in Bork's draft opinion. Tachau wanted to see if the parties had raised the issue of standing, so he looked through the files for copies of the briefs. Instead, he found a copy of the judges' summary of the basis for their decision, which stated that the plaintiffs "had standing to bring this suit, but [the court] would dismiss the case on other grounds."[47] Tachau was pleased to find this summary because he thought it would now be easier to persuade Gordon to reject Bork's opinion.

Tachau showed Gordon the summary of the judges' decision and asked why the rationale for the *Vander Jagt* ruling had been changed. Gordon expressed concern that Bork's draft was contrary to the panel's decision in March, and he wondered whether the reason for the change was that Judge Robb had changed his mind. Gordon asked Tachau to call Robb's chambers and find out whether Robb had changed his position. Tachau spoke with Joseph Lee, who told him that Judge Robb was in the hospital but that the matter would be taken up with him.[48]

Within the next week, Gordon received a telephone call from his old friend, Judge Wilkey, who told him that Robb did not agree with Bork's "standing rationale" and that he was very unhappy with the direction the opinion had taken. Wilkey, who was a colleague of Robb and Bork on the court of appeals, said that Robb wanted Gordon to draft an opinion which would recognize the plaintiffs' standing to sue but would dismiss their claim on the basis of "remedial discretion." Gordon told David Tachau about this discussion and asked him to draft an opinion along those lines.[49]

Judge Gordon's account may help to explain Gordon's annoyance with Bork. It does not, however, prove that Bork was dishonest or deceitful in dealing with him and Robb. Judge Tyler, in writing the ABA report on Bork's nomination to the Supreme Court, said that "even accepting Judge Gordon's recollection of the events, the [ABA] committee did not believe the matter was serious, particularly since it happens once in a while in . . . the best of circumstances."[50] Obviously, the ABA panel concluded that misunderstandings and failures of communication happen from time to time, even without any deception. Moreover, it is hard to believe that Bork would have tried to sneak an opinion past his colleagues, since he could hardly assume that they would sign the opinion without reading it or, at least, having it reviewed by their law clerks. Finally, as Bork pointed out in his letter to the Judiciary Committee, the opinion would also be circulated to the other judges on the court of appeals, any one of whom might raise the matter with Judge Robb or with other colleagues.[51] It is not surprising, therefore, that Judge Bork's opponents were unable to get much mileage out of Bork's role in the *Vander Jagt* case.

14
THE MEDIA CAMPAIGN: POLLING AND ADVERTISING IN THE CONFIRMATION PROCESS

Public opinion polls and media advertising played an unprecedented role in the battle to defeat the Bork nomination. Polling results signaled that Bork was beatable and thereby encouraged potential opponents to exert greater efforts to defeat the nomination. Bork's opponents were also able to use polls to learn which issues would be most effective in their advertising campaign. Finally, polls were used at the end of the process to convince senators that it was politically wise to vote against Bork's confirmation.

Early polls showed that despite widespread publicity, most people had never heard of Robert Bork. Among those who had heard of him, public opinion was closely divided. In a *Washington Post-ABC News* poll conducted in August, 45 percent of this group approved the nomination and 40 percent disapproved.[1] However, a majority of all of those interviewed in the poll said that they had not read or heard anything about Judge Bork.[2]

The early polls also suggested that it would be politically feasible for the Senate to expand on its traditional role in Supreme Court confirmations. In the *Washington Post-ABC News* poll of August 3–5, 46 percent said the Senate should consider only Bork's background and qualifications in deciding whether to confirm him, but 51 percent said the Senate should also consider Bork's legal views.[3] And in the Martilla & Kiley poll conducted for AFSCME, a labor union representing state and municipal employees, a large majority expressed the view that the Senate would be justified in rejecting a nominee who was "committed to a narrow philosophy" or who "does not seem to be a fair-minded person."[4] By framing the question in this way, the pollsters clearly suggested that Judge Bork was committed to a narrow philosophy and was not fair minded. This made it more likely that interviewees would favor Senate consideration of Bork's judicial philosophy. If the public could be persuaded that Bork's legal philosophy was wrong headed, voter sentiment would then be used to generate pressure on members of the Senate.

The polling data clearly showed Bork's vulnerability with important segments of the Democratic Party, which was still in control of the U.S. Senate. The Martilla & Kiley poll showed that Bork was generally supported by a majority of whites, males, and Republicans but that he was opposed by most blacks, women, and Democrats.[5] Opponents of the Bork nomination were able to exploit this information because a number of southern senators had been elected with only a minority of white votes and an overwhelming majority of black votes. By demonizing Bork among black voters, opponents could bring enormous pressure to bear on these senators. The key was to find issues with which to persuade voters that Bork's judicial philosophy would be harmful to them.

The Martilla & Kiley poll showed that voters could be persuaded to oppose the Bork nomination if they became convinced that Bork was not "fair minded" and that the best way to increase voter skepticism would be to show that Bork was unsympathetic to civil rights.[6] The pollsters also learned that many people believed that Bork had made antiabortion statements but still did not think that *Roe v. Wade* would be overturned. When informed that Bork's confirmation could result in a change in abortion rulings, more people were willing to oppose Judge Bork.[7] On the other hand, the poll showed that the Watergate issue might not work against Bork; voters simply were no longer very interested in Watergate.[8]

After obtaining the results of the Martilla & Kiley poll and of some focus-group sessions, lawyers and media specialists gathered together, trying to develop the issues that would be most effective against Bork. They wrote a three-page memorandum that listed five major themes: (1) that Bork would turn back the clock on many Supreme Court decisions, (2) that he opposed civil rights, (3) that Bork supported big business and big government, (4) that he opposed women's rights and the Supreme Court's decision in *Roe v. Wade*, and (5) that Bork would restrict First Amendment rights.[9]

By the beginning of September, just before the committee hearings began, a *New York Times-CBS News* poll showed that 14 percent of respondents supported Judge Bork's confirmation, 13 percent opposed it,
and a staggering 66 percent were undecided.[10] Nan Aron, director of the
Alliance for Justice, said that Bork opponents were heartened by this poll
because it demonstrated that they were "getting [their message] across
and that people weren't blindly supporting Bork. It wasn't that it demonstrated that [people] were opposed, but that they were open and that
our campaign had had results."[11]

Bork's testimony before the Judiciary Committee, and the publicity
attending it, marked a major turning point in voter sentiment. A *New
York Times-CBS News* poll showed Bork's support to be eroding after his
appearance before the committee. The *New York Times-CBS News* poll
conducted during the week of September 21 showed 26 percent of the
people surveyed to have an unfavorable opinion of Judge Bork, 16 percent with a favorable opinion, and 57 percent undecided or having no
opinion. When the same question was asked ten days earlier—just before
the committee hearings—11 percent had a favorable opinion and 12 percent had an unfavorable opinion.[12] A *Washington Post-ABC News* poll
conducted during and after Bork's testimony showed that Bork was opposed by eight out of ten blacks. Furthermore, opposition among southern whites had risen from 25 percent to 41 percent since the previous
Washington Post-ABC News poll conducted in August.

To make matters worse, some of Bork's opponents manipulated their
polling techniques in order to magnify Bork's political vulnerability. A
Lou Harris poll, conducted between September 17 and September 23,
showed that 57 percent of respondents believed Bork should not be confirmed, while only 29 percent believed he should be confirmed, with 14
percent not sure. But the Harris survey was clearly slanted against Bork.
Before being asked whether they supported or opposed confirmation,
survey participants were provided with two pro-Bork and two anti-Bork
statements and were invited to comment on them. The statements that
ostensibly favored Bork were: (1) "Judge Bork seems well informed, and
such qualifications are worth more than where he stands on giving minorities equal treatment, protecting the privacy of individuals, or other
issues;" and (2) "If President Reagan says that Judge Bork is totally qualified to be on the Supreme Court, then that's enough for me to favor the
Senate confirming his nomination."[13] On the other hand, the anti-Bork
statements were much more alarming and gave far stronger reasons

for opposing the nomination than the pro-Bork statements gave for supporting it.[14] One anti-Bork statement quoted Judge Bork as saying that "when a state passes a law prohibiting a married couple from using birth control devices in the privacy of their own home, there is nothing in the Constitution that says the Supreme Court should protect such married people's right to privacy" and added, "that kind of statement worries me." The other anti-Bork statement was that "Judge Bork seems to be too much of an extreme conservative, and, if confirmed, he would do the country harm by allowing the Supreme Court to turn back the clock on rights for minorities, women, abortion, and other areas of equal justice for all people."[15]

But the poll that seemed to signal the end of Bork's chances for confirmation was a survey of voters in twelve southern states, conducted by the Roper Organization for the *Atlanta Journal-Constitution*. It showed 51 percent of respondents were opposed to Bork's confirmation, 31 percent were in favor of it, and 18 percent were undecided.[16] Bork's opponents used the poll to help win the swing votes in the Senate—the southern Democrats. Nan Aron of the Alliance for Justice confirmed that their strategy was to target the southern senators, particularly the five freshmen Democrats elected with large black majorities.[17] Senator John B. Breaux, one of the freshmen Democrats, remarked that the people who had supported him were the ones who felt most strongly about the Bork nomination. Breaux added that if he decided to vote for confirmation, he would need to have "a hell of a good reason."[18]

Although polling results had a considerable impact on the outcome, it should be noted that many southern Democrats were predisposed against the Bork nomination from the beginning. Southern Democrats were no longer the conservative senators of an earlier era.[19] Furthermore, they were unwilling to give much deference to President Reagan's nomination of Bork, after Reagan had campaigned against them on the issue of retaining Republican control over judicial appointments. Walter Dellinger, a law professor at Duke who worked closely with Senator Biden, pointed out that southern Democrats had conducted a cloakroom ballot early in the confirmation process and that the vote was overwhelmingly against Bork. This led Dellinger to conclude that if the senators had voted without regard to political considerations, Bork would have been defeated.[20] But of course, senators live in the real world, where politics are all important, and the polling results gave them the political cover they needed. As Bork himself noted, his decline in public opinion polls "proved devastating to holding the southern senators."[21] The polling results also opened the door to a massive advertising campaign against Senate confirmation.

Bork's opponents were skillful in using the information learned from the polls to help structure their media campaign against confirmation. Advertisements, news releases, interviews, and grassroots lobbying were focused on the issues identified by the polls as being of greatest concern to the voters. People for the American Way spent close to $2 million on its advertising campaign, more than any other group in the anti-Bork coalition. In absolute terms, this was not a large amount for such a campaign, but the Bork opposition was also able to capture a great deal of free media coverage.

Several times a week throughout the campaign, People for the American Way sent memos to some seventeen hundred news reporters and editorial boards in an effort to generate favorable news stories.[22] In addition, news feeds were given to radio stations to enable them to paint Bork in the most unfavorable light possible.[23] The media and the coalition opposing Bork had a symbiotic relationship. The coalition needed the media to publicize its portrait of Judge Bork. The media, on the other hand, used coalition members much like a library resource. Because the coalition had gathered so much data on Bork, reporters were eager to get information from them.[24]

The coalition's effort to manage the news was well coordinated. The coalition held meetings every morning, at which its media people would get the "line of the day." They would then do what they could to incorporate that line into their public messages.[25]

Bork's opponents also ran a number of television and radio ads in order to get their point across when free media were unavailable. The most prominent of the advertisements, run by People for the American Way, featured Gregory Peck with a young family on the steps of the Supreme Court before the frieze "Equal Justice for All." Peck accused Bork of opposing civil rights, privacy, and much free speech protection. Peck concluded by stating: "Robert Bork could have the last word on your rights as citizens, but the Senate has the last word on him. . . . Please urge your senators to vote against the Bork nomination, because if Robert Bork wins a seat on the Supreme Court, it will be for life—his life and yours." David Kusnet, vice president of People for the American Way, told the *Boston Globe* that "the ad showed two positive symbols, the Court and

the American family, interacting. Juxtaposed on top of them was a loom-
ing [figure of Judge] Bork, threatening the people and the institution."[26]

People for the American Way also ran ads in major newspapers around
the country accusing Bork of "sterilizing workers, billing consumers for
power they never got," undermining privacy, and supporting big business.[27] Planned Parenthood ran ads stating that if Bork were confirmed,
"you'll need more than a prescription to get birth control. It might take a
constitutional amendment."[28] Of course, it would "take a constitutional
amendment" only if local legislators enacted a prohibition on the sale or
use of contraceptives and local prosecutors actually enforced the prohibition. There was virtually no chance that this combination of events—
which had not occurred before—would come to pass in the late twentieth century, but the ad was successful in trading on the fears of anxious
listeners.

Bork was clearly upset that his supporters had not done more to counteract the media campaign against him, a campaign, he later said, that
"reached new lows in mendacity, brutality and intellectual vulgarity."[29]
Judge Bork remarked that this was the first national campaign against a
Supreme Court nominee and the only one in which just one side took
part.[30] But A. Raymond Randolph, a friend and adviser, said that running ads to counter the opposition would have been questionable because
Bork was a sitting judge. Randolph added that it would have cost a lot
and that this meant Bork would need to raise money, thereby creating
additional problems.[31] It is not clear, however, why conservative groups
operating independently of Bork could not have done the fund-raising.

Tom Korologos, another Bork adviser, said that he objected to the
Gregory Peck ad but did not want to get down in the mud with Bork's
opponents to run the kind of advertising campaign that they ran. He did
not think confirmations should be fought that way. Korologos admitted
that some conservatives at the Heritage Foundation and elsewhere
thought that more media buys were needed.[32] Yet in the end, most of
Bork's supporters opted for more traditional approaches, such as writing
letters, paying courtesy calls on senators, and publishing op-ed pieces.[33]

A few conservative groups, however, were willing to run a high-profile
campaign. Pat McGuigan and others raised money from grassroots supporters and ran radio and newspaper ads.[34] Conservative activists also
made the rounds of radio talk shows, arguing for Judge Bork's confirmation, and evangelical groups put out the word in their monthly newslet-
ters.[35] But without White House support and a broadly based coalition,

they could not hope to mount as effective a campaign as the anti-Bork side. John Bolton, who worked closely with Bork and Korologos in attempting to shepherd the nomination through the Senate, admitted that his side was outmanned. Bolton said that after each session of the hearings, the opposition groups would be "working the press" and putting their spin on how the session had gone. According to Bolton, the opposition was "getting coverage and setting the agenda."[36]

Complaints about the anti-Bork ads surfaced in many quarters. Senators Simpson, Grassley, and Hatch sharply criticized the misleading nature of the ads. Hatch said Bork was portrayed in ads by People for the American Way as "a bedroom-invading bigot."[37] For Bork, perhaps the most outrageous ad was one run by Planned Parenthood, describing Bork as an "ultraconservative judicial extremist" who used an obscure judicial philosophy. The ad charged that Bork believed people could not make changes in their own living arrangements without government approval. It went on to describe how Bork had upheld a local zoning law that effectively banned a grandmother from living with her children and grandchildren. As Bork pointed out at a Federalist Society dinner in 1988, the case in question did not arise in his jurisdiction, he had nothing to do with the decision, and he had never written about or discussed the case before Planned Parenthood ran its ad.[38]

After the Gregory Peck ad had aired a few times without drawing much attention, White House spokesman Marlin Fitzwater complained: "[T]he liberal special-interest groups . . . are producing slick, shrill, advertising campaigns that not only purposely distort the judge's record, they play on peoples' emotions as only propaganda campaigns can. To say that Americans will lose their freedoms, as these ads claim, is patently outrageous and deliberately untrue."[39] After that, the Peck ad was aired repeatedly for free on news programs of every sort.[40]

When the confirmation battle was over, the two sides continued to disagree on whether the ads were misleading and on what their impact had been. Bork's friend, A. Raymond Randolph, said a good deal of misinformation came out during the Bork hearings, not all of it generated by the left. He added that it is easy to attack someone who is espousing a philosophy of judicial neutrality and to paint him as an "ogre" because of the legal results that he reaches; it is much more difficult to run an ad in his favor because of the subtleties involved in a philosophy of neutrality.[41]

Irene Natividad, former president of the National Women's Political Caucus, when asked whether the media campaign had distorted Bork's record, stated that whenever you emphasize different things, it "looks like distortion." Natividad said the coalition chose to focus on the people who might not otherwise know what the consequences of Bork's confirmation would be. She insisted that it was all done with proof from Bork's own writings and added that Bork thinks the liberal media distorted his record, but he "lent himself to this."[42]

The impact of the ads has also been the subject of much disagreement. After the Senate vote on confirmation, Bork stated that the blitzkrieg of misleading media ads was one of the two major factors that led to his defeat—the other being the so-called southern strategy, which appealed to blacks in states where they were largely responsible for their senators' elections.[43] Similarly, in an appearance on ABC's *Nightline*, Senator Alan Simpson claimed that while Bork's testimony before the Judiciary Committee was seen by about 4 million people, perhaps "60 million, 70 million, 150 million saw Gregory Peck in full flower. . . . "

On the other hand, Kenneth Bass, an adviser to Senator Biden, argued that Judge Bork's own presentation and testimony "did him in."[44] Similarly, Arthur Kropp, executive director of People for the American Way, said: "To blame Robert Bork's inability to get past the Senate on a series of commercials isn't true. It's because of what he said for 20 to 30 years, what he said about privacy, what he said about standing, what he said about civil rights. To bring it down to some ad campaign that distorted him is just ridiculous."[45]

But contrary to the claims of partisans on each side, both the advertising campaign and Bork's own testimony contributed to his defeat. The ads were not decisive, but they were significant. As Nan Aron remarked, opinion polls showed that Bork's opponents were "getting [their message] across" and that "our campaign had had results."[46] The advertising campaign also had an impact on the type of press and television coverage that Bork received. *Media Monitor*, a publication of the conservative Center for Media and Public Affairs, found that of "381 source judgments [which] clearly indicated praise or blame, 63% were negative" and that network coverage on Bork's judicial ability was only slightly positive (averaging 53 percent), while negative assessments of Bork's judicial philosophy were widespread (about 82 percent).[47]

Bork's own testimony was also significant because it failed to allay public concerns, and in some ways it exacerbated those concerns. Even

Bork's most avid supporters recognized that his television appearances were damaging to his chances for confirmation. A. Raymond Randolph, who was unhappy with Bork's first day of testimony, said "the cosmetics were not good."[48] Tom Korologos initially stated that Bork was defeated in spite of his outstanding performance during the hearings.[49] But later, after seeing how successful Judge Kennedy had been, Korologos remarked that Bork was hurt by his "Einstein-like" answers, delivered in staccato fashion, in contrast to the pleasant-sounding answers given by Kennedy.[50] As television critic Tom Shales put it, Bork came across on television as a "dazzling intellect" who lacked compassion.[51]

Professor A. E. Dick Howard of the Virginia Law School remarked that the Bork nomination was not defeated by opinion polls or media advertising. But the crucial issue is not whether media advertising was decisive in defeating the nomination. The question is what a campaign of this sort will do to the confirmation process, regardless of whether it changes the outcome in a particular case. The use of opinion polls and media campaigns creates a risk of turning Supreme Court confirmation struggles into national plebiscites, with sixty-second commercials operating as the coin of the realm. Because of the complexity of many legal issues, these matters usually cannot be reduced to television sound bites without serious distortion. In addition, massive media campaigns may help to turn confirmation battles into full-scale political contests in which nominees are pressured, as Judge Bork was, to make campaign promises in search of confirmation votes. In the long run, this may result in a loss of judicial independence if judges feel bound by their promises and in a loss of judicial credibility if they do not.

PART THREE

ACTION BY THE SENATE

15
MOUNTING PRESSURE: THE UNCOMMITTED SENATORS

The battle over the Bork nomination generated extraordinary political pressure, and those receiving the most pressure were the so-called uncommitted members of the Senate Judiciary Committee. At one point, Howell Heflin said his arms had "been twisted by both sides 'so much that they're both ready for transplants.'"[1] Arlen Specter's office reported that Specter received two phone calls threatening his life if he did not vote the caller's way on the Bork nomination. One caller was pro-Bork; the other was anti-Bork.[2] The pressure on senators took many forms: personal letters, telephone calls, advertisements, petitions, and behind-the-scenes politicking. Although some senators later denied that political considerations had influenced their vote on Judge Bork, a few were candid enough to admit that the numerical strength and the intensity of the Bork opposition were significant factors in their decision to vote against confirmation.

The offices of Senators DeConcini, Heflin, and Specter were inundated with letters and telephone calls. Senator Specter received fifty thousand pieces of mail before the end of September. By October 6, the date set for the Judiciary Committee's vote on the nomination, Heflin's office had also received fifty thousand mailings.[3] However, the impact of these mailings on Heflin was somewhat limited. First, according to Heflin's press aide, Jerry Ray, less than 15 percent of Heflin's communications were from Alabama; most of the calls and letters came from California and Texas. Second, many of the communications consisted of unsigned letters that had been generated by a few committed volunteers.

And some of the phone calls were simply "canned" messages solicited by the National Conservative Political Action Committee (NCPAC).[4] The Alabama version of the NCPAC tape, which requested a contribution to NCPAC "to help win this important battle," asked voters to call Senator Heflin or Senator Shelby and deliver a telephone message urging the senator "to resist the politicization of our court system."[5] On the opposite side, various civil rights groups, such as the Southern Christian Leadership Conference (SCLC) and the NAACP, urged their members to write letters to senators asking that they oppose the Bork nomination.[6]

Nonmembers of the Judiciary Committee also received thousands of pieces of mail and telephone calls. Many senators, including Bennett Johnston and James Sasser, said that initially their mail was heavily in favor of Bork's nomination but that after the confirmation hearings, they received more mail opposing Bork than supporting him. Apparently, Bork's own testimony helped to turn the tide against confirmation.[7]

Both supporters and opponents of Judge Bork conducted petition drives, though the anti-Bork forces were more active in this area. Reverend Joseph Lowery of the SCLC presented petitions to Senator Sam Nunn with the names of eleven thousand people opposed to Bork.[8] The Atlanta branch of the NAACP delivered cards and petitions to both Georgia senators, urging them to oppose confirmation. The petitions were collected across the state of Georgia in schools, businesses, and in some cases, by door-to-door canvassing.[9]

Lobbyists and politicians also met personally with key senators. Joe Reed, head of the Black Alabama Democratic Conference, had a meeting with Senators Heflin and Shelby and urged them to vote against confirmation.[10] Reverend Jesse Jackson also met with Shelby and Heflin and asked that they vote against Bork "because he is divisive."[11] Jackson reminded Heflin of all the black voters that Jackson helped to register, who had voted for Heflin in overwhelming numbers.[12] Heflin had been reelected in 1984 with 46 percent of the white vote and 81 percent of the black vote.[13] Senator Shelby, noting that Bork was opposed by civil rights groups and supported by fundamentalist Christian groups, said that the organized lobbying groups canceled each other out. However, Shelby was impressed by professionals, many of them "with Republican leanings," who had watched the Bork hearings and then told him, "Don't vote for Bork."[14]

On Friday, October 2, Senator Heflin was called to the White House to discuss the Bork nomination directly with President Reagan. The following Tuesday, just hours before the Judiciary Committee's vote on confirmation, Reagan lobbied Heflin again. There were rumors at that time, apparently emanating from the Justice Department, that Clement Clay Torbert Jr., chief justice of the Alabama Supreme Court and a close personal friend of Senator Heflin, was being considered for a seat on the federal court of appeals for the eleventh circuit. Justice Department spokesman Stephen Markman denied that there was any connection between the consideration of Torbert and Heflin's vote on Bork, and Heflin acknowledged that the Torbert matter was not raised by President Reagan in their private meetings.

Nevertheless, the circumstances surrounding Torbert's consideration raise serious questions about whether this was a subtle attempt to influence Heflin. First, interviews with Torbert began in mid-July, shortly after the Bork nomination was announced. Second, none of Reagan's seventy-odd appointments to the court of appeals had been Democrats, like Torbert.[15] Third, at the time that Torbert came under consideration, there was not even a vacancy on the eleventh circuit, although there was some prospect—realized later that year—that Judge John C. Godbold would leave the court. Finally, this type of quid pro quo was not unprecedented in the Reagan administration. In 1986, Senator Slade Gorton, after having committed himself to vote against the confirmation of Daniel Manion to the federal court of appeals, was persuaded to change his mind when informed that the White House, after months of inaction, was ready to accept Gorton's recommendation to nominate William A. Dwyer for a district court judgeship in Washington State.[16]

In the end, all of the "undecided" members of the Judiciary Committee voted against the Bork nomination. Arlen Specter was the first of these members to announce his opposition and was the only Republican on the committee to oppose Bork's confirmation. After reaching his decision, Specter telephoned White House Chief of Staff Howard Baker, lobbyist Tom Korologos, and Bork himself to explain his decision. Korologos told Specter: "You don't have to explain. Your votes are decided by conscience, constituents and colleagues."[17] Korologos later said that Specter's decision was crucial and that "Specter hit the game-winning RBI."[18]

On Thursday, October 1, Specter took the Senate floor to explain the basis for his decision. After acknowledging how difficult the decision was and how many hours he had spent discussing his concerns with Judge Bork, Specter said that his conclusion was based "on the totality of [Bork's] record," with emphasis on how he was likely to apply traditional constitutional principles of free speech and equal protection. Specter elaborated:

> I am further concerned by his insistence on Madisonian majoritarianism in the absence of an explicit constitutional right to limit legislative action. Conservative Justices have traditionally protected individual and minority rights without a specifically enumerated right or proof of original intent when there are fundamental values rooted in the tradition of our people. . . .
>
> These conceptual concerns might be brushed aside if it were not for his repeated and recent rejection of fundamental constitutional doctrines. Over the years, Judge Bork has insisted that equal protection applies only to race as originally intended by the framers. As recently as 1 month before his nomination, he said equal protection should have been kept to things like race and ethnicity. His view of the law is at sharp variance with more than a century of Supreme Court decisions which have applied equal protection to women, aliens, illegitimates, indigents, and others.
>
> For the first time at his confirmation hearings, Judge Bork said he would apply equal protection broadly in accordance with the Court's settled doctrine under Justice Steven's reasonable basis standard. Without commenting on the various technical levels of scrutiny, I have substantial doubt about Judge Bork's application of this fundamental legal principle where he has over the years disagreed with the scope of coverage and has a settled philosophy that constitutional rights do not exist unless specified or are within original intent.
>
> Similarly, Judge Bork had, prior to his hearings, consistently rejected the "clear and present danger" test for freedom of speech even though a unanimous Supreme Court had accepted it as an ingrained American value for years. Justice Holmes' famous dictum that "time has upset many fighting faiths," expressed the core American value to listen to others and permit the best ideas to triumph in the marketplace of free speech, short of a clear and present danger of imminent violence. . . .
>
> In raising these doubts about Judge Bork's application of settled law on equal protection and freedom of speech, it is not a matter of questioning his credibility or integrity, which I unhesitatingly accept, or his sincerity in insisting that he will not be disgraced in history by acting contrary to his sworn testimony, but rather the

doubts persist as to his judicial disposition in applying principles of law which he has so long decried.[19]

On Wednesday, September 30, immediately after the close of the committee hearings, Senator DeConcini said he would decide on the Bork nomination over the next weekend. However, DeConcini already appeared to be leaning strongly against confirmation. He stated that he was "really concerned" about how Bork would decide equal protection cases using his reasonableness test.[20] He also repeated his strong disagreement with Bork's view that there is no constitutionally protected right of privacy. After hearing these statements, Senator Alan Simpson remarked that he "never had Dennis DeConcini as undecided. . . . After the first few days I just put him in the 'no' column."[21] Nevertheless, DeConcini denied charges appearing in *Policy Review*, a conservative publication of the Heritage Foundation, that DeConcini had huddled with feminist groups two months earlier to plot strategy against Bork.[22]

On Monday, October 5, DeConcini and another previously undecided member of the committee, Majority Leader Robert Byrd, announced their opposition to Bork's confirmation. DeConcini said he was "more concerned than ever about [Bork's] lack of compassion. . . . I do not believe the U.S. Senate can take the risk that putting Judge Bork on the Supreme Court entails. His entire career indicated a lack of understanding of the effect of judicial decisions on real people. Judge Bork views the Constitutions [*sic*] as a bloodless and sterile contract instead of a bond between diverse and competing people to use common sense and consideration of each other as a framework to build a nation."[23]

During the Senate debate two weeks later, DeConcini made a point of saying that he had read Bork's writings, had talked with hundreds of Arizonans, and had listened carefully to all except one day of testimony before deciding how to vote. Perhaps protesting a bit too much, DeConcini added that his decision was based on the merits and that he had "excluded considerations as to [what] it might mean to [him] politically . . . one way or the other."[24] The latter comment is not easily reconciled with DeConcini's apparent concern for the views of "hundreds of Arizonans" or with his insistence on waiting until Bork's fate was virtually sealed before deciding how to vote.

Senator Byrd, too, had remained on the fence as long as he could. As late as September 29, Byrd stated that he would vote against either a positive or negative recommendation in the Judiciary Committee and would support only a neutral "no-recommendation" motion.[25] However, by October 5, Byrd could see which way the wind was blowing, and he announced that he would vote against Bork's confirmation. Byrd stated that "[t]he nomination is just too controversial to go forward with" and that "there's a great deal of unease and distrust" about it.[26] In order to avoid giving Republicans an opportunity to score political points from the controversy, Byrd urged President Reagan to withdraw the nomination.[27] For the same reason, Byrd later tried to speed up the vote on Bork's confirmation and have the Senate turn to other matters.

Howell Heflin was the last of the "undecided" to announce his opposition to Bork, waiting until just before the vote in the Judiciary Committee. Heflin said that although he would prefer a conservative appointee, he was concerned that Bork's writings and speeches "reveal extremism on a number of issues." Bork's "life and lifestyle," according to Heflin, "indicate a fondness for the unusual, the unconventional, and the strange." Heflin concluded:

> I am in a state of quandary as to whether this nominee would be a conservative justice who would safeguard the living Constitution and prevent judicial activism or whether, on the other hand, he would be an extremist who would use his position on the Court to advance a far-right, radical, judicial agenda.
>
> The question is difficult. Frankly, I am not sure that I have the answer. I am reminded of an old saying, "when in doubt, don't." I see a great deal of wisdom to this warning. A life-time position on the Supreme Court is too important to risk to a person who has continued to exhibit—and may still possess—a proclivity for extremism in spite of confirmation protestations. Because of my doubts at this time and at this posture of the confirmation process, I must vote no.[28]

But because Heflin waited so long to announce his position, he had much less influence on other senators than most of the pundits predicted. Senator Bennett Johnston, among others, had already lined up many of the southern Democrats to vote against Bork, after reminding them of the debt they owed their black constituents. Johnston played a major role in explaining the political realities to a group of young Democratic senators from the South that included Richard Shelby of Alabama, Wyche Fowler of Georgia, John Breaux of Louisiana, and Terry Sanford of

North Carolina. Johnston told Senator Shelby, "You're going to vote against [the Bork nomination] because you're not going to turn your back on 91 percent of the black voters in Alabama who got you here." Johnston also explained that southern whites were not coming to Bork's defense in the manner expected by the Reagan administration. These senators paid close attention to Johnston, who is well respected for his knowledge of politics.[29]

The vote in the Judiciary Committee was 9 opposing confirmation (eight Democrats and one Republican) and 5 supporting it (all Republicans). Since no nominee in this century who lost a majority of votes in committee had won confirmation in the Senate, the committee vote on Bork seemed virtually to doom his nomination. Within a few days, enough undecided senators announced their opposition to Bork's confirmation to make his defeat almost certain. The anti-Bork forces were able to create a sense of momentum by arranging for staggered announcements by senators of decisions to oppose confirmation. For example, on Tuesday, October 6, the *Los Angeles Times* reported that Senate Majority Leader Robert Byrd and three other senators announced their opposition to Bork.[30] Two days later, the *Washington Post* reported that as many as ten previously undecided senators were now prepared to vote against confirmation.[31] The die clearly had been cast at that point. Perhaps Senator Heflin put it best when he compared Bork's chances of confirmation to "a Christmas turkey that has been in the oven four hours too long. No matter where you put your thumb and push, it's done."[32]

16

THE STRUGGLE OUTSIDE

Even as public opinion and the number of committed senators moved inexorably against confirmation, President Reagan was being urged to attack Democratic liberals and the "special interests" that had led the opposition to Bork. Conservatives like Terry Eastland, spokesman for the Department of Justice, believed that the battle for the Judiciary Committee had been lost by default and that the pro-Bork forces should not surrender without firing a shot.[1] Bork himself met with White House aides in late September and criticized them for not doing enough to support his cause.[2] The struggle outside the Senate would soon be joined, in anticipation of the debate on the Senate floor.

Some of President Reagan's advisers encouraged him to make a major television address vigorously criticizing the special interests that had "lynched" Robert Bork during the committee hearings. But the president decided on a more low-key approach. Rather than undertake a major ideological fight on the principles that Judge Bork represented, Reagan praised Bork as a moderate and hailed his firmness on crime and victim's rights, even though Bork had rarely spoken out on these issues.[3] In a brief comment on October 6, Reagan said Bork's opponents had "made this a political contest by using tactics and distortions that I think are deplorable."[4]

It was not until it became clear that the Bork nomination had no chance of succeeding and the question was how to minimize the political damage of the impending defeat that Reagan adopted a more strident approach. In an address to the nation on October 14, he said, "The confirmation process became an ugly spectacle, marred by distortions and innuendoes, and casting aside the normal rules of decency and honesty."[5] The new approach was partly a reaction to criticism from conservative senators that the White House had not done enough for Judge Bork.

Senator Grassley, a strong Bork supporter, had said that the White House was "asleep at the switch" and that "while Ron and Nancy were riding horses in August, the opposition was gaining."[6]

Initially, there were at least two reasons for moderating the counter-attack. First, Chief of Staff Howard Baker believed that a more aggressive approach would jeopardize Reagan's relations with Capitol Hill and make it more difficult for Reagan to complete his legislative agenda. Second, there was some concern that Reagan's lame-duck status, coupled with the loss of political capital that could attend a prolonged battle over Bork, would jeopardize the confirmation of the next Supreme Court nominee. One White House adviser said that Reagan wanted to avoid a bloody ideological fight, "[b]ut the right wing has never been able to accept that fact."[7]

Bork himself received conflicting signals. On the one hand, "Reagan had given strict orders that at no time should anyone pressure" Bork to withdraw.[8] On the other hand, White House aides continued to receive visits from Republican senators who urged that Bork's nomination be dropped.[9] The aides then circulated the senators' suggestion that it might be best if Bork withdrew.

After the vote in the Judiciary Committee, Bork began feeling rather despondent about his prospects for confirmation and about the fact that his record had been badly distorted. The portrayal of him as a "racist" was particularly upsetting. Bork met with a group of some sixteen Republican senators who encouraged him to "hang in there." Alan Simpson, one of Bork's strongest supporters, was alone in arguing that Judge Bork should not let the nomination go to the floor of the Senate. Simpson said that there would be over sixty votes against the nomination and that he "didn't think a recorded vote like that would be good for Judge Bork."[10]

Despite the urging of his friend Leonard Garment, who told him not to be a "quitter," Bork went into the White House on Wednesday, October 7, and advised Reagan that he was inclined to ask that his nomination be withdrawn. When told that by pressing on he could put his opponents' feet to the fire, Bork said: "I'm not a politician . . . I don't really understand the business of making them pay a price. I've got a life to lead." Reagan replied that he would understand if Bork decided to withdraw.[11]

The next day, Bork began writing a withdrawal statement at his office in the court of appeals. He did not relish the prospect of more emotional turmoil, and he knew the Judiciary Committee's negative vote made confirmation almost impossible. Bork's situation was similar to that of Abe Fortas after the Senate refused to invoke cloture during the debate on Fortas's nomination to be chief justice. Seeing that his prospects were doomed, Fortas had asked President Johnson to withdraw the nomination the day after the cloture vote.[12] Similarly, Representative Richard H. Poff of Virginia declined an "almost certain" nomination to the Supreme Court during the Nixon administration, after Senator Robert Byrd gave him a friendly warning that his nomination would be opposed and possibly even filibustered by liberals.[13] Like Fortas and Poff, Judge Bork saw defeat as inevitable, and he was ready to ask that his nomination be withdrawn.

Then Bork received an encouraging telephone call from Senator Alan Simpson, who said he had been rethinking his position and now believed that Bork "ought to stand up for the principles involved if you think you can do it."[14] In addition, Bork received strong encouragement from his family to stay in the battle, and he decided they were right. He set about, with the help of his sons, to draft a statement explaining his reasons for fighting it out.[15]

On Friday, October 9, Bork met with President Reagan in the Oval Office to inform him of his decision. Also present were Vice President Bush, Chief of Staff Howard Baker, and Baker's deputy Kenneth M. Duberstein. Bork came right to the point. He told Reagan he wanted to stay in the race in order to educate the public and set the record straight. Bork gave Reagan a copy of his speech and then went into the rose garden, where he shocked official Washington by announcing his decision to remain in an apparently losing battle. His voice laden with emotion, Bork stated that he harbored "no illusion" about his prospects for success but that he would not withdraw and that "there should be a full debate and a final Senate decision." He said it was not only "the fate of Robert Bork" but rather "a crucial principle [that] is at stake." Bork believed that if he withdrew now, the "public campaign of distortion . . . would be seen as a success" and would be "mounted against future nominees. For the sake of the federal judiciary and the American people, that must not happen."[16] Bork added that "the tactics and techniques of national political campaigns have been unleashed in the process of confirming judges" and that such a campaign was "unprecedented" and "dangerous." He nevertheless concluded by asking that "voices be lowered" as the confirmation process continued.[17]

Inside the White House, reactions to Bork's decision were mixed. President Reagan and White House Counsel Edwin Meese strongly approved of his decision, as did Gary Bauer, assistant to the president for policy development. Bauer said the decision showed "political courage . . . rarely seen in Washington." He suggested somewhat wistfully that there could be a backlash against the tactics used by the anti-Bork forces, with the possibility that votes could switch to Bork's favor.[18] On the other hand, some White House officials continued to believe that a prolonged fight would jeopardize Reagan's political agenda. Nevertheless, because of Reagan's edict against pressuring Bork to withdraw, those officials consistently refused to be quoted for the record.[19]

After Bork's decision to stay in the race, conservative Republicans became even more vocal in urging a prolonged and vigorous fight. Some hoped to generate enough pressure on senators to turn the confirmation vote around. However, this was a faint prospect at best. More realistically, conservatives hoped to make it more difficult for senators to oppose Reagan's next nominee to the Supreme Court. They also expected to inflict some political damage on Bork's opponents by forcing a public debate on the tactics they had used against Bork. Finally, many Republican senators honestly believed that Bork had been victimized by a McCarthy-like smear campaign, and they wanted to set the record straight.

Ironically, this strategy posed a problem for Republicans like Senator D'Amato and Senator Cohen, who favored Bork but could be politically vulnerable if they voted for confirmation.[20] Senator Cohen called Bork after he had made his decision to vote for him. He urged Bork to give up because the atmosphere had been poisoned and "the Senate was not well served and the country was not well served by having this really get ugly." Bork rejected Cohen's plea, saying he wanted a chance to vindicate himself and to see the process through.[21]

On October 13, 1987, Reagan planned to deliver a blistering attack on "a few liberal special interests" who had "declared a war of conquest on the American system of justice." In these remarks, Reagan would also have stated that Bork had "been the victim of a sophisticated campaign of smears and lies."[22] White House press spokesmen announced that the criticism was toned down after Bork requested that voices be "lowered" in the debate over his confirmation. The revised speech said: "Judge Bork and I agree that there are no illusions about the outcome of the vote in the Senate, but we also agree that a crucial principle is at stake. That principle is the process that is used to determine the fitness of those men and women selected to serve on our courts—and the ultimate decision will impact on each of us and each of our children."[23] Despite the measured rhetoric, Reagan could not resist adding some off-the-cuff remarks in which he called the confirmation process "a political joke" and promised to choose a new Supreme Court nominee who would upset Democrats "just as much" as Judge Bork did.[24] These remarks may have reflected Reagan's true feelings on the matter. In any event, the discrepancy between Reagan's speech and his subsequent remarks is illustrative of the internal conflict in the White House over an endgame strategy in the Bork controversy.

The next day, Reagan took a hard-line approach in a ten-minute address to the nation. Reagan stated that when he announced the Bork nomination, he thought the process would proceed "with a calm and sensible exchange of views. Unfortunately, the confirmation process became an ugly spectacle marred by distortions and innuendoes and casting aside the normal rules of decency and honesty."[25] In the Democratic response, Senator Terry Sanford said that the "President's confrontational approach is not becoming to the constitutional process in which we are engaged." He added that senators opposing Bork's nomination "are tired of having our integrity impugned. We are tired of having our intelligence insulted."[26]

The presidential address was offered to all the major television networks, but only CNN was willing to carry the entire broadcast live. White House press spokesman Marlin Fitzwater complained: "The American people deserve to hear their national leaders discuss an issue of such importance. Having devoted hours of broadcast time to the Senate hearing, they have suddenly gone blind to the President's address. That view of their public responsibility is sadly inadequate."[27] Officials at ABC, NBC, and CBS characterized the speech as "political," not newsworthy, and refused to air it live.[28]

In the end, the struggle over the Bork nomination became a battle about which side would get the most mileage out of the excesses of its opponents and what precedents would be established for future Supreme Court confirmation disputes. During the Senate debate that followed, these matters became paramount.

17
THE SENATE DEBATE: BATTLING FOR HISTORY'S VERDICT

Shortly after the Judiciary Committee voted, the Senate began its debate or, as Bork termed it, "non-debate," since virtually all Senators had publicly declared their positions and were unlikely to change their minds.[1] Three subjects dominated the discussion: (1) whether Judge Bork was "outside the mainstream" of lawyers and judges, (2) whether the Senate's role in the appointments process should be broadly construed, and (3) whether the confirmation process had been fair to Judge Bork. There was disagreement on all of these questions, but it was the third issue that proved to be most explosive.

The debate began with explanations from various senators for their vote in favor of or in opposition to the confirmation of Judge Bork. Senators favoring confirmation pointed to Bork's intellect and integrity[2] and argued that Judge Bork's judicial philosophy was well within the mainstream. These senators emphasized that Bork had a record as solicitor general, and later as a federal judge, in support of civil rights. Senator Grassley said that Bork had "used his position as solicitor general to argue more pro-civil rights cases than any Supreme Court nominee since Thurgood Marshall."[3] Similarly, Senator Mark Hatfield observed that Bork had participated in some four hundred cases as a member of the court of appeals and that he voted with the so-called liberal group 75 percent of the time and with the plaintiff in seven of ten cases involving issues of race, sex, or age discrimination.[4]

Senator Hatch pointed out that legal scholars and respected jurists, many of whom have been considered "moderate" or "liberal," agreed with various positions that Judge Bork had taken over the years.[5] For example, Senator Hatch noted that Professor Philip Kurland of the University of Chicago Law School "stated that *Griswold v. Connecticut* and *Roe v. Wade* are examples of 'blatant usurpation[s] of the constitution-making function.'"[6] Hatch also cited an opinion by Justice Black, which rejected a generalized right of privacy and stated: "The Court talks about a constitutional 'right of privacy' as though there is some constitutional provision or provisions forbidding any law to be passed which might abridge the 'privacy' of individuals. But there is not. . . . I like my privacy as much as the next one, but I am nevertheless compelled to admit that government has a right to invade it unless prohibited by some specific constitutional provision."[7]

Senator Hatch was effective in showing that many of the views for which Bork was criticized had been embraced by mainstream judges and scholars. Hatch did not address the question of whether a judge who embraced all the positions taken by Judge Bork would be considered mainstream. But it seems clear that even when taken in their totality, Bork's views are no more "extreme" than those of other members of the Supreme Court, both past and present.[8]

More important, however, than the question of whether Hatch was right or wrong in his characterization of Judge Bork is that Senator Hatch succeeded in framing the terms of the debate. His focus was on Bork's claim to the "mainstream," and the question later asked of Judge Kennedy and other nominees was whether they were "in the judicial mainstream." This focus tends to facilitate confirmation, since it is much more difficult to show that a nominee is outside the mainstream than it is to take exception to the nominee's views in particular cases.

Judge Bork's supporters also argued that Bork's philosophy of judicial restraint would give proper respect to the democratic process by not allowing a judge to substitute his personal preferences for those of elected representatives. For example, Senator Hollings, one of only two Democrats voting for confirmation, stated that "Judge Bork's respect for separation of powers is the source of his philosophy of judicial restraint" and that the power to make public policy "rightly belongs in the Congress and the other elected representatives, not to unelected judges."[9] Similarly, Senator Nickles of Oklahoma, explaining his support for Judge Bork, stated: "I fall on the same side of the issue as Judge Bork in saying that the Court should interpret the Constitution, should interpret the law as written, and allow elected officials, whether it be the Congress or the

State Legislatures to make the laws. That is the proper check and balance system established in the Constitution."[10]

Judge Bork's opponents, like his supporters, focused on the question of whether Bork was outside the judicial mainstream. Some argued that Bork had "radical views derive[d] from a constricted view of the individual rights upon which this country was founded, a view that we should bind our civil and individual liberties in a straight-jacket called original intent."[11] Others said Bork was outside the mainstream on questions of privacy and equal protection. Few senators openly expressed their concern about abortion rights. Instead, they continued to discuss the issue in terms of procreation and the right to privacy.

Senators also expressed concern about whether Bork would protect women's rights. Bork's earlier position that the equal protection clause should be limited to the areas it was originally intended to cover, such as race and ethnicity, drew heavy fire, even though Bork testified at the hearings that he now believed the equal protection clause applied to other areas as well. In fact, the change in his position raised questions about his candor and predictability. Senator Tom Daschle said that Bork's "confirmation conversion has come as a surprise to many of my colleagues. Expecting a dogmatically staunch defender of his much espoused, ultraconservative philosophy, the Senate witnessed an equivocal, nebulous and unconvincing nominee seemingly willing to explain away almost anything to satisfy his skeptics."[12] Similarly, Senator Breaux, in explaining his opposition to Bork, stated that "[a] lifetime of political writings and speeches by Judge Bork, followed now by his public testimony discounting these former views, clearly suggests a lack of predictability."[13] Bork could find no way out of this dilemma: If he adhered to his earlier position, he would be accused of being outside the mainstream; but when he modified his previous views, he was charged with confirmation conversion. Attempts to avoid the dilemma by insisting that Bork's writings were intended to be "tentative" and to provoke academic debate fell largely on deaf ears.

Some of Judge Bork's opponents argued for an expansive view of the Senate's role in judicial appointments. Senator Dodd said the Framers intended an active role for the Senate but left it to each senator to determine "the acceptable criteria in judging a Supreme Court nominee." In his view, senators must determine whether confirmation of the nominee is in the best interest of the United States. To answer that question, Dodd believed senators should consider (1) whether the nominee possesses the necessary legal skills, (2) whether he or she has character and personal integrity, and (3) whether the nominee is committed to upholding the individual rights and liberties guaranteed by the Constitution. "We must ask whether the nominee has the commitment and judicial temperament to give life and real-world meaning to our Constitution's guarantees. We may disagree about the meaning of the various provisions of the Constitution, but the nominee's views must be within an appropriate range, and his or her approach must reflect a deep commitment to our Nation's constitutional ideals."[14]

Senator Sarbanes and Senator Mitchell also urged a broad role for the Senate in the appointments process. Mitchell said: "The constitutional role of the Senate is as an equal participant with the President in appointments to the judiciary. The Senate is not a rubber stamp."[15] Sarbanes said: "[A] judicial nominee, becomes a member, upon confirmation, of the third independent branch of our National Government. I believe, therefore, we [are] called upon to make a more independent judgment with respect to such nominees—particularly given that, once confirmed, they serve for life."[16]

But even some liberal Democrats, recognizing that their party would regain the White House in the foreseeable future, rejected a Senate role as "equal participant" in judicial appointments. For example, Senator Metzenbaum, a strong opponent of Judge Bork, believed that "senators [should] defer to the President unless there is an extraordinary case." In his view, Judge Bork's nomination presented such an extraordinary case.[17] Not surprisingly, Bork supporters also urged a limited role for the Senate in the appointments process. Senator Grassley said:

> As the Senate's role has evolved over time, the Senate has limited its analysis to the nominee's objective qualifications regarding his or her experience, and integrity. However, as any witness to the Bork confirmation process knows, the Senate departed from its customary role. . . .
>
> I am very troubled that the questioning of the nominee was too specific and too detailed. In effect, committee members were extracting campaign promises from the nominee who gave them under oath. In doing this the Senate is seeking to control the result of Supreme Court deliberations. In my opinion, this compromises the independence of the judiciary and infringes on the separation of

powers. We have no business trying to get a nominee to decide cases our way.[18]

Similarly, Senator Mitch McConnell, a strong Bork supporter, believed the Senate should base its decisions about Supreme Court nominees solely on "competence, achievements, temperament, conduct and integrity."[19] But he warned that if others applied a broader standard, then in the future he, too, would "carefully scrutinize the judicial philosophy of every nominee, perhaps even to the point of passing over the nominee's excellent credentials and unimpeachable character."[20]

There was a wide difference of opinion between Bork's supporters and opponents over the fairness of the confirmation proceedings, and it was on this issue that the Senate debate was most acrimonious. Bork supporters attacked the special interest groups that, they said, had "lynched" Robert Bork. In particular, they pointed to false and misleading advertisements and accused the opposition of "white-collar McCarthyism."[21] Senator Biden said that one senator went so far as to walk out of the U.S. Senate and verbally attack two other senators "in the most scurrilous way. . . . I could not believe when I heard it. I do not believe he meant it. I believe he was angry and he said it, but I must tell you that two members on this side are not likely to forget it, as much as they want to be good, decent people. Those things leave scars."[22]

Senators Hatch and Armstrong spent a considerable amount of time detailing the errors and exaggerations contained in various anti-Bork advertisements. Some senators replied that the ads were irrelevant because no senator would decide whether to support or oppose the nomination on the basis of advertisements.[23] But, of course, advertising could affect public opinion; and no one suggested that public opinion would be ignored by members of the Senate.

The debate became especially heated when Senator Humphrey characterized as "villainy" Senator Kennedy's earlier statement that in Judge Bork's America, women would be forced into back-alley abortions, and blacks would be made to sit at segregated lunch counters. Humphrey also charged that an aide to one senator had engaged in Ku Klux Klan tactics by intimidating a black law professor into not testifying, for fear that he would be humiliated if he testified.[24]

Senator Metzenbaum responded by defending his aide, Linda Greene, who, he said, was close to the professor and was simply giving him friendly advice. Metzenbaum pointed out that the professor later wrote to the committee, stating that he had not been intimidated.[25] Metzenbaum also criticized Senator Humphrey for having injected into the discussion a kind of invective that had not been used by other senators.

On October 23, Senator John Danforth took the floor and did his best to elevate the debate. But at the same time, Danforth set out a stinging indictment of the way Judge Bork had been treated. Danforth noted that "even before Judge Bork was nominated, Kate Michelman of the National Abortion Rights Action League said, 'We're going to wage an all-out frontal assault like you've never seen before on this nominee, assuming it's Bork.' That's what it became. . . . It became an all-out frontal assault on Judge Bork, including the ginning up of interest groups just the way we do it here in the Senate" when important legislation is pending.[26]

Danforth, like Senator Humphrey, was critical of Ted Kennedy. But Danforth's criticism was low key and free of rancor, making it, of course, all the more powerful. Danforth said that even people "who believe in abortion criticize the Supreme Court's reasoning in Roe v. Wade. It does not mean you want to have back-alley abortions. You can be for or against legalized abortion and criticize Roe." Nevertheless, Danforth believed Kennedy's attack, like those contained in television ads, was both effective and insidious: "Blacks were frightened. . . . Women were frightened. But a lot of other people were frightened, too. . . . So the polls . . . began to turn and the momentum to shift."[27]

Senator Danforth was concerned about the consequences of requiring a judicial nominee to make promises in order to be confirmed. "I would suggest," he said, "that the precedent we are setting in the U.S. Senate by our vote against Judge Bork is a precedent which is contrary to the principle of an independent judiciary." Danforth was also concerned that the confirmation process had been grossly unfair to Robert Bork. He closed his speech with an eloquent statement on that point:

> Mr. President, what has happened to Robert Bork is wrong. . . . It is wrong. And, Mr. President, we are responsible here in the Senate. The man has been trashed in our house. Some of us helped generate the trashing. Others of us yielded to it. But all of us, myself included, all of us have been accomplices to it. All of us who have not spoken out have been accomplices to it. All of us who have sat there . . . and let this trashing go on and let this good man be charac-

terized as some sort of a Frankenstein's monster without raising a
voice against it, all of us are accomplices. . . . I hope that we would
resolve that we are never going to let this kind of thing happen
again.[28]

Four years later, Senator Danforth would be intimately involved in an
effort to prevent one of President Bush's nominees from being brought
down by another public trashing.

The ultimate vote on Bork's confirmation was anticlimactic, since defeat was certain by that point. Nevertheless, Bork's wife, Mary Ellen, and
his two sons sat in the gallery as the final speeches were delivered. They
left shortly before the vote. The final count was 42 to 58. By party break-
down, there were 40 Republicans and 2 Democrats supporting the nomination and 52 Democrats and 6 Republicans opposing the nomination.
All the Democratic freshmen senators voted against Bork's confirmation.[29]

After the conclusion of the debate, Bork issued a brief statement of
gratitude for the support he received from President Reagan and from his
own family. He said that although voices were not lowered, as he had
wished, he was "glad the debate took place." Bork added that "[t]here is
now a full and permanent record by which the future may judge not only
one, but the proper nature of a confirmation proceeding."[30]

18

THE NEW NOMINEES:
GINSBURG AND KENNEDY

When the Bork hearings ended, it was widely believed that the hearings had established a precedent which would require vigorous questioning of Supreme Court nominees by the Senate Judiciary Committee and detailed responses from the nominees about their judicial philosophy. As Senator Leahy remarked shortly after the vote rejecting the Bork nomination, "So many people got so interested [in the Bork hearings] and so sensitized that they're not going to let their senators get away with not giving the next nominee a great deal of scrutiny."[1] Senator Biden and others agreed that future nominees would be subjected to in-depth questioning that would force them to share their judicial views in the same way that Judge Bork had done.

These assertions of senatorial prerogative were to be tested quickly and repeatedly. Over the next several years, confirmation hearings would be held for five nominees to the Supreme Court. Action on those nominations reveals much about the meaning of the Bork precedent and the new senatorial prerogatives.

The immediate task for the Reagan administration, after Judge Bork's nomination had been defeated, was to find a confirmable successor to Justice Powell. The list of potential nominees was quickly narrowed to fewer than half a dozen candidates. Two of the candidates, Anthony Kennedy and Douglas Ginsburg—both then serving on federal courts of appeals—emerged as the leading contenders. Kennedy had a clearly conservative record during more than a decade of service as a federal judge. He was nevertheless perceived to be a "moderate" conservative who could win easy confirmation.

Ironically, the perception of Judge Kennedy as a moderate who was readily confirmable seemed at first to work against his nomination rather than in favor of it. President Reagan had promised a crowd of supporters that he would nominate someone the senators will "object to just as much as the last one." Even more important, the Bork hearings had been so contentious that political nerves were rubbed raw on all sides. In this atmosphere, the prospect of support for Kennedy from opponents of Judge Bork was bound to be viewed with suspicion, if not alarm, in some quarters.

As the hour of decision approached, several conservative Republicans, including Senators Humphrey, Grassley, and Helms, threatened to oppose Kennedy, and Senator Helms went so far as to suggest a possible filibuster. In addition, Attorney General Meese and former Attorney General William French Smith spoke favorably of Ginsburg in private conversations with President Reagan. Since Reagan had long hoped that his nominees would have a lasting impact on the Supreme Court, the fact that Ginsburg was only forty-one years old became a positive attribute rather than a cause for concern. On the surface, all of these factors argued for a Ginsburg nomination, and at this time, the administration did not proceed far beyond the surface. On October 29, the president announced his intention to nominate Judge Ginsburg for the seat vacated by Justice Powell.

Ginsburg met with almost immediate opposition. Many liberals believed that he had been chosen because he was a Meese-like conservative or, as one put it, a "Borklet." Senator Kennedy, who had praised Ginsburg only a year earlier as an "open-minded [person] with a sense of compassion," now dismissed him as "an ideological clone of Judge Bork."[2] Arthur Kropp, executive director of People for the American Way, said the nomination "just makes your stomach turn."[3] And Senator Cranston, the Democratic whip, urged the Judiciary Committee to "take its own sweet time" in considering the nomination.[4]

Soon Ginsburg's record, both as a public servant and as a private citizen, provided opponents with ample ammunition for use in a confirmation battle. On November 2, four days after his nomination was announced, Judge Ginsburg was accused of having participated in efforts by the Justice Department to deregulate the cable industry at a time when Ginsburg himself owned $140,000 of stock in a Canadian cable company that was doing business in the United States. An amicus brief had been prepared under Ginsburg's supervision, urging the Supreme

Court to rule that the First Amendment protected cable operators from government regulation. Although Ginsburg did not own stock in the company litigating before the Court, he could profit indirectly from a favorable ruling. Critics argued that there was an apparent conflict of interests and that Ginsburg had acted improperly in failing to have his participation in the case cleared with the Office of Government Ethics.

Judge Ginsburg was also attacked for having sat on a federal case arising out of actions in which he had been personally involved two years earlier as a policy maker in the Office of Management and Budget (OMB). It was reported that Ginsburg had participated in preliminary rulings in the case and that he was scheduled to hear oral arguments, when a court clerk advised an attorney that one of the judges was mentioned in an exhibit. Ginsburg then recused himself, but the fact that he had apparently been willing to judge a case arising out of matters in which he had been a direct participant gave added credence to charges of ethical insensitivity.

Since ethics charges have been used successfully against other Supreme Court nominees, the cable and OMB controversies could not be lightly dismissed. Nevertheless, these attacks, like the criticisms of Ginsburg's legal philosophy and lack of judicial experience, were leveled by individuals believed to have opposed the Ginsburg nomination from the very beginning. More threatening were the assertions, soon to come, that Ginsburg was vulnerable on core issues of abortion and drug use, which were of pivotal importance to his own conservative supporters. Republicans were already in the minority in the United States Senate; if Ginsburg's own base of support could be significantly eroded, it was doubtful that the nomination could survive.

By November 3, reports began to surface that Ginsburg's wife had performed abortions and that Ginsburg himself had once recommended abortion services for a victim of rape. Dr. Hallee Morgan, Judge Ginsburg's wife, admitted that she had performed abortions as part of her medical training but said she did not plan to continue to do so. Judge Ginsburg denied having recommended an abortion, and his ex-wife, who had initially released the information, then called a reporter and said, "I think I messed up."

The abortion controversy, together with the ethics questions, caused some Republicans to begin to distance themselves from the nominee of their own party. Senator Robert Dole, the Senate minority leader, signaled the growing Republican discomfort with Ginsburg's nomination when he was asked why he did not give a wholehearted endorsement to the nominee. "I want to find out about the cable thing," Dole told reporters. He added that he had "only met the guy for five minutes."[5] Apparently, someone else would have to assume responsibility for Judge Ginsburg's confirmation.

The final blow came on November 5, when it was disclosed that Ginsburg had illegally used marijuana while serving on the faculty at the Harvard Law School. Ginsburg tried to put the best face on a difficult situation. He issued a statement admitting that "once as a college student in the 60's, and then on a few occasions in the 70's, I used marijuana. That was the only drug I ever used. I have not used it since. It was a mistake, and I regret it."[6] The statement was quite misleading. It gave the impression that Ginsburg's use of marijuana was a youthful indiscretion, although the facts showed that Ginsburg had used marijuana while employed as a law professor and had done so in public.

But no explanation, accurate or misleading, could now save the Ginsburg nomination. Senator Warren Rudman, a New Hampshire Republican who had voted for Judge Bork, told reporters that the White House would "have to seriously consider whether they have a major problem." He added, "Quite frankly, they've had a problem from day one."[7]

The administration moved quickly to make Judge Ginsburg realize how desperate his position had become. William Bennett, the secretary of education, acting with the president's knowledge, called Ginsburg and told him that his campaign was no longer winnable and was very damaging to the administration.[8] Other officials advised Ginsburg that some twenty to thirty senators had concluded that he could not be confirmed. The nominee was left with little choice. At about 11:30 A.M. on November 7, just nine days after he was chosen for the Court, Judge Ginsburg called President Reagan to ask that his name be withdrawn.

After the failure of a second judicial candidate, the administration faced a serious dilemma. It had promised Republican conservatives that it would nominate non-activist jurists to the Supreme Court; but with a national election only a year away, time would soon run out for confirming a new nominee. These two considerations—the desire for a conservative justice and the need for speedy confirmation—argued powerfully for the nomination of Judge Kennedy, who had lost out to Ginsburg less than two weeks earlier. Kennedy had a strong conservative record as a member of the court of appeals, but his language and demeanor were moderate enough to provide political cover for senators who had voted against Robert Bork.

Kennedy's name moved quickly to the top of the list of candidates. Howard Baker, the president's chief of staff, gave those who had opposed Kennedy only a few days "to come up with a viable rival."[9] Meanwhile, Attorney General Edwin Meese went to Capitol Hill to lobby for Kennedy among conservative Republicans. With Baker and Meese agreeing on the choice of Kennedy, there was little chance for an alternative candidate to emerge. On November 11, President Reagan announced that Judge Kennedy would be nominated to the Supreme Court.

There was much at stake as the Kennedy nomination headed toward hearings before the Senate Judiciary Committee. Most important, of course, was the impact that a Kennedy seat would have on the Supreme Court. If Judge Bork could tip the ideological balance on the Court, the confirmation of a like-minded justice would have a similar effect. Second, assuming that the Bork hearings established new ground rules for Senate confirmation rather than an idiosyncratic exception, the Kennedy hearings would presumably make clear just what the new rules would be. Finally, the outcome of the hearings might well influence future confirmation battles. The war over Judge Bork had been fought on ideological grounds. In order for that fight to be considered worthwhile, it was essential that Kennedy be perceived as someone who was vitally different from Robert Bork.

Although a new nominee was now before the Judiciary Committee, the issues of primary concern—privacy, affirmative action, and civil rights—were the same ones that had driven the Bork hearings. Among these issues, it was the right to privacy that became the focal point for distinguishing Judge Kennedy from Judge Bork. Senator Biden asked Kennedy whether he had "any doubt that there is a right of privacy." Kennedy's response was carefully drawn. "It seems to me," he said, "that most Americans, most lawyers, most judges, believe that liberty includes protection of a value that we call privacy."[10] When asked by Senator DeConcini whether "you have concluded . . . that there is a fundamental right to privacy," Kennedy repeated, "I prefer to think of the value of privacy as being protected by the [liberty] clause . . . and maybe that is a semantic quibble, maybe it is not."[11] Asked more pointedly whether the *Griswold* case "was properly reasoned," Kennedy became quite reticent. "I really think I would like to draw the line and not talk about the

Griswold case, so far as its reasoning or its result."[12] When pressed further, Kennedy stated that there is a "marital right to privacy," but he did not say where that right was found nor suggest what its contents might be.[13]

The Judiciary Committee's report on the Kennedy nomination would later cite Judge Kennedy's position on privacy as a basis for distinguishing Kennedy from Judge Bork.[14] But, in fact, Kennedy's testimony revealed very little about his position on privacy. Judge Kennedy's repeated insistence that "privacy values" are protected by the liberty clause of the Fourteenth Amendment tells us virtually nothing. It was established long ago that the Fourth Amendment's safeguards against unreasonable searches and seizures are included in the liberty clause, and no one doubts that those safeguards are designed to protect "privacy values." To the extent that Kennedy viewed Fourth Amendment values as constitutionally protected, he could not be distinguished from Judge Bork or any other recent nominee to the Supreme Court. To be sure, Kennedy also said there is a marital right of privacy that would extend beyond the Fourth Amendment's protection against searches and seizures. But he refused to say anything about the scope of that right. Furthermore, Kennedy soon added an addendum that left his views on the constitutional right of privacy quite uncertain. Only a few moments after Kennedy said there was a marital right of privacy, he was asked whether courts should recognize "the right to marry, to establish a home [and to] bring up children."[15] Kennedy replied: "Again, I think that most Americans think that they have those rights, and I *hope* that they do. Whether or not they are fully enforceable by the courts . . . is a matter that remains open."[16] In short, Judge Kennedy distinguished sharply between the existence of a right to marry, for example, and the question whether any such "right" could be enforced by a court of law. Since the legal debate over privacy has focused precisely on the issue of judicial enforceability, Kennedy's testimony disclosed relatively little about the nominee's position on the critical issues in that debate.

The hearings also revealed very little about Judge Kennedy's views on other important issues, like affirmative action and free speech. Senator Biden asked Kennedy for his views on affirmative action, but the judge declined to answer. "The issue has not come before me in a judicial capacity as a circuit judge, and might well as a Supreme Court Justice, so I would not commit myself on the issue."[17] That was enough for Senator Biden, who declared himself "not sure, quite frankly, how to fairly pursue the issue further with you without getting into areas that you might have to decide on."[18] If this meant that a nominee could be asked only about positions he had previously taken and not about positions he might later take, it suggested that nominees who had taken no position on serious constitutional questions need not have much to say to the committee. President Bush and the next Supreme Court nominee, David Souter, would soon show that they had learned the lesson of this exchange between Biden and Kennedy.

The committee was no more demanding on the issue of free speech. Senator Specter asked Kennedy whether there was "any question in your mind about the propriety of the longstanding rule in the Supreme Court of the United States about the clear and present danger test or freedom of speech."[19] Kennedy replied that the Court gives more protection to free speech than the clear and present danger test requires and that the *Brandenburg* case in particular "goes a little further than the clear and present danger test."[20] Kennedy added that he knew of "no substantial, responsible argument which would require the overruling of that precedent."[21] Senator Specter seemed satisfied. Neither Specter nor any other committee member pressed Judge Kennedy about his view, expressed in *Singer v. United States Civil Service Commission*, that a federal employee could be fired for "the open and public flaunting *or advocacy* of homosexual conduct."[22] Judge Kennedy's position in the *Singer* case seems inconsistent with *Brandenburg*, and the judgment in *Singer* was eventually vacated by the Supreme Court. Yet, the testimony from Kennedy, suggesting his support for *Brandenburg*, went unchallenged; and despite *Singer*, his commitment to free speech went unquestioned.

But it was in the area of civil rights that Kennedy's record was most revealing and that the committee's questioning, if one assumes the propriety of ideological inquiry, was most seriously flawed. The record showed that Judge Kennedy had repeatedly taken positions which would sharply restrict the application of federal civil rights laws. In at least four instances, the Supreme Court by lopsided votes had rejected the positions taken by Judge Kennedy.

In one case, Kennedy had ruled that a parent who transferred her handicapped child to a private school was entitled to no reimbursement for the tuition costs incurred during administrative review of her claim that the child was placed in an inappropriate educational setting.[23] Two years later, the Supreme Court ruled unanimously that if a parent prevailed in her claim of inappropriate educational placement, she would be entitled to full reimbursement for expenses incurred while her claim was under review.[24] Justice Rehnquist, who wrote the Court's opinion, noted that a denial of reimbursement would undermine the child's right to an appropriate educational placement. When asked about this case at his confirmation hearings, Judge Kennedy said, "I have absolutely no problem with the Supreme Court's decision."[25] But obviously he did have a problem with that point of view when his vote counted and when the pending issue was not his confirmation by the Senate but the plea of an anguished parent before his court.

In another case, Judge Kennedy voted to allow an employer to discharge an employee for writing a letter to some members of Congress, opposing a policy position taken by the employer.[26] Two years later, the Supreme Court ruled that federal law protected such communications and that employees could not be fired for making them.[27] When asked about the case at his confirmation hearings, Kennedy again announced that he was "fully satisfied with the decision of the Supreme Court."[28]

The pattern continued. Judge Kennedy had authored an opinion holding that a civil rights organization could not bring suit to challenge racially discriminatory practices of real-estate brokers who "steered" home buyers into segregated neighborhoods. Kennedy said that because the plaintiffs were not seeking homes for themselves and complained only of being denied the benefit of living in an integrated community, they had no standing to sue.[29] Three years later, the Supreme Court rejected Kennedy's view and ruled that standing to sue against racially discriminatory housing practices could not be limited to those who sought homes for themselves.[30] When asked about the case, Kennedy told the Senate Judiciary Committee, "I certainly have no quarrel with the [Supreme Court's] decision."[31]

He also had no quarrel with a Supreme Court decision that vacated a ruling by Judge Kennedy that would have required each individual member in a class action to intervene in the proceedings in order to prevent the statute of limitations from defeating a claim.[32] The Supreme Court rejected Kennedy's position by a unanimous vote. Yet, no one on the Judiciary Committee accused Kennedy of being "outside the mainstream," as they had said of Judge Bork. Nor did anyone accuse Kennedy of having a confirmation conversion when he remarked that he was "quite willing to accept the decision of the Supreme Court," which had overturned his own decision in the matter.[33]

Judge Kennedy clearly received only the most cursory kind of scrutiny from the Senate Judiciary Committee. Joseph Rauh Jr., who testified against Kennedy on behalf of Americans for Democratic Action, accused the committee of "playing patty cake with Judge Kennedy." Rauh was surely right. Responses that had produced great skepticism when delivered by Robert Bork could be offered by Kennedy without causing a ripple. The committee praised Judge Kennedy for having "a broad vision of 'original intent'"[34] because Kennedy had testified that original intent should not be limited to "what the Framers . . . actually thought" they were doing[35] but referred to "the legal consequences of their acts," rather than to their subjective motivations.[36] Judge Bork had said much the same thing, but he was condemned for having a "narrow vision" of original intent. And Judge Kennedy was never questioned seriously about his record in civil rights cases, even though the repeated rejection of his views by lopsided majorities in the Supreme Court suggested that on matters relating to federal civil rights statutes, it was he, more than Judge Bork, who was vulnerable to the charge of being outside the judicial mainstream.

The easy confirmation of Judge Kennedy, in the face of this record, strongly suggests that a president who is persistent can secure the confirmation of someone who shares his legal philosophy. Equally important, the hearings showed that the Judiciary Committee would not follow a consistent practice of vigorously questioning judicial nominees. The Senate, like the rest of the country, had grown tired of the months of debate over approval of a new justice. It was ready to confirm someone who might vote largely like Judge Bork, if only the new nominee was somewhat smoother around the edges and did not talk like Bork.[37] If necessary, the committee would simply look the other way when confronted with the nominee's civil rights record or would "play patty cake" with the nominee. But if the Senate was willing to acquiesce in the appointment of Judge Kennedy because of the bloody and protracted battle over Robert Bork, there is little reason to believe that it will act differently in future cases, after rejecting other nominees on ideological grounds.

PART FOUR

JUDICIAL CONFIRMATIONS IN THE POST-BORK ERA

19
JUDGE SOUTER:
A STEALTH NOMINEE

The Bork and Kennedy hearings showed that even when the Senate seems to be focused on judicial ideology, one Supreme Court nominee may be confirmed while another with a similar judicial philosophy is denied confirmation. The Senate's exhaustion with the protracted Bork proceedings, combined with Kennedy's pleasant and noncombative style, made the Kennedy confirmation almost inevitable, despite the nominee's clear conservative record on the bench. But if it is apparent that one way for the president to secure confirmation of his judicial nominees is to wear down the opposition, this is certainly not the only way. When President Bush was given his first opportunity to nominate a Supreme Court justice, he took the relatively nonconfrontational course of nominating a judge with almost no record of public pronouncements on major constitutional issues. The candidate was soon viewed as a judicial conservative who would be reluctant to "legislate from the bench," as the president put it, but who had left almost no tracks and would not be an easy target for Senate liberals.

On Friday, July 20, 1990, William Brennan announced his retirement as an associate justice of the Supreme Court. Of course, the announcement immediately triggered speculation as to who would be Brennan's successor. President Bush moved quickly to short-circuit efforts by various activists to advance the prospects of their favorite candidates.

The Bush administration had inherited a list of more than fifty potential Supreme Court nominees from the files of the Reagan White House. This list had been pared down to fewer than twenty names by the time that Justice Brennan announced his retirement. Less than twenty-four hours later, the list was reduced to eight, and half of those were considered longshots. The four front-runners—all judges who had been appointed to the federal court of appeals by Reagan or Bush—were Edith Jones, David Souter, Laurence Silberman, and Clarence Thomas. Attorney General Thornburgh and White House counsel C. Boyden Gray told Bush that Thomas, who had less than a year of judicial experience, should acquire more seasoning before being considered for the Supreme Court. The President himself removed Silberman from the list without stating his reasons for doing so. The result was that just two days after Brennan's announcement, the list of potential nominees had been narrowed down to Edith Jones and David Souter. Both candidates were invited to Washington to meet with the president.

Jones and Souter were each taken to a "safe house," where they could spend Sunday night quietly, without attracting the attention of the Washington press corps. Edith Jones stayed at the home of John Schmitz, a deputy to White House counsel C. Boyden Gray. On Monday morning, Schmitz took her through a back door in the White House to meet with Attorney General Thornburgh. Later, she was escorted to the family quarters, where she met with the president in his private office. After about thirty minutes, she was turned over to staff members, who would entertain her during the day while she awaited a decision from President Bush.

David Souter, who had spent the night at the home of Michael Luttig, the acting assistant attorney general in the Office of Legal Counsel, met on Monday morning with Gray and Thornburgh. At 1:30 in the afternoon, Souter was taken to President Bush's office, where he and the president talked for about forty-five minutes. Then Souter was whisked away, like Jones, to wait for the President's decision. Bush met with Thornburgh, Gray, Chief of Staff Sununu, and Vice President Quayle to discuss the two candidates. After the meeting, the president spent an hour alone writing a brief that listed the pros and cons of each candidate. A short while later, Bush announced that Souter would be his nominee. C. Boyden Gray was dispatched to deliver the news to Edith Jones and to put her on a plane back to Texas.[1]

The unexpected selection of Judge Souter sent reporters and other observers scurrying in all directions to learn what they could about Souter's public record and even about his private life. Souter was quickly seen as a "conservative" jurist who was committed to judicial restraint but whose record was generally free of controversial statements and positions.[2] As a member of the New Hampshire Supreme Court, on which he served for seven years, Souter had written that the court's interpretive task was to determine the meaning of constitutional language "as it was understood when the Framers proposed it and the people ratified it" in the eighteenth century. That statement was as conservative as any that Judge Bork had made for enforcing the "original understanding" of the Framers rather than leaving judges free to put their own imprint on the Constitution, as they thought best. Reporters also pointed out that Judge Souter had been on President Reagan's list of finalists when a replacement was sought after Bork's nomination had failed. Although New Hampshire Senator Warren Rudman was largely responsible for placing Souter's name on that list, the fact that Judge Souter could emerge as a potential nominee during the Reagan administration was used to send a signal to conservatives who might otherwise have been uncertain about the nominee.

Nevertheless, Judge Souter's record was free of strident attacks on the Warren Court or on decisions revered by liberal senators. In some areas—most notably, abortion and civil rights—Souter seemed to have said little or nothing on the public record. Accordingly, he was soon dubbed the "stealth nominee," and some critics suggested that Souter had been nominated precisely because he had no clear record on many controversial issues. One columnist was moved to recommend his eighteen-year-old son for the next vacancy on the Supreme Court, noting as his qualifications that the young man had a searching intellect and no paper trail. "To my knowledge, he has published nothing on the law."[3]

Before long, the stealth nominee had disappeared entirely from the political radar screen, displaced by important international events in the Persian Gulf that seemed to make domestic issues pale by comparison. In early August, Iraq attacked the tiny state of Kuwait and stood poised to extend its aggression to Saudi Arabia and the United Arab Emirates. A judicial nomination could command little attention in an atmosphere permeated by threats of war, oil shortages, and economic dislocation.

On the eve of the Souter confirmation hearings, Senator Biden attempted to refocus attention on the nominee's views on major constitutional issues. Referring to the confirmation proceedings, Biden said, "At this fateful moment in our history, we have a right to know—and a duty to discover—precisely what David Hackett Souter thinks about the great constitutional issues of our time."[4] Measured by that standard, the hearings were destined to fail. The committee was not only unable to discover "precisely" what Judge Souter thinks about great constitutional issues; it, in fact, learned very little about Souter's thinking on any significant question.

The issue that had been "on everyone's mind and everyone's lips since the moment of [Souter's] nomination" was, of course, abortion.[5] But Judge Souter flatly refused to answer any questions from the committee about a woman's right to obtain an abortion. Instead, he offered the committee an anecdote, relating how he had counseled a pregnant woman about abortion twenty-four years earlier and had "learned that afternoon what was at stake."[6] Beyond this, Souter would only express general support for a concept of "marital privacy," which he would not define except to remark that it included the right to have children. Souter refused not only to say whether *Roe v. Wade*[7] should be overruled but even to comment on the Court's reasoning in that case or on the legal standard that should be applied to abortion. Such comments, he said, would be "inappropriate" because there was "a likelihood" that the Court would reexamine the *Roe* decision.[8] Yet, Judge Souter was quite willing to discuss the standard of review in cases of religious freedom and gender discrimination, even though there certainly was a likelihood that the Court's rulings in those areas would be reexamined. Souter's refusal to answer questions on abortion seemed to have less to do with compromising his independence as a judge than with compromising his viability as a nominee.

However, the most striking feature of Souter's testimony was not the overt refusal to answer questions but rather the nominee's ability to give responses that seemed reassuring but which, in fact, were largely or wholly devoid of content. Judge Souter's reply to questions about affirmative action provides a good example. The issue was a delicate one for Souter not only because it is highly controversial but more especially because Souter had been quoted as saying in a speech that affirmative action is really affirmative discrimination. Souter told the committee that he hoped this "was not the exact quote because I don't believe that." The speech, he said, was intended to refer only to discrimination "having nothing to do with any remedial purpose but [adopted] simply for the sake of reflecting a racial distribution."[9] Souter then commented on other forms of affirmative action:

[T]here will be a need—and I am afraid for a longer time than we would like to say—a need for the affirmative action which seeks out qualified people who have been discouraged by generations of societal discrimination from taking their place in the mainstream. . . . I think it also goes without saying that when we consider the power of the judiciary to remedy discrimination which has been proven before the judiciary, the appropriate response is not simply to say "stop doing it." The appropriate response, whenever it is possible, is to say "undo it". . . . And as I said a moment ago, one of the developments in American constitutional law which is at the stage, I would say, of exploration now is the development about the particular power of Congress to address a general societal discrimination. . . . That is a concern which will be played out in constitutional litigation for some time ahead of us."[10]

These remarks were widely perceived as demonstrating Souter's support for affirmative action.[11] But affirmative action in the form of the outreach program described by Souter has never raised any serious constitutional problems, since such programs do not discriminate on the basis of race. Moreover, Souter's support for undoing acts of proven discrimination simply accepted the existing law on the subject and said nothing about the extent to which remedies for discrimination could include racial preferences, as opposed to racially neutral judicial relief. Finally, even the congressional authority to legislate affirmative action, upheld by the Supreme Court only a few months earlier because of the special powers conferred on Congress in this area, was placed in some doubt by Souter's statement that this issue was at a "stage . . . of exploration" and would be "played out in constitutional litigation for some time." The net result was that Souter's testimony on affirmative action, which led the press to believe that he was supportive of such action, actually left the nominee entirely uncommitted on the issue.

Judge Souter was equally elusive in dealing with other issues. Senator Simon asked him whether the power of Congress to enforce Fourteenth Amendment rights was "fairly sweeping." Souter appeared to agree that it was, but he carefully described the power as "unprecedented," rather than "sweeping."[12] Senator Simon was satisfied, but there is a substantial difference between the senator's characterization of congressional power and Judge Souter's characterization of it. Congress's power—which, after all, was conferred by constitutional amendment—could obviously be called "unprecedented." But Simon had asked how broad or sweeping the power was, and Souter's measured response said absolutely nothing on that issue. Souter thus showed himself to be adept not simply at giving nonresponsive answers to important questions but also at appearing all the while to have said exactly what the senators had hoped to hear. His responses, as one columnist remarked, "served the same function as a senator's answer to a constituent's letter: not to define his own views, but to soothe and reassure. . . . Souter [was] shrewd enough to know that the senators could be appeased with a little indulgence, letting them pretend they were fulfilling their obligation to rigorously inspect the nominee [while] he furnished them with evidence of his warm, fuzzy side . . . and with achingly sincere bromides on the role of the Supreme Court. . . . "[13]

Even when Judge Souter had a clear record on the subject under inquiry, he managed to elude committee scrutiny. As noted above, Judge Souter had insisted, while serving on the New Hampshire Supreme Court, that "[t]he court's interpretive task is . . . to determine the meaning of [constitutional] language as it was understood when the Framers proposed it and the people ratified it. . . . "[14] It was just this type of statement—which tied constitutional meaning to the language of the text and the intent of the Framers—that had created so much difficulty for Judge Bork, who was found, because of such statements, to have too narrow a vision of the Constitution. When asked about his approach to constitutional interpretation, Souter seemed, according to Senator Biden, to have "categorically rejected the archconservative judicial philosophy of 'original intent.'"[15] But, in fact, Souter had simply redefined the concept of original intent in such a way that most observers would feel obliged to reject the version he described: "When I speak of original intent, I am talking particularly about [the] view that the meaning . . . or the application of [a] provision should somehow be confined to those specific instances or problems which were in the minds of those who adopted and ratified the provision, and that the provision should be applied only to those instances or problems. I do not accept that view."[16] Neither would Judge Bork accept that view; he strongly endorsed court orders to desegregate public schools, for example, even though he believed that school segregation was not one of the specific problems in the minds of the Framers.[17] At another point in his testimony, Souter stated more cogently that "when we look for the original meaning, we are looking for meaning and for principle. We are not confining ourselves simply to immediately intended application."[18] Judge Bork had said exactly the same thing during his testimony before the committee, but at that time, Bork's view was thought to place him outside the mainstream of constitutional scholars.

The lesson of the Souter hearings is not that Judge Souter misled the Judiciary Committee by his testimony on original intent or other issues but rather that he had little difficulty in sidestepping the committee's inquiries. The ease with which he was able to do this tells much about the effectiveness of the confirmation process. The fact of the matter is that a skillful witness can readily frustrate that process under most circumstances. As one writer observed: "Supreme Court confirmation hearings used to be uninformative because no one particularly cared what the nominee thought or else figured it wasn't permissible to ask him. Now they are uninformative because, though everyone is dying to know what the nominee thinks, no one has found a way to extract a truthful confession."[19] In Souter's case, as in Judge Kennedy's, the upshot was that the Judiciary Committee engaged in no vigorous questioning of the nominee. In the Kennedy hearings, the committee showed that it would vote to confirm a nominee with views similar to those of Judge Bork; and in the Souter hearings, the committee showed that it was willing to confirm a nominee whose views were almost entirely unknown. After the experience with the Souter and Kennedy proceedings, the public was becoming skeptical about the confirmation process. The hearings for the next Supreme Court nominee would strongly reinforce that view.

20
CLARENCE THOMAS: ROUND ONE

When Justice Thurgood Marshall decided to retire, President Bush instructed his staff to compile a list of possible nominees and, more specifically, to include the names of those who had been finalists in the selection process a year earlier. This meant that Edith Jones would be on the list, as would Laurence Silberman. But, from the beginning, Bush leaned toward nominating Judge Clarence Thomas of the federal court of appeals for the District of Columbia.

After a preliminary list of about a dozen prospects had been compiled, Bush asked the staff to concentrate on "non-traditional" candidates. The list was then pared down to Emilio M. Garza, an Hispanic judge on the court of appeals, and Clarence Thomas. Chief of staff John Sununu reportedly favored Garza. Sununu thought that the appointment of Garza would help Republicans win a greater percentage of the Hispanic vote but that the appointment of Thomas would not help with the black vote.[1] On the other hand, C. Boyden Gray, Bush's chief legal adviser, supported Thomas with an almost fanatical fervor. Gray, who was quite influential in the Bush White House, believed that Thomas would be a strong conservative voice on the Court.[2]

For a number of reasons, President Bush followed his initial instincts and nominated Clarence Thomas. First, Bush believed that Thomas was the most conservative of the candidates under consideration.[3] Thomas's appointment would therefore enable the president to satisfy the right wing of his party, for whom abortion and Supreme Court appointments were all important. Second, Bush believed that it would be easier for a conservative African-American to gain confirmation than it would be for some other conservative. Senators who had voted to confirm nominees like Antonin Scalia and Anthony Kennedy could not easily explain a vote against the confirmation of Clarence Thomas. And some Democratic senators, who had a strong base of support among black voters, would find it hard to vote against Thomas if their black constituents favored him.[4]

Third, as Timothy Phelps and Helen Winternitz have reported, Benjamin Hooks of the NAACP had confidentially informed Arch Parsons, a black reporter for the *Baltimore Sun*, that he "wouldn't draw the line against Thomas."[5] This meant that the civil rights community would not form a united front against Thomas, as it had against Judge Bork. Hook's statement was relayed to Lee Liberman in Boyden Gray's office, and Bush was promptly briefed on this development.

Finally, Senator John Danforth, for whom Thomas had worked years earlier, told Vice President Quayle that he would act as Thomas's sponsor and would do all he could to achieve confirmation if Thomas became the nominee. In effect, Danforth agreed to play the same role for Thomas that Senator Rudman had played for Judge Souter. Quayle passed this information along to Bush, which had the effect of cementing Thomas's nomination. Because of Danforth's opposition to the president's civil rights bill and his support for a compromise plan favored by Senate moderates, Bush believed Danforth would have great credibility on the question of Thomas's confirmation.[6]

In short, Judge Thomas was nominated to the Supreme Court as a result of shrewd political calculations and not, as President Bush would later suggest, because no one else was as well qualified as Thomas.[7] After the appointment of a stealth nominee the previous year, Bush needed a jurist with well-recognized conservative credentials—one who was qualified but not necessarily "the most qualified candidate," as Bush would call Clarence Thomas. But what the Thomas nomination illustrates most clearly is that a president who is determined to bring someone to the Supreme Court with a particular ideological disposition can usually succeed in doing so if he is sufficiently careful in the nominating process.

SPIN CONTROL

Once Judge Thomas was nominated, Senator Danforth and Kenneth Duberstein made sure there was plenty of favorable publicity about him and that any negative stories were quickly rebutted. One highly publicized part of the confirmation effort was the so-called "Pin Point strategy."[8] Numerous stories appeared in the media, describing the poverty that Thomas had endured during his youth in Pin Point, Georgia, and suggesting that he had "pulled himself up by his bootstraps" to reach the pinnacle of success. The Citizens Committee to Confirm Clarence Thomas, chaired by Gary Bauer, paid the travel expenses of Thomas's friends and relatives in Pin Point so that they could lobby for his confirmation.[9] Judge Bork, appearing as a commentator on *Court TV* during the Thomas hearings, remarked wistfully that he wished the White House had gone to such lengths for him.

White House strategists were determined not to repeat the mistakes that had been made during the Bork proceedings. Gary Bauer told the *Washington Post* that the White House now recognized that the failure to respond quickly to attacks on Bork had been a "disaster."[10] Accordingly, whenever charges were leveled against Thomas, one of his supporters would put together a rapid response. For example, when the press learned that Thomas had once kept a confederate flag on his desk, supporters responded that it was the state flag of Georgia that had adorned Thomas's desk.[11] And when the Congressional Black Caucus held a press conference to announce its opposition to Thomas, Congressman Gary Franks, at the urging of the Bush administration, called his own press conference to emphasize that many blacks like himself supported Judge Thomas.[12]

Significantly, the media campaign by conservative groups was much more vigorous than it had been during the Bork proceedings. While liberal groups were in disarray for most of the summer, the Christian Coalition was spending over $1 million on Thomas's behalf.[13] One ad, run jointly by L. Brent Bozell III and Floyd G. Brown, attacked the ethics of Senators Kennedy, Biden, and Cranston and asked pointedly, "Whose values should be on the Supreme Court, Clarence Thomas's or Ted Kennedy's?"[14] The ad was so strident that Judge Thomas and President Bush felt obliged to denounce it. Sununu phoned Bozell and said it was his job to tell Bozell to pull the ads. But Floyd Brown said that, privately, Sununu loved the ad.[15] As a result of the furor, Bozell garnered a huge amount of free publicity by appearing on various television programs to discuss the ad campaign.

Yet, no substantial television campaign was run against Judge Thomas. Although Arthur Kropp of People for the American Way claimed that a shortage of money prevented his organization from running ads against Thomas, the real reason for inactivity may have been fear of a political backlash.[16] Some liberal groups felt that they simply could not afford to alienate Thomas's black supporters by attacking Thomas.

A HOUSE DIVIDED

As expected, the Thomas nomination divided the civil rights community. The Southern Christian Leadership Conference (SCLC), which had been founded by Reverend Martin Luther King, supported Thomas. The SCLC's president, Reverend Joseph E. Lowery, stated at a news conference: "Our choice for the Court is not between Thomas and a proven progressive . . . but between Thomas and an appointee like [the] arch-conservative members of the present Court, whose votes have turned back the clock on civil rights, freedom of speech and the criminal justice system."[17] Lowery added that instead of risking another conservative nomination, "we'd rather take a chance on an emerging Thomas."[18] The Congress of Racial Equality, the Fraternal Order of Elks, and other black organizations also decided to support Thomas, while the National Urban League remained officially neutral.

On the other hand, the Congressional Black Caucus voted 19 to 1 to oppose the Thomas nomination.[19] Also opposed to Thomas were the NAACP Legal Defense Fund and the National Baptist Convention.[20] Ultimately, the NAACP also came out against Thomas but not until many weeks had elapsed. The very fact that the NAACP was neither early nor strong in its opposition was a reflection that the black rank and file had been divided over whether Thomas should be confirmed, with a majority favoring confirmation. Consequently, some southern Democratic senators and even a few northern Democrats who had a large base of support among black voters decided that it would be politically risky to oppose Thomas.[21] Earl Shinhoster of the NAACP admitted: "[A] white nominee with the same credentials and the same political views, expressed in a similar manner, would have been vilified in the black community at large, but people have been very restrained in attacking Clarence Thomas. . . . There are people who say 'he may be a devil but he's our devil,' and I understand that."[22]

THE SEPTEMBER HEARINGS

At his confirmation hearings, Judge Thomas tried, like David Souter a year earlier, to suggest that he had an open mind on virtually all subjects.

But because Thomas had been so vocal during his years of service for the Reagan administration, this was a much more difficult task for him than it had been for Souter. On issues of abortion, affirmative action, and natural law, members of the Judiciary Committee wanted to know where Judge Thomas stood and where he would try to take the Supreme Court.

Abortion

Senator Leahy, aware that Thomas would not commit himself on the question of whether *Roe v. Wade*[23] should be overruled, tried to find out how Thomas had reacted to *Roe* when the case was decided. Thomas replied that he did not remember discussing *Roe v. Wade*, and he flatly denied that he had ever "debated" the *Roe* decision.[24] Ralph Neas and Joseph Rauh later placed ads in publications like the *Legal Times*, asking for anyone to come forward who ever had a conversation with Thomas about abortion. Unbeknownst to Neas and Rauh, conservative activist Paul Weyrich apparently believed that Thomas had indeed expressed views on abortion. Phelps and Winternitz reported that at one point, Weyrich was so upset by Thomas's "lack of candor" in testifying about abortion that he considered withdrawing his support for Thomas.[25] But ultimately, Weyrich was persuaded by Tom Jipping to say nothing because Thomas had not perjured himself and "had at least preserved his integrity."[26]

Nevertheless, Thomas's noncommittal posture on abortion was called into question by a speech he gave in 1987 to the Heritage Foundation. In that speech, Thomas said that "Louis Lehrman's article against the right to choose was a splendid example of applying natural law."[27] Lehrman, then a candidate for governor of New York, had argued that under natural law, a fetus has a right to life that cannot be taken away. Thomas also had signed onto a position paper prepared by Gary Bauer, calling for the appointment of more Supreme Court justices who would vote to overturn *Roe v. Wade*.

Under close questioning from Senator Leahy, Thomas insisted that he had not read Bauer's memorandum. He also said that he had intended only to praise Lehrman in a general way, because he was in the Louis Lehrman Auditorium and was searching for unifying principles that would make his conservative audience more receptive to civil rights for minorities. Thomas emphasized that he had not intended to praise Lehrman's views on abortion and added that Lehrman's use of natural law with respect to abortion was inappropriate.[28] But many observers believe that Thomas's credibility was not enhanced by these statements nor by those concerning his prior discussion of *Roe v. Wade*. Senator Simon, for example, said that Thomas's assertion that he could not recall discussing *Roe v. Wade* "invited disbelief."[29] Nevertheless, White House operatives were apparently convinced that the optimum strategy for securing confirmation was for Thomas to say as little as possible on this issue.[30]

Affirmative Action

Judge Thomas was somewhat more comfortable in dealing with issues of affirmative action. On this subject, it was the committee members who were reticent to speak, fearing that they might be portrayed in the media as "pro-quota." Senator Specter was thus the only member of the committee to question Thomas in any depth on these issues.[31]

Specter asked Judge Thomas why he resisted group-based efforts to put minorities in the position they would have enjoyed, absent racial discrimination. Thomas said he did not believe in preferences, goals, or quotas. He took this position because he thought the main value expressed in the 1964 Civil Rights Act was fairness to every individual, and he did not want to undermine the self-respect of minority people by giving them token positions that they did not deserve on the basis of merit.

Specter asked Thomas about affirmative action in law school admissions, since Thomas himself was apparently the beneficiary of affirmative action at the Yale Law School.[32] Specter suggested that minority applicants with lower test scores than white applicants should perhaps be given a preference if they have the potential to blossom. Thomas thought it appropriate for law schools to consider the obstacles an applicant has overcome in determining whether he is qualified to compete with other students. Thomas admitted that this was a subjective judgment, but he favored this approach because it was not based on race.

Specter then asked why the same type of preference should not be used in an employment setting. Thomas replied somewhat vaguely that we should look for "avenues of inclusion," adding that he had aggressively called for minorities to be given the opportunity to develop their potential.[33] After a request for clarification from Senator Biden, Thomas hedged his position: "From a policy standpoint, I agreed with affirmative action policies that focused on disadvantaged minorities and disadvantaged individuals in our society. I'm not commenting on the legality or the constitutionality. I have not visited it from that standpoint."[34]

Senator Specter later defended Judge Thomas against charges that Thomas had deliberately delayed the release of an opinion he wrote for the court of appeals in *Lamprecht v. FCC*.[35] The opinion reportedly would overturn a decision of the Federal Communications Commission (FCC) that granted a broadcast license to a woman under an affirmative action policy. The case had been argued on January 25, 1991, but an opinion was not handed down until thirteen months later, *after* Thomas's nomination to the Supreme Court had been confirmed. Some observers speculated that the release of the opinion was delayed by Thomas in order to avoid any adverse effect on his prospects for confirmation.[36]

On September 27, just before the Judiciary Committee's vote on Thomas, Senator Specter told the committee that he had spoken with the nominee and that Thomas "categorically denied withholding any opinion."[37] Specter said he had reviewed allegations that Thomas withheld the opinion in *Lamprecht*, and he did "not believe that there is any basis for those charges."[38] Although some committee members expressed concern about this story, it did not appear to affect the vote of any of the senators.

Natural Law

Some Democratic senators, especially Biden and Metzenbaum, were concerned about Judge Thomas's apparent interest in natural law. In a speech at the Pacific Research Institute, Thomas had said, "I find attractive the arguments of scholars, such as Stephen Macedo, who defend an activist Supreme Court that would strike down laws restricting property rights." Senator Biden asked what Thomas found attractive about Macedo's arguments. Thomas replied that it had been some time since he had read Macedo's work and that his interest in this work was limited to abstract political philosophy. Thomas added, "I don't see a role for the use of natural law in constitutional adjudication."

But Senator Metzenbaum quoted Thomas's 1989 article in the *Harvard Journal of Law and Public Policy*, which said: "The higher-law background of the American Constitution, whether explicitly appealed to or not, provides the only firm basis for a just, wise and *constitutional* decision."[39] Since Thomas had put the word "constitutional" in italics, Metzenbaum thought it was clear that he supported the use of natural law in constitutional decision making. Thomas replied that the Framers of the Constitution believed in natural law but that they had reduced to written law various principles like liberty which were important to them. He noted, however, that "when it's in the Constitution, it's not a natural right; it is a constitutional right."

Senator Biden tried to show that Thomas's views on natural law could be relevant to his interpretation of the Constitution by asking Thomas how a judge knows what "liberty" means, as that term is used in the Fourteenth Amendment.[40] Thomas admitted that ascertaining this meaning was a very difficult task, and he said it is necessary to look at the country's history and tradition to learn the meaning of liberty intended by the Framers. Biden asked Thomas what he meant when he said that "[e]conomic rights are protected as much as any other rights in the Constitution." Thomas replied that although property rights are protected, this did "not necessarily mean that in constitutional adjudication the protection would be at the same level that we protect other rights."[41] Senator Hatch then asked if there was any shred of evidence that Thomas would be a judicial activist. Thomas said "no" and stressed that "the Court [should] not serve . . . as the super-legislature to second guess" the political branches of government.

OTHER WITNESSES

By the time Thomas completed his testimony, most committee members realized that public opinion was decidedly in his favor. Accordingly, many senators, as well as members of the press and the general public, decided to tune out the three days of testimony by other witnesses. Those who continued to pay some attention saw four black law professors urge that Thomas be rejected because of his positions on constitutional law. Professor Christopher F. Edley Jr. of Harvard asked the committee to focus on Thomas's legal views rather than on his character. Similarly, Patricia King of Georgetown described her own roots in poverty but argued that it was important to examine a nominee's views and not simply his background. Professor Charles Lawrence of Stanford called Thomas a "loyal foot-soldier" for the Reagan-Bush administrations. Lawrence said, "One cannot help but wonder what this history of accommodation has done to Clarence Thomas's character."[42]

However, the testimony of these academics seemed to be largely offset by an endorsement from Dean Guido Calabresi of the Yale Law School, who had known Thomas at Yale. Calabresi, although disagreeing with many of Thomas's legal views, believed that his "history of struggle and his past openness to argument, together with his capacity to make up his own mind, make him a much more likely candidate for growth than others who have recently been appointed to the Supreme Court."[43] Calabresi thought there was a "significant chance that he would be a powerful figure in the defense of civil rights. . . . "

Erwin Griswold, former dean of the Harvard Law School and later solicitor general of the United States, took a more skeptical view of Judge Thomas's potential. Griswold said that Thomas lacked depth and had "not yet demonstrated any clear intellectual or professional distinction." He added that this raised a "frightening prospect" because Thomas was only forty-three years old and could serve another forty years on the Court.[44]

In the end, the Judiciary Committee was deadlocked 7 to 7 on the issue of Thomas's confirmation. This was somewhat surprising, since most observers believed the committee would vote heavily in favor of confirmation. Thomas seemed to have lost some votes because of his unwillingness to answer numerous questions. For example, Senator Herbert Kohl, a new member of the Judiciary Committee, said that he was initially inclined to vote for confirmation but that Judge Thomas "was less than forthcoming and often not responsive to the questions he was asked."[45] Kohl also said that Thomas had engaged in "oratorical opportunism," telling various groups what he thought they wanted to hear, only to repudiate those statements before other audiences. And Senator Howell Heflin said that some of "Judge Thomas's responses suggest to me deceptiveness, at worst, or muddle-headedness, at best."[46] Yet, despite this erosion of support within the committee, Thomas still seemed to be headed for an easy victory in the Senate, where he was thought to have at least sixty votes in favor of confirmation. All of this would change dramatically with the appearance of Anita Hill.

21

CLARENCE THOMAS: ENTER ANITA HILL

On October 5, just three days before the Senate's scheduled vote on the Thomas nomination, Timothy Phelps of Long Island's *Newsday* broke a story involving charges of sexual harassment against Clarence Thomas. The gist of the story was that Thomas, while heading the Equal Employment Opportunity Commission (EEOC), had talked to Anita Hill—then a member of his staff and later a law school professor—about various sexual matters and had repeatedly invited her to go out with him.[1] Within hours, Nina Totenberg of National Public Radio broadcast a similar version of Hill's charges, followed by an interview with Professor Hill. These charges would soon provoke an explosive national debate over Judge Thomas's confirmation.

The White House, in conjunction with Republican leaders in the Senate, promptly began to circulate reports that Hill's story had been fabricated with the help of special interest groups opposed to Judge Thomas. It was also said that a Democratic senator or staff member had leaked the story at the eleventh hour—after the committee had considered the harassment allegations—in order to subvert the process and defeat the Thomas nomination. From the other side, women's groups accused the Judiciary Committee of not responding quickly or strongly enough to Anita Hill's charges. In order to determine which of these claims might be well founded, it is necessary to examine the genesis of those charges.

EMERGING CHARGES OF SEXUAL HARASSMENT

Early in the confirmation process, the Alliance for Justice received a tip, emanating from a Washington dinner party, that "a teacher at the

University of Oklahoma . . . left the EEOC because Thomas had harassed her." It was an easy matter to determine that the person in question was Anita Hill. The Alliance for Justice gave its information to William Corr, chief counsel to a subcommittee on antitrust chaired by Senator Metzenbaum,[2] although the subcommittee clearly had no jurisdiction over the Thomas matter. Corr asked Gail Laster, counsel to Metzenbaum's subcommittee on labor, to look into the charges, even though that subcommittee likewise had no jurisdiction.[3]

Laster reached Professor Hill on September 5 and mentioned allegations of sexual harassment against Judge Thomas. Hill replied that Laster should look into those allegations. Laster then contacted Ricki Seidman, chief investigator for the Labor and Human Resources Committee chaired by Senator Kennedy. Seidman spoke with Hill on September 6 and again three days later. After some initial reluctance, Hill agreed to talk about the harassment issue but said she "had not yet decided how far she wanted the information to go."[4] Hill described the sexual harassment only in brief terms and told Seidman that someone else could corroborate her account. Seidman suggested that Hill might be more comfortable speaking with James Brudney, who had known Hill at Yale Law School and was now chief counsel to Senator Metzenbaum's labor subcommittee.[5]

Brudney called Hill on September 10. Professor Hill indicated that she did not wish to testify publicly and was concerned about whether she would be believed if no other women came forward. In another conversation the same day, Hill told Brudney that she was willing to proceed through Senator Biden's staff, although she was still unwilling to testify in public.[6]

On September 12, Hill made her first contact with the staff of the Judiciary Committee, speaking with Harriet Grant. Hill repeated her concern for confidentiality and said she did not want Judge Thomas to be told her name. Senator Biden was briefed on this conversation and, in a meeting with staff members, decided that nothing more could be done unless Hill agreed for Thomas to be informed about her charges.[7]

Susan Hoerchner, an administrative law judge in California, called the committee staff on September 17. She provided few details but did make it clear that Hill had told her about sexual harassment at work in 1981. However, Hoerchner wanted to remain anonymous because of her position as an appointed judge.[8]

Hill contacted Grant again on September 19 and said she was willing to have the full committee told about her charges and that her name could be used, if necessary.[9] The next day, Grant called Hill to say that her allegations would be given to the FBI for investigation and that she and Thomas would be interviewed. Hill replied that she would have no problem talking with the FBI but wanted to think about the "utility" of doing so.[10]

On September 22, Brudney spoke with Hill again and learned that she had still not decided whether to submit to an FBI interview but that she had drafted a written statement setting forth her charges of sexual harassment.[11] The next day, Hill telefaxed the statement to the committee. At Brudney's request, Hill also telefaxed an unsigned copy to him.[12]

Senator Biden provided a copy of Hill's statement to Strom Thurmond, the ranking Republican on the committee. Biden and Thurmond held meetings with their respective Senate leaders, George Mitchell and Bob Dole. Then, through communications with the White House, an FBI investigation was initiated.[13] The FBI promptly interviewed Hill, Thomas, and Susan Hoerchner, but it apparently found little objective evidence to help determine who was telling the truth.[14]

Hill called Harriet Grant on September 25 and asked that her written statement be circulated to the members of the Judiciary Committee. Grant told Hill that her information would be made available to committee members but that she could not guarantee members would see the statement itself.[15] Hill was evidently upset by Grant's noncommittal response.

After Phelps and Totenberg ran stories on the harassment allegations, Hill felt she had no choice but to testify in support of her charges. She held a press conference at which she stated that it was always her intent for committee members to know about the charges. Hill also said that she had "given a statement to a member of staff and I was assured at that point that the committee would take it into account. . . . I called back to confirm that that was the case, and I was told that no, it was not the case because they wanted to protect my confidentiality."[16]

There is plenty of blame to go around for the mishandling of the Hill-Thomas controversy. The members of the Judiciary Committee bear substantial responsibility. No Senate investigators were sent to the EEOC to investigate the charges, and no Senator except Paul Simon even bothered to speak to Professor Hill.[17] Moreover, the committee voted on Judge Thomas's confirmation without holding any hearings on Hill's charges, even though she apparently would have been willing to appear before the committee in closed session. Finally, the procedures ultimately employed to air the controversy provided insufficient time for a thorough inquiry, and they forced Thomas and Hill into open hearings that were likely to sully the reputation of one, or perhaps both, of them.

Anita Hill also bears some responsibility, especially for failing at times to make clear the degree of confidentiality that she required. But Hill was new to the intricacies of committee politics and could reasonably have expected some help from the people in whom she confided and from those who espouse support for women's rights. Hill had made known to Nan Aron and others that she did not want to "go public."[18] In fact, "every witness who had contact with Hill during the time leading up to the [Phelps-Totenberg] disclosures" reported that "Hill had no desire to go public with her allegations and indeed feared that possibility."[19] Yet, someone who was opposed to Judge Thomas deliberately forced Hill into the glare of unwanted publicity by leaking her written statement in order to undermine the Thomas nomination. Anita Hill, like Paula Jones some years later, learned that concern for her interests could be quickly overwhelmed by concern for a greater political agenda.

Peter Fleming, the special independent counsel who investigated the matter, was unable to identify the person responsible for leaking Professor Hill's statement, although Fleming believed that the leak came from inside the Senate.[20] The *Washington Times* speculated in an editorial that James Brudney must have leaked his copy of Hill's statement because all of the other copies were closely held.[21] Glenn Simpson, a reporter for Washington's *Roll Call*, also concluded that Brudney had been the source of the leak. Since Nina Totenberg had gone to great lengths to verify the authenticity of the statement in her possession,[22] Simpson reasoned that Totenberg must have been working from an unsigned copy, which is exactly what Brudney had in his possession.[23] Furthermore, as Fleming noted in his report, Brudney offered "no explanation for why he retained his copy of Hill's statement—obviously a sensitive document—after its purpose had been exhausted with the completion of his memorandum on sexual harassment on Wednesday, September 25."[24] Fleming was unable to find direct evidence of communications between Brudney and Totenberg.[25] However, his investigation was frustrated by the Senate's refusal to allow him to subpoena the phone records of Totenberg and

Phelps or to cite them for contempt when they refused to answer questions about the source of their stories.

DEMANDS FOR A NEW ROUND OF HEARINGS

In the Senate, the political impact of publicizing Hill's charges was felt almost immediately. Democrats, hoping to defeat the Thomas nomination, argued vigorously for a substantial delay, while Republicans initially opposed any delay at all. The Senate had earlier agreed, by a unanimous consent resolution, that it would vote on Thomas's confirmation on October 8, at 6:00 P.M. Because of this resolution, the only way to delay the scheduled vote was to secure the agreement of all one hundred Senators.

Democrats like Barbara Mikulski and James Exon argued that additional hearings were needed to determine whether Anita Hill was telling the truth. Several Democrats also suggested that a new round of hearings would give Thomas a chance to clear his name so that he would not have to take his seat on the Supreme Court with a cloud over his head. On the other hand, Senator Hatch argued that "[f]urther hearings . . . , further dialogue is not going to solve the problem for anybody. All it is going to do is continue this process of nastiness that has been going on."[26] Senator Hatch said that Judge Bork's opponents had succeeded in a smear campaign, but he and others were determined not to let Judge Thomas's opponents do the same thing.

Despite all the argument and finger pointing, the question ultimately came down to who had the votes on the issue of confirmation. On the day of the scheduled vote, Senator Dole counted only 41 firm votes for confirmation and 16 to 17 votes uncertain.[27] After Senator Dixon, who had previously announced his support for Judge Thomas, said it would be a "major mistake" for the Senate to vote as originally scheduled, the Republican leadership decided that Thomas would have a better chance to be confirmed if the vote were delayed.[28] Most of the wrangling behind closed doors was then over the length of the delay. Senator Danforth apparently proposed a forty-eight-hour postponement.[29] Similarly, Senator Specter reluctantly concluded that a brief delay would be appropriate, although he did not think it would change any votes.[30]

The issue was eventually presented to Judge Thomas, who acquiesced in a short delay. With that, the Senate unanimously agreed to postpone consideration of Thomas's nomination for one week, until October 15. Senator Biden made clear that the new round of hearings would be limited to the issue of whether Thomas had engaged in sexual harassment.[31] Biden also agreed to a request that Judge Thomas be permitted to deliver an opening statement before Anita Hill testified and to give a second statement after Hill testified. This arrangement, together with the decision to limit the hearings to a only a few days, gave Thomas a distinct tactical advantage.[32]

OPENING STATEMENTS

When Judge Thomas returned to the Judiciary Committee for the second round of hearings, the atmosphere had completely changed. There was no longer any light-hearted banter between Thomas and the senators. The smile that had been on Thomas's face through most of the earlier sessions was replaced by an angry frown. Thomas began his opening statement by saying that he was "surprised, hurt and enormously saddened" when told about Hill's allegations on September 25. He testified that he had no idea what he could have said or done to cause Anita Hill to make these charges against him. He then proceeded to deny all of Hill's allegations.

Thomas gave a chronology of his relationship with Hill and emphasized his aversion to sexual harassment. Then, he discussed the great pain that the confirmation process had brought to him and his family:

> Enough is enough. I'm not going to allow myself to be further humiliated in order to be confirmed. I am here specifically to respond to allegations of sex harassment in the workplace. I am not here to be further humiliated by this committee or anyone else, or to put my private life on display for prurient interests or other reasons. I will not allow this committee or anyone else to probe into my private life. . . .
>
> Confirm me if you want, don't confirm me if you are so led, but let this process end. . . . I never asked to be nominated. . . . Little did I know the price, but it is too high. . . . I am comfortable with the prospect of returning to . . . the U.S. Court of Appeals. . . . I want my life and my family's life back and I want them returned expeditiously.[33]

Some observers thought Thomas was about to withdraw from the confirmation process. But, Thomas quickly showed that he would not be pressured into withdrawing his name and later said that he would "rather die than withdraw."

Before questioning Judge Thomas, Senator Biden stated that Professor Hill continued to ask for confidentiality with respect to her statement and, therefore, his questions would necessarily be limited. At that point, Senator Hatch angrily interjected that it would be a "travesty" to allow Hill or her attorneys "to tell us what can or cannot be used now that this man's reputation has been very badly hurt."[34] Hatch even threatened to resign from the committee if Thomas were deprived of the right to confront his accuser.

The committee telephoned Hill during an adjournment called to work out an acceptable procedure. Hill and her lawyers were adamant that she be permitted to deliver her statement personally rather than have it read to the public. They rightly feared that the statement would lose much of its impact if Hill did not present it herself, when the statement was first aired. Accordingly, by agreement of the committee, Professor Hill was permitted to testify first, and Judge Thomas was scheduled to respond later in the day.

In her opening statement, Professor Hill said that after she had worked with Clarence Thomas for about three months at the Department of Education, Thomas asked her out on a date and that he persisted after she repeatedly declined. Hill also testified that Thomas began to talk about sexual acts: "He spoke about acts that he had seen in pornographic films involving such matters as women having sex with animals and films showing group sex or rape scenes. He talked about pornographic materials depicting individuals with large penises or large breasts involved in various sex acts. On several occasions, Thomas told me graphically of his own sexual prowess."[35]

When Thomas became Chairman of the EEOC, he asked Hill to move to the agency with him. Professor Hill explained her decision to accept the offer, testifying that she thought Thomas's offensive behavior had ended and that her job at the Department of Education was in jeopardy. But, according to Hill, Thomas again began to make inappropriate remarks after a few months at the EEOC. He commented on whether her attire made her sexually attractive and repeatedly asked for an explanation as to why she would not go out with him. Hill recounted an episode involving a can of coke: "I remember . . . an occasion in which Thomas was drinking a Coke in his office. He got up from the table at which we were working, went over to his desk to get the Coke, looked at the can and asked, 'Who has put pubic hair on my Coke?' On other occasions, he referred to the size of his own penis as being larger than normal, and he also spoke on some occasions of the pleasures he had given to women with oral sex."[36]

Professor Hill maintained that after leaving Washington in 1983 to teach at Oral Roberts University, she had little contact with Thomas. Hill knew Republicans would argue that her continuing contacts with Thomas belied the claim that he had harassed her. However, her attempt to minimize these contacts was not successful, and many people could not understand why a woman would stay in contact with someone who had sexually harassed her.

COMMITTEE QUESTIONING OF HILL

Senator Biden asked Hill to focus on incidents that occurred in Thomas's office. Hill said that Thomas discussed pornography in his office at least once and that the conversation included "a reference to an individual who had a very large penis and he used the name . . . Long Dong Silver."[37] When Biden asked which incident was the most embarrassing, Hill mentioned Thomas's "discussion of pornography involving women with large breasts and engaged in a variety of sex with different people or animals." Hill said Thomas seemed to have enjoyed pornographic films and had encouraged her to see them also.

Biden asked Hill about her decision to move with Thomas to the EEOC. Hill said, "After some consideration of job opportunities in the area, as well as the fact that I was not assured that my job at Education was going to be protected, I made a decision to move to the EEOC."[38] Hill added that she assumed Thomas's replacement would want to hire his own assistant, and she was worried about rumors that the Department of Education might be abolished.

Later, Senator Specter asked Hill if she did not realize that as a Schedule A attorney, she could have kept her job at the Department. Hill insisted that her understanding had been that she might lose her job, although she did not attempt to verify this understanding. Specter also questioned Hill about a telephone log that showed that she called

Thomas's office more often than she had admitted and that sometimes she "just called to say hello." Hill conceded the accuracy of the log, saying she did not want to burn bridges with Thomas and "could not afford to antagonize a person in such a high position."[39]

QUESTIONING OF THOMAS

When Judge Thomas returned to the hearings later the same day, Senator Biden gave him the opportunity to make another statement before submitting to questions from the committee. Thomas categorically denied all of Professor Hill's charges. He then launched a stinging attack on the hearing process itself:

> I think that [what happened] today is a travesty. . . . It is disgusting. . . . This hearing should never occur in America. This is a case in which this sleaze, this dirt, was searched for by staffers of members of this committee, was then leaked to the media, and this committee . . . validated it and displayed it at prime time over our entire nation. How would any member on this committee, any person . . . like sleaze said about him or her in this fashion? Or this dirt dredged up and this gossip and these lies displayed in this manner? How would any person like it? . . . This is not an opportunity to talk about difficult matters privately or in a closed environment. This is a circus. It's a national disgrace.
>
> And from my standpoint as a black American, . . . it is a high-tech lynching for uppity blacks who in any way deign to think for themselves, . . . and it is a message that unless you kow-tow to an old order, this is what will happen to you. You will be lynched, destroyed, caricatured by a committee of the U.S. Senate rather than hung from a tree.[40]

With this reference to the "lynching [of] uppity blacks," Thomas managed at once to play on white guilt, to reinforce his support among blacks, and perhaps most important, to silence his critics on the Judiciary Committee.

When the questioning began, Thomas continued to respond aggressively. Asked whether he had watched Hill's testimony, Thomas said, "No, I've heard enough lies."[41] Senator Heflin then wanted to know whether Thomas could disprove Hill's allegations. Judge Thomas replied angrily that it was impossible for him to prove a negative and that he could only deny the allegations. Heflin wondered what could have motivated Professor Hill to make such allegations. Thomas replied that he did not know and that "you should ask the people who helped concoct this ... what the motives were." Thomas asked rhetorically how committee members would like to have uncorroborated allegations leaked to the press and then to be "dragged before a national forum of this nature to discuss those allegations that should have been resolved in a confidential way."

Senator Hatch focused on the allegations concerning pornographic films and Thomas's discussion of sexual acts. In response to a series of leading questions, Thomas agreed that the allegations concerning his physical attributes and sexual prowess reflected black stereotypes. He said this added to the difficulty he had in defending himself: "Once you pin that on me I can't get it off. . . . This [process] plays into the most bigoted, racist stereotypes that any black man will ever face."[42]

Senator Hatch also presented a theory, suggested to him by a Justice Department lawyer, to explain Hill's testimony about Long Dong Silver. He cited a sexual harassment case in which a woman testified that the defendant had handed her a photograph of Long Dong Silver, a black male with an elongated penis. Hatch implied that Hill used this case to fabricate Thomas's alleged reference to Long Dong Silver. Finally, Hatch claimed that the "Coke can" incident was reminiscent of a scene from *The Exorcist*, which contained a passage about pubic hair floating in a glass of gin.

Judge Thomas supported his denial of Hill's charges by pointing to the fact that he had worked with hundreds of women, and Hill was the only one who alleged sexual harassment. He said, "If you really want an idea of how I treated women, then ask the majority of the women who worked for me. . . . Give them as much time as you have given one person, the only person who has been on my staff who has ever made these sorts of allegations about me."[43] Several women who were former employees of Thomas later testified to how well Thomas had treated them.

But Angela Wright, the one witness who might have given support to Hill's charges and undermined Thomas's credibility, was not called to testify. Wright had told Senate staff members that while she worked for Judge Thomas, he had tried to date her and once appeared at her apartment uninvited. This statement seemed to contradict Thomas's assertion that he never tried to socialize with his employees. Wright also reported that at an out-of-town seminar, Thomas complimented her on her dress and asked her about her breast size.

Although Wright's statement was placed in the committee record, Democrats were reluctant to call her as a witness. Both Thomas and Phyllis Berry-Myers had testified that Wright was not a good worker and that Thomas had ordered Myers to fire Wright after she called someone a "faggot." Wright had also been fired by Democratic Congressman Charlie Rose after she had walked out of his office, yelling about some alleged "unfairness." A number of Hill's supporters were also concerned because Wright planned to testify that while she found Thomas's conduct strange, she did not consider it "harassment." In the end, Democrats on the committee were unwilling to run the risk of calling Angela Wright.

THE POLYGRAPH EXAM

After Republican senators launched attacks on Professor Hill's credibility, Hill and her advisers began to think seriously about a polygraph examination. During her FBI interview, Hill had said she would be willing to submit to a polygraph exam, and her advisers now concluded that this would be the best way to bolster her credibility.[44] On the last day of hearings, Anita Hill took a polygraph test, administered by Paul Minor, formerly an FBI polygrapher. An announcement that Hill had passed a lie detector test was made at a press conference that afternoon.[45]

Thomas's supporters immediately tried to downplay the polygraph examination. Senator Hatch used part of the time allocated to him for questioning witnesses to challenge the results of the examination. As coauthor of the Polygraph Protection Act, Hatch said he was "highly offended" that Professor Hill's "handlers" would resort to a polygraph. He suggested that "you can find a polygraph operator for anything you want to find them for" and later remarked that asking Hill take a polygraph test was exactly what a "two-bit slick lawyer" would do.[46] In the end, Senator Biden ruled that the committee would not accept the polygraph results because it had "'nothing to do' with ordering the test" and the committee could not vouch for the credentials of the examiner.[47]

SUPPORTING WITNESSES

Four witnesses—John Carr, Joel Paul, Susan Hoerchner, and Ellen Wells—were called to corroborate Professor Hill's charges. Each of the witnesses described statements that Professor Hill had made years earlier concerning incidents of sexual harassment to which she had been subjected at the EEOC or the Department of Education. John Carr, a partner in a Washington law firm, said that he saw Hill socially in 1983 and spoke with her several times by phone. During one of these conversations, Hill sounded troubled, and Carr asked what was wrong. Hill replied that her boss "asked her out on dates and showed an unwanted sexual interest in her." Hill cried during the phone call and did not want to go into detail. Carr did not remember whether Hill had identified Clarence Thomas by name, but he was sure she was referring to Thomas and had thought at the time that sexual harassment by the Chairman of the EEOC was outrageous.[48]

Professor Joel Paul of American University Law School met Hill at a conference in 1987. At the time, Hill wanted to conduct research in Washington, and Paul arranged for her to work at American University. Over lunch that summer, Paul asked Hill why she had left the EEOC. Paul testified, "Professor Hill responded reluctantly and with obvious emotion and embarrassment that she had been sexually harassed by her supervisor at the EEOC."[49] Paul recalled that after his conversation with Hill, he consulted Susan Dunham, an employment discrimination lawyer, who told him that what Hill described was a case of "the fox guarding the hen house." When Hill's allegations were publicized, Dunham reminded Paul of this conversation and independently confirmed his memory of the events.

Judge Susan Hoerchner said she met Hill when they were first-year law students at Yale and had known her for thirteen years. During a phone conversation, she asked Hill how things were at work. Hill responded that her boss was sexually harassing her by continuing to ask her out after she repeatedly declined. Hoerchner did not ask for details because it was painful for Hill to discuss the subject.[50]

Several committee members pointed out that these witnesses were unable to corroborate many of Hill's specific allegations. Senator Specter asked whether Hill had told Hoerchner about pornographic films and about other allegations. Hoerchner replied, "I do not have a specific memory of that, and that would be very much in keeping with her reserved character."[51] Later, Specter asked Hoerchner whether she could corroborate Hill's allegations about the Coke can incident or about Thomas's discussion of his sexual prowess and of women having sex with animals. To each of these inquiries, Hoerchner replied, "no."

Nevertheless, the testimony of these four witnesses was strongly supportive of Professor Hill because it indicated that she was not simply fabricating a story for the purpose of defeating Judge Thomas's nomination. As Senator Kohl remarked pointedly, "If there was a plot afoot, it must have originated ten years ago." Furthermore, since the four witnesses did not know one another, there was little likelihood of collusion among them.

The first panel to testify for Judge Thomas consisted of four women who worked for him at the EEOC: J. C. Alvarez, Nancy Elizabeth Fitch, Diane Holt, and Phyllis Berry-Myers. All of these witnesses spoke very highly of Thomas. Alvarez said that Thomas never exhibited the slightest tendency to harass anyone. She emphasized that she was highly sensitive to such conduct because she had experienced sexual harassment herself.[52]

When the panel was asked what motive Hill might have for lying, Phyllis Berry-Myers said that Hill spoke about Thomas in "highly admirable terms . . . that didn't just indicate a professional interest." She suggested at one point that Hill may have had a "crush" on Thomas.[53] But Nancy Elizabeth Fitch, a historian and former special assistant to Thomas at EEOC, had a somewhat different view. She thought Hill felt very friendly toward Thomas but had no romantic interest in him: "[S]he saw him as a person who was going places, and both of us felt that we wanted to do whatever we could to help him do that."[54] Fitch suggested that both Thomas and Hill might believe their own testimony, but she herself believed Thomas because of the way he treated her.

Another panel of witnesses raised questions about Anita Hill's credibility. One witness, former Dean Charles Kothe, had hired Hill to teach at Oral Roberts Law School after Thomas submitted a favorable recommendation for her. Kothe testified that Hill spoke of Thomas in such glowing terms that it would have been utterly incongruous for him to have done the things that she alleged.[55]

Perhaps the most unusual member of the cast of supporting witnesses was John Doggett. The thrust of Doggett's testimony was that Hill had fantasized about a relationship with him, and he suggested that her charges of sexual harassment might be the product of a fantasized relationship with Thomas.[56] Doggett said he first met Hill in Washington while jogging near her apartment. Hill initiated a conversation with him and suggested that since they were neighbors, they should have dinner sometime. Apparently, each expected the other to call, and the dinner never took place. Doggett did not see Hill again until her going-away party, when she allegedly asked to speak with him in private. According to Doggett, she said: "I'm really very disappointed in you. You really shouldn't lead women on and then let them down." Doggett found this statement to be "absolutely bizarre" because he had given her no indication that he was interested in her.[57]

Senator Biden, however, found it bizarre for Doggett to think this incident was enough to show that Hill had fantasized about him. Senator Metzenbaum later tried to air Doggett's own dirty laundry by reading an unsworn statement submitted to the committee by Amy Graham. In this statement, Graham asserted that on her first day as a secretary at a law firm, Doggett approached her, kissed her on the mouth, and said she would enjoy working with him. Graham also alleged that Doggett would rub her shoulders while she was at the copying machine and that his conversations had sexual overtones.[58] Doggett denied these allegations, and Senator Biden said it was unfair for Doggett to be asked about unsworn, uncorroborated accusations.

Doggett's main role seemed to be to provide a motive for Professor Hill's charges and, perhaps, to explain why she sounded credible and why she had passed a polygraph test. Although Democrats might have undermined this effort through a careful cross-examination, Senator Metzenbaum's attack on Doggett backfired because it reinforced the claim that Democrats were engaged in unfair tactics designed to defeat the Thomas nomination. Even so, Doggett's fantasy theory gained few adherents.

After another panel of eight women made short statements on Thomas's behalf,[59] the committee decided not to call any other witnesses. Neither Thomas's supporters on the Judiciary Committee nor his detractors had come across well during the second round of televised hearings. Republicans were criticized for being too aggressive, while Democrats were attacked for not being aggressive enough. As one Senate aide remarked, "At that point there was only one desire, and it was shared by every member of the committee, Democratic and Republican: 'Shut this damn thing down!'"[60]

SENATE DEBATE

The mood of the Senate debate on confirmation was tense and, at times, unpleasant. Senators tried not so much to convince their colleagues as to justify their own position to constituents at home. A brief sampling reveals the tenor of the debate.

Senator Robert Byrd emphasized his initial support for Thomas and explained why he had changed his mind. Byrd said he had observed Anita Hill's demeanor and found her to be credible. In addition, Byrd complained about "stonewalling" by Judge Thomas, who "wanted to clear his name, but . . . did not even listen to the principal witness, the only witness against him." Finally, Byrd was offended by Thomas's characterization of the committee proceedings as a "high-tech lynching," which Byrd considered "an attempt to fire the prejudices of race hatred."

Senator Specter took the floor to explain why he did not believe Professor Hill's charges. Hill had testified that she was never told that her statement alleging sexual harassment might cause Judge Thomas to withdraw and make additional hearings unnecessary. But later the same day, Hill testified that one of the possibilities she discussed with James Brudney was that information would be presented to the nominee, which might prompt him to withdraw at some point. Specter said that Hill had made this correction in order to avoid being charged with perjury. Hill denied that her statements were inconsistent, arguing that her earlier testimony addressed only the question of whether her "affidavit" by itself would force Thomas's withdrawal. And Senator Kennedy, who had been criticized by liberal groups for sitting on his hands during the Thomas hearings, defended Professor Hill: "There is no proof that Anita Hill has perjured herself—and shame on anyone who suggests that she has."[61] Later, Senator Specter responded with a caustic reference to Kennedy's own indiscretions: "We do not need characterizations like 'shame' in this Chamber from the Senator from Massachusetts."

No part of the Senate debate seemed to affect the final vote, which was 52 to 48 in favor of confirmation. But, as in the Bork proceedings, public opinion polls had a significant impact. Initially, public opinion was sharply divided over whether Judge Thomas or Professor Hill was more credible. Many people called their senators to urge that they support or oppose the Thomas nomination.[62] In the end, however, a *New York Times*/CBS poll found the public believed Thomas's account more than Hill's account by a margin of 48 to 35 percent.[63]

No doubt, the differences in approach taken by Republican and Democratic committee members played a part in shaping public opinion. As Andrew Rosenthal observed in the *New York Times*, the Republican members of the committee embarked on a "scorched-earth" effort to discredit Professor Hill. On the other hand, Democratic members avoided any vigorous cross-examination of Judge Thomas, perhaps out of fear of a political backlash from black voters.[64] Equally important, Thomas and his supporters were able, because of the committee's procedural decisions, to dominate the airwaves during prime time on the last two days of hearings.[65]

22

JUDGE GINSBURG:
A DEMOCRAT FACES THE
CONFIRMATION PROCESS

On March 19, 1993, Justice Byron White announced that he would retire in June, at the end of the Supreme Court's Term. White's resignation meant that a Democratic President would appoint a member of the Supreme Court for the first time in a quarter of a century. There was speculation that President Clinton might try to counteract the appointment of conservative justices during the Reagan-Bush administrations by nominating a committed liberal to succeed Justice White. The assumption was that because the Democratic Party controlled both the Senate and the White House, the president would have a free hand in making the appointment. But as many of Judge Bork's opponents would soon discover, the effects of the battle over Robert Bork could not be confined to nominations by conservative Republicans. In the new atmosphere of Supreme Court appointments, a committed liberal was likely to find the confirmation process as daunting as would a committed conservative.

During the 1992 presidential campaign, Bill Clinton had suggested in an interview on MTV that Governor Mario Cuomo of New York would be an ideal choice for the Supreme Court. In view of the fact that New York was a critical state for Clinton in the November election, this suggestion was certainly understandable, even if it did not necessarily reflect any firm intention on Clinton's part. Following White's announcement, there was predictable speculation that Cuomo would be nominated. However, after a great deal of hemming and hawing by Cuomo and some noticeable silence from Clinton, Governor Cuomo withdrew his name from consideration, saying that he was too young to retire to the cloistered world of the Supreme Court. Clinton thought briefly about nominating his friend Education Secretary and former Governor Richard Riley of South Carolina. But when Riley, too, indicated that he wanted no part of a Supreme Court nomination, Clinton staffers went to work on a list of some forty-two candidates produced by White House counsel Bernard Nussbaum.

From the beginning, it was understood within the Clinton administration that the nominee would have to be someone who was widely perceived as a judicial "moderate." Clinton's campaign promise to name justices who supported abortion rights had drawn sharp criticism from members of the president's own party. Senator Biden said, "It was very inappropriate for Bill Clinton to indicate on the record during the campaign that he would impose a litmus test on the abortion issue, because that will polarize opinion in the Senate."[1] Another Democratic member of the Judiciary Committee predicted that an attempt to keep the president's campaign promise would guarantee "a blood bath" in the United States Senate. Republicans issued similar warnings. Senator Robert Dole, the minority leader, said that "[i]f the President nominates a litmus-test liberal, all bets will be off." And Senator Orrin Hatch, now the ranking Republican on the Judiciary Committee, pointedly advised Clinton to choose judges who will "neutrally and objectively interpret and apply the laws, not judges who will impose their own policy preferences."[2]

Shortly after Justice White's announcement, sources close to the president began to spread the word that Clinton would most likely choose "a moderate politician or judge rather than a legal scholar" for the Supreme Court. They said flatly that the president would "steer clear of any candidate so clearly identified with an ideological camp that he could become a lightening rod for conservative opposition."[3] The message could hardly have been clearer. President Clinton would not risk a confrontation in the Senate, even though his own party was in control there. A majority of the Senate had blocked the confirmation of Robert Bork; now it seemed that even a minority, if determined to battle and perhaps to filibuster a nomination, could defeat the prospects of a candidate who was ideologically unacceptable.[4]

Clinton's problem was aggravated by the difficulties he had experienced with earlier nominations. He had nominated Zoe Baird for the post of attorney general, only to be forced to withdraw her name after a political firestorm erupted, when it was revealed that Ms. Baird had hired undocumented aliens and failed to pay social security taxes for them. A similar fate befell Judge Kimba Wood, whose formal nomination was withheld when it was learned that she had hired undocumented aliens, even though it was legal for her to do so at the time. The Clinton administration defended its decision on Wood by saying that she had not been forthcoming about the fact that undocumented aliens had worked for her. Later, the president would also be forced to withdraw the nomination of Lani Guinier to be assistant attorney general for civil rights. Ms. Guinier, a law professor at the University of Pennsylvania, had written two articles—one in the *Virginia Law Review* and another in the *Michigan Law Review*—in which she argued that more than a simple majority of votes should sometimes be necessary to prevail in a legislative body. In this way, minority voters who were able to elect three out of seven members of the city council, for example, could still have their agenda satisfied a "fair" percentage of the time. Relying on these articles, Clint Bolick, vice president and director of litigation at the Institute for Justice, a conservative think-tank, dubbed Guinier the "quota Queen" in an op-ed piece in the *Wall Street Journal*.[5] His organization began circulating her articles, and he appeared on a number of television news shows to oppose her nomination. In the end, conservatives were so successful in characterizing her position that they were able to do the same thing to Lani Guinier that liberals had done to Robert Bork. President Clinton was forced to withdraw her name from consideration when it became apparent that she had the support of only ten to twenty senators.

To avoid a confrontation over Justice White's successor, the White House stayed in close contact with Republican Senators Robert Dole and Orrin Hatch, as well as with Senate leaders of the president's own party. In a further effort to avert opposition, the administration floated the names of two front-runners for the Supreme Court—Interior Secretary Bruce Babbitt and Judge Stephen Breyer of the federal court of appeals. Babbitt's name drew considerable fire. Environmentalists complained that the loss of Babbitt as secretary of the interior would be a serious blow, and Babbitt later joked that his friends were more of a problem than his enemies. But it was hardly plausible for the administration to suggest that an interior secretary was indispensable, while a Supreme Court candidate could be easily replaced. In the end, it seemed clear that it was not his Democratic friends but his Republican opponents, who delivered the fatal blow to Bruce Babbitt. The *New York Times* reported that Senator Hatch "said it would be unacceptable to nominate

Mr. Babbitt, a former Arizona Governor and onetime Democratic Presidential contender who has never been a judge."[6] Hatch had expressed concern "about putting another political figure on the bench, who might substitute his or her own visceral or personal beliefs for the law, instead of interpreting the law that is made by elected representatives of the people."[7] Senator Dole also complained that Babbitt was merely a politician who lacked prior judicial experience. Of course, many former justices, including Brandeis, Frankfurter, and John Marshall, lacked judicial experience before their appointment to the Supreme Court. The real concern of the Republican opposition was that Babbitt, whose background was in politics, might view the Court as merely another political forum and therefore be prone to "judicial activism."

As a result of these criticisms, Babbitt's prospects receded, and Breyer became the apparent front-runner. On Friday, June 11, Breyer's nomination was reported to be imminent. Breyer, though still suffering the effects of a bicycle accident, was flown to Washington for lunch with the president. However, Clinton seemed to have some reservations after talking to Breyer. His concerns were heightened when the *Washington Post* reported that Breyer had failed to pay social security taxes for his once-a-week housekeeper, who was already collecting social security benefits. Breyer apparently had not realized that taxes were owed, but after the Zoe Baird controversy, he checked with the IRS and paid all of the back taxes, which amounted to about $4,000. In many respects, Breyer's case resembled that of Washington attorney Charles Ruff, whose nomination for deputy attorney general had been withdrawn after it was learned that he had earlier failed to pay social security taxes for a part-time housekeeper.[8] As a result of the public outcry over Zoe Baird, members of the Senate were highly sensitive to this type of problem. Democratic Senators David Boren and Tom Harkin raised concerns about the application of a double standard that would sink female nominees like Zoe Baird and Kimba Wood but might let a male nominee slide through.[9] Unfortunately for Breyer, one of the best things he had going for him was that he was well liked by senators on both sides of the aisle and his confirmation promised to be easy. After the social security flap arose, that was no longer certain, and the administration turned to another possible nominee.

On Sunday, June 13, President Clinton met for ninety minutes in the White House residence with Judge Ruth Bader Ginsburg of the federal court of appeals for the District of Columbia. The meeting was evidently a great success. Unlike Breyer, who had discussed antitrust law with Clinton, Judge Ginsburg told the president the story of her life. Clinton was moved by the tragedies that Ginsburg had endured. Her mother had died the day before Ginsburg's high school graduation, and Ginsburg did not attend the ceremony.[10] Later, her husband was diagnosed with cancer shortly after his graduation from Harvard Law School, and he was thought to have only a few months to live. After two operations and extensive radiation therapy, he was cured, but the Ginsburgs were told that they would have no more children. Ten years later, Ruth Ginsburg was surprised to learn that she was pregnant with her second child.[11]

At 11 P.M. on the evening of the Ginsburg interview, Bernard Nussbaum called Judge Ginsburg and asked her to stay up because the president wanted to talk with her. About half an hour later, immediately after watching a basketball game on television, Clinton called Ginsburg at her apartment in the Watergate complex. Because the telephone connection was bad, Clinton told her he would call back. "If I'm going to propose," he said, "we might as well have a good line."[12] The president then dialed Ginsburg and offered her a seat on the Supreme Court. Twenty minutes later, he called Judge Breyer and, immediately afterward, Secretary Babbitt to inform them of his decision.

On Monday, June 14, 1993, President Clinton announced from the Rose Garden that he would nominate Ruth Bader Ginsburg to fill Justice White's position on the Supreme Court. The announcement was a surprise to many, who still believed that Breyer had cinched the nomination. Nevertheless, there were sound political reasons for Clinton to nominate Judge Ginsburg. First, Senators Hatch and Dole were known to support Ginsburg. After her nomination was announced, Senator Hatch said: "I don't think we want people in judicial robes legislating from the bench, and I don't think that Judge Ginsburg will do that. I do not believe she will be an activist judge in the sense of substituting her own policy preferences for what the law really is."[13] Second, Ginsburg, as a Jewish woman, would add to the Court's diversity, which was a matter of some importance to Democratic constituencies. Third, Ginsburg was highly respected in legal circles for having been one of the leaders of the women's rights movement. She had argued six major cases in the United States Supreme Court and won five of them, establishing a precedent along the way that the Court would give heightened scrutiny to gender-based action by government. Senator Daniel Patrick Moynihan quoted former Dean Erwin Griswold of the Harvard Law School as saying that Ginsburg was to gender equality what Thurgood Marshall had been to racial equality.[14] Lastly, Ginsburg had the reputation of being a "moderate" and a consensus builder, something that Clinton strongly desired. On the court of appeals, Ginsburg was considered the most judicially conservative of the Democratic appointees to that court.[15] A statistical analysis of her decisions in 1987 showed that she voted with the conservative block of the court, led by Robert Bork, more often than any of the other liberal Democratic judges. Judge Bork, however, was somewhat skeptical of her ability to build a consensus on the Supreme Court. Bork said that "it's such a divided Court, I don't know how possible it is to be a consensus builder. . . . I think Ruth will be amiable and reasonable enough to convince some people. But I don't see her going from chamber to chamber or taking people out to lunch to try to build a consensus."[16]

After being introduced by the president in the Rose Garden ceremony, Judge Ginsburg delivered a highly moving statement about her nomination. She said her nomination was significant "because it contributes to the end of the days when women, at least half the talent pool in our society, appear in high places only as one-at-a-time performers."[17] Then, in an emotional tribute, she thanked her mother, "the bravest and strongest person I have known, who was taken from me much too soon. I pray that I may be all that she would have been had she lived in an age when women could aspire and achieve, and daughters are cherished as much as sons."[18] At that point, Clinton threw the meeting open to reporters' questions. However, the first question turned out to be the last. Brit Hume of *ABC News* had the temerity to ask the president to "walk us through" the decision-making process, which he characterized as having "a certain zigzag quality."[19] Clinton responded in a huff: "I have long since given up the thought that I could disabuse some of you turning any substantive decision into anything but political process. How you could ask a question like that after the statement she just made is beyond me."[20] He then stormed off without taking any more questions. The next day, trying to undo some of the political damage, he joked with Brit Hume about the announcement of Hume's engagement.

Because of the bipartisan support that Ginsburg received, Senator Biden was able to schedule the confirmation hearings to begin just five weeks after the nomination was announced, a marked contrast to the delay of two and a half months that Judge Bork encountered after his nomination. Moreover, the outcome of the Ginsburg hearings was virtually a foregone conclusion. Senator Biden noted at the outset that the nomination had generated so little controversy that on the day the confirmation hearings began, the first mention of the hearings in the *New York Times* was buried on page 15.[21] And the mood of senators on the Judiciary Committee was very different from the mood during the Bork and Thomas hearings. In his opening statement, Senator Heflin said: "What a change of atmosphere from the recent past. Congeniality prevails over confrontation; back-slapping has replaced back-stabbing. Inquiry is the motivation rather than injury."[22] It was a revealing commentary on what had transpired at the Bork and Thomas hearings.

Ginsburg was praised from both sides of the aisle. Nearly everyone applauded her academic and judicial performances. Republicans were pleased that Ginsburg had not been an activist on the court of appeals. On the other hand, many Democrats hoped that once freed from the obligation of strict adherence to Supreme Court precedents, Ginsburg would become more of a judicial activist. The only senator who tried to dampen the enthusiasm was Arlen Specter, who had recently returned to the Senate, following a brain operation. Specter said that "a coronation in advance is not in the best interest of the system," and he criticized colleagues—without naming them—who had endorsed Ginsburg before the confirmation hearings even began.[23]

The hearings themselves were uneventful. Judge Ginsburg testified about her childhood as a daughter of first and second generation Americans, whose ancestors had been victims of pogroms in Eastern Europe. She recalled seeing signs as a child, reading "no dogs or Jews."[24] She also elaborated on the difficulty she had in finding a job, despite the fact that she was graduated at the top of her class at the Columbia Law School. In many ways, her discussion of family life and personal privation was reminiscent of what Judges Scalia and Thomas had told the committee about their own family histories, which had created favorable impressions for them.

Since Judge Ginsburg's confirmation was a foregone conclusion, several senators used their time not trying to discover what her views were but trying instead to convince Ginsburg to embrace the senators' own views. For example, Democratic senators like Biden and Metzenbaum urged her to take an expansive view of her role and of the protections afforded by the Constitution. Biden, in particular, tried to show that constitutional safeguards should be interpreted to evolve over time and should not be confined to the meaning originally intended by the Framers. Ginsburg told Biden that she believed in an evolving Constitution, since women otherwise would still be treated as second-class citizens. But she did not explain what she meant by an "evolving Constitution." As earlier noted, Judge Bork had no difficulty concluding that school segregation was unconstitutional even though the Framers had not embraced that conclusion; for Bork, the crucial point was that the Framers had enacted a principle of racial equality, which he interpreted to require school desegregation. Judge Ginsburg could reason similarly that although the Framers did not endorse gender equality, they clearly embraced a principle of equal protection, and the Court's decisions in sex discrimination cases—which Ginsburg helped to fashion as an advocate before the Court—enforced that general principle. Thus, her statement to Senator Biden did not commit her to go far beyond Judge Bork, and it revealed relatively little about her views on constitutional interpretation.

On the other side of the aisle, Senators Hatch and Grassley argued against judicial activism. Senator Grassley said that judges "are not elected nor are they accountable to the people [and they] need to exercise restraint and not endeavor to reform society."[25] Hatch likened the Court's decision in *Roe v. Wade* to the *Dred Scott* case,[26] which required a slave in a free territory to be returned to his master in a slave state. Senator Carol Moseley Braun interjected that as a descendant of slaves, she was offended by this discussion, which, she thought, suggested that there was some defense for slavery. She asked if Hatch could use some other method to question the witness. Hatch assured Senator Moseley Braun that he was not defending *Dred Scott*; in fact, he said that it was a terrible decision and that he felt the same way about *Roe v. Wade*.[27] In the end, Judge Ginsburg appeared to be unmoved by the pleas of the senators on either the left or the right, although she was quite diplomatic and expressed sympathy for their concerns.

Even Judge Ginsburg's announcement that she supported a constitutional right to an abortion hardly caused a ripple at her confirmation hearings. Ginsburg was the first nominee to announce to the Senate her position on the abortion question. She apparently felt some need to "clarify" her views on abortion because of a recent speech, in which she had criticized *Roe v. Wade* and raised considerable concern among women's groups.[28] Judge Ginsburg's speech observed that *Roe v. Wade* "halted a political process that was moving in a reform direction and thereby . . . prolonged divisiveness and deferred stable settlement of the issue."[29] A narrower ruling, she said, limiting the decision to the particular statute involved in *Roe*, "might have served to reduce rather than to fuel controversy."[30] Ginsburg's announcement of support for abortion rights was enough to quiet criticism from the left. Nevertheless, her speech made it quite clear that if she had written for the Court in *Roe v. Wade*, Ginsburg would have produced a very different opinion from the one authored by Justice Blackmun.

The only real controversy at the hearings stemmed from Judge Ginsburg's unwillingness to answer substantive questions on matters that might come before the Supreme Court. In her opening remarks, Ginsburg staked out a rather wide range of discretion to decide which questions she would answer: "Because I am and hope to continue to be a judge, it would be wrong for me to say or preview in this legislative chamber how I would cast my vote on questions the Supreme Court may be called upon to decide. . . . Were I to rehearse here what I would say and how I would reason on such questions, I would act injudiciously."[31]

Ginsburg was criticized by some committee members for her unwillingness to answer certain questions. At the start of the hearings, Senator Biden said the country was past the point of asking whether it is legitimate for the committee to inquire about a nominee's judicial philosophy. But Senator Cohen took issue with that assertion. Cohen said the Senate should determine the competence and judicial temperament of a nominee. Beyond this, he agreed that some examination of judicial ideology is permissible but only to determine whether the nominee's philosophy is "so extreme that it might call into question" the usual requisites of competence and judicial temperament.[32] Barring such an extreme case, he said, the question of philosophy was inappropriate for committee review. This was a sensitive and thoughtful analysis of the Bork precedent. Biden did not respond to Senator Cohen, but he expressed frustration with Judge Ginsburg's unwillingness to answer some of his inquiries. Later in the hearings, after checking the record of other recent Supreme Court nominees, Biden said that Ginsburg answered no more but also no less than other nominees.[33] This was probably true, but since it would be difficult to answer much less than Judge Souter, for example, Biden's observation was not very meaningful.

Senator Hatch was somewhat exasperated when Judge Ginsburg refused to tell him whether the death penalty is, in all circumstances, unconstitutional under the Eighth Amendment; and Senator Specter became mildly frustrated with her unwillingness to state whether, for legal purposes, the Korean conflict was a war—a question that Judge Souter also refused to answer. Specter asked for clarification of what she would answer, suggesting that perhaps she had not been entirely consistent about when she answered and when she did not. Judge Ginsburg pointed out that a nominee's independence could be compromised by "discussing or giving hints about votes in particular cases." Ginsburg added that she felt perfectly comfortable explaining what she had written but did not want to speak about other matters that might come before her at the Supreme Court.[34]

Nevertheless, when it came to hot-button issues like gay rights, Ginsburg was extremely cautious, even though she had given a speech in which she stated that discrimination on the basis of sexual orientation is "wrong." She indicated at the hearings that "rank discrimination" against anyone "is against the tradition of the United States and is to be deplored." When asked by Senator Cohen to clarify the meaning of "rank discrimination," she stated that this term meant "discrimination against some person for reasons that are irrelevant to that person's talent or ability."[35] When Senator Cohen pressed her by asking if that applied to sexual orientation, she said: "Senator, you know that that is a burning question that at this very moment is going to be before the Court, based on an action that has been taken. I cannot say one word on that subject that would not violate what I said had to be my rule about no hints, no forecasts, no previews."[36]

In the end, like most nominees, Ginsburg answered the questions that she thought would help her win confirmation. Given that her nomination was assured, Ginsburg did not need to answer very many. The committee, therefore, learned little about Ginsburg, although not less than it had learned about Judge Souter or Judge Thomas.

Most of the witnesses testifying after Ginsburg were supportive of her confirmation. Few senators were present during the testimony of these witnesses, and there were almost no questions. Representatives of the ABA reported that the Standing Committee on the Judiciary was unanimous in awarding Judge Ginsburg its highest rating—"well qualified." The committee had interviewed more than six hundred people and had used three reading groups, led by distinguished law professors, to review all of Judge Ginsburg's opinions, articles, and speeches. Senator Hatch, who had been critical of the ABA in the past, praised the committee's work and expressed satisfaction with the structural changes made by the committee in order to avoid a politicization of the process. After the ABA representatives appeared, the Judiciary Committee received testimony in support of Ginsburg from Judge Patricia Harris, former Judge Shirley Hufstedler, and a number of noted lawyers and scholars, including William Coleman, Ira Millstein, Professor Gerald Gunther, and Dean Herma Hill Kay.

The only group to oppose Ginsburg was a panel composed of right-to-life activists and Howard Phillips of the Conservative Caucus. The panel argued that Judge Ginsburg's position in support of abortion rights disqualified her from eligibility for a seat on the Supreme Court. Senator Hatch told them that in view of the fact that Bill Clinton won the election, Judge Ginsburg was the best nominee they were likely to get and that "this senator rejects the concept that any single litmus test disqualifies anyone from serving on the Court."[37] The witnesses opposing Ginsburg were under no illusion that their testimony would affect her confirmation, but the hearings gave them a forum to publicize their views free of charge.

The Ginsburg hearings also included, for the first time, a closed session designed to permit questioning of the nominee about any sensitive personal charges that might have been leveled against her. If necessary, such charges could later be aired in a public forum. All senators would have access to transcripts of the closed session, and Judiciary Committee staffers would be available to brief senators on sensitive matters. Senator Biden planned to make such sessions a standard part of all future Supreme Court confirmation proceedings. He hoped in this way to avoid the problems that arose during the Thomas hearings, when some members of the Judiciary Committee complained that they did not learn about Anita Hill's charges until shortly before the vote and Biden was criticized for not handling the charges properly.

Ginsburg's closed-door session took only twenty minutes, and apparently nothing of substance was discussed. Only one question of an ethical nature had arisen, and it did not pose a serious problem. The question centered around the fact that the Montauk Golf Club had waived an initiation fee of $25,000 for Ginsburg and other judges who joined the club. Senator Grassley noted that a federal statute and the Canons of Judicial Conduct required judges to report gifts, loans, or favors, other than those under $50, now $100. Judge Ginsburg had taken the position that the waiver of the initiation fee was not a gift or favor because a judge's membership included no voting rights, was labeled a "special membership," and could be terminated at will by the club. Nevertheless, Ginsburg later admitted in a letter to Grassley that she probably should have reported the waiver of the initiation fee.[38] That ended the matter for Senator Grassley, who said that this was not a "disqualifier." Comparing this incident with Judge Thomas's admission that he smoked marijuana as a youth, Senator Grassley noted that his earlier comment about Judge Thomas—that "we weren't confirming . . . [him] for sainthood, we were confirming him for the Supreme Court"—was equally applicable here.[39]

On Thursday, July 29, 1993, just six days after the conclusion of its hearings, the Judiciary Committee voted unanimously in favor of Judge Ginsburg's confirmation. Both conservative and liberal members of the committee justified their votes by arguing that Ginsburg would be their type of justice. Liberals pointed to Judge Ginsburg's pathbreaking work as an advocate for women's rights and to her support for abortion and the protection of minorities. Conservatives pointed to her work on the bench as a judge who believed in judicial restraint, who adhered to precedent, and who sometimes was in agreement more with Judges Bork and Scalia than with liberal appointees like Judge Patricia Wald.[40] After a brief debate, the full senate approved the Ginsburg nomination by a vote of 96 to 3. The only negative votes came from conservative Republicans Jesse Helms, Don Nichols, and Robert Smith. Senator Helms said he voted against her because of her support for abortion rights and because he believed that she would support the "homosexual agenda." Some liberals were also disappointed with Judge Ginsburg, but like many conservatives who had supported Judge Souter, they found themselves with nowhere else to turn. A year later, liberal activists would try again to place a true believer on the Supreme Court.

23
JUDGE BREYER REVISITED

When Justice Blackmun announced his retirement in April 1994, it came as no surprise. Privately, Blackmun had told President Clinton that this would be his last term at the Supreme Court. Moreover, he had publicly signaled his intention to retire quite soon in his concurring opinion in *Planned Parenthood v. Casey*.[1]

The search for Justice Blackmun's successor was essentially a replay of the nominating process a year earlier. First, there was a brief flirtation with a prominent political figure—this time, Senate Majority Leader George Mitchell. Later, Bruce Babbitt seemed to re-emerge as the Clinton favorite. Then when opposition to Babbitt surfaced among Senate conservatives, as it had the previous year, Clinton backed away from Babbitt in favor of a candidate who would be easily confirmed. Finally, the president announced his intention to nominate another judicial moderate— Judge Stephen Breyer—who had substantial support among Republicans on the Senate Judiciary Committee and elsewhere.

Initially, the apparent front-runner for Justice Blackmun's seat on the Supreme Court was Senator George Mitchell. While campaigning for office, Clinton had made it clear that he wanted a Supreme Court nominee who had significant political experience as, for example, Earl Warren did before he became chief justice. Mitchell, who had just announced his plans to retire from the Senate, seemed to satisfy all of Clinton's requirements. Not only was he a seasoned politician but as Senate majority leader, he had experience in putting coalitions together, experience that Clinton thought would be valuable at the Supreme Court. Finally, Senator Mitchell seemed a safe bet for easy confirmation. Senatorial courtesy has such a long tradition that there was little likelihood that serious opposition would be mounted against Mitchell.

Nevertheless, two potential problems emerged. First, there was a technical issue under the emoluments clause of the Constitution, which provides that no senator "shall, during the Time for which he was elected, be appointed to any civil Office . . . the emoluments whereof shall have been encreased during such time."[2] Mitchell had been serving his last term in the Senate when the salary of federal judges was increased, and the question was whether the emoluments clause would preclude his appointment. It seemed possible that Congress would enact legislation setting Mitchell's salary as a Supreme Court justice at a lower level for a period of time in order to deal with the emoluments problem. However, when President Reagan considered nominating Senator Hatch after Judge Bork's nomination was defeated, the Office of Legal Counsel had concluded that the emoluments problem could not be solved by passing legislation to lower the salary for the office.[3] Even so, most senators did not seem greatly concerned with this issue. Indeed, the issue had been finessed when Senator Lloyd Bentsen was nominated to be secretary of the treasury; Congress simply passed a joint resolution that lowered his salary as treasury secretary until the end of the term for which Bentsen had been elected.[4] Concern for the emoluments clause, it seems, may depend on whose ox is gored.

A more serious question was whether Senator Mitchell could guide a health care bill through the Senate—a matter about which both Clinton and Mitchell cared very deeply—while Mitchell simultaneously prepared for and attended Senate confirmation hearings.[5] There was concern that Mitchell's effectiveness with Senate colleagues would be undermined by the fact that his appointment to the Supreme Court was imminent, and he would therefore need their support more than they needed his.

On April 12, Senator Mitchell withdrew his name from consideration for the Supreme Court. Mitchell said he believed Congress had "a rare opportunity to pass historic [health care] legislation in the months ahead" and that he was "unwilling to do anything that might detract from that effort."[6] Clinton then told his aides to assemble a list of possible nominees.

White House aides, headed by Lloyd Cutler, put together a dozen names, including some that had been considered a year earlier. The list was soon whittled down to five leading candidates: Jose Cabranes, an Hispanic federal district court judge; Amalya Kearse, a black female judge on the federal court of appeals in New York; Chief Judge Richard

Arnold of the court of appeals in Arkansas; Secretary of Interior Bruce
Babbitt; and Chief Judge Stephen Breyer of the court of appeals in Boston.[7] Inevitably, political considerations became significant factors in the
decision making. Just as Woodrow Wilson had appointed Brandeis in the
hope of winning the Jewish vote in New York[8] and Eisenhower had appointed William Brennan in the hope of getting the Catholic vote, so
Clinton's advisors believed the president could attract Hispanic votes in
1996 by appointing Jose Cabranes. But while Cabranes was backed by
most Hispanic organizations, he did not enjoy their universal support. La
Raza and the Mexican American Legal Defense Fund refused to appear
with the Congressional Hispanic Caucus, when the caucus endorsed him.
There was much concern about a decision by Cabranes in which he refused to grant parole to fifty-one Haitians while their applications for
political asylum were under review.[9] In addition, Cabranes did not have
a proven track record on many of the issues that were of interest to Clinton. When it became apparent that the appointment of Cabranes would
create too many risks, Clinton asked his advisers whether there were any
other Hispanics whom he could appoint. None seemed to satisfy the
needs of the president.

The appointment of Amalya Kearse would have enabled Clinton to
take credit for naming the first black woman to the Supreme Court.
Kearse, a pro-choice Republican, may have been viewed as tainted because her name originally surfaced during President Bush's search for a
Supreme Court nominee, even though she was unlikely to be considered
a serious candidate by Bush in light of her pro-choice views. Kearse
seems to have had the misfortune of being too liberal to be appointed
by a Republican and, perhaps, too conservative to be appointed by a
Democrat.

That left three finalists. Richard Arnold, an Arkansas friend of the
president, posed some problems for Clinton. First, the Arkansas connection was troublesome because Clinton had already been charged with
cronyism for other political appointments and was haunted by the
Whitewater scandal, which had its roots in Arkansas. There was
some risk that more dirty laundry from Arkansas might be aired in
confirmation hearings for Arnold. In addition, Judge Arnold had been
criticized by some women's groups for opinions that he had written at
the court of appeals. In a case involving the Jaycees, he had ruled that a
Minnesota statute that effectively prohibited gender discrimination in

the membership policies of certain private groups was unconstitutional because it abridged the Jaycees' rights of free speech and association.[10] That view was later rejected by the Supreme Court, which ruled that the First Amendment claims of the Jaycees were overridden by Minnesota's compelling interest in eradicating discrimination against women.[11] In another controversial decision, Arnold had joined a 7 to 3 majority that sustained the constitutionality of Minnesota's abortion statute.[12] It is not clear that Arnold's judicial rulings themselves would have been sufficient to derail his nomination, since he had also written a number of opinions favoring civil rights plaintiffs and supporting free speech.[13] However, Judge Arnold, who had recently been treated for lymphoma, faced a serious health problem. Clinton took the unusual step of speaking personally to Arnold's doctors, but they could not assure him that Arnold would be able to serve fifteen to twenty years on the Court.

That left the choice between Babbitt and Breyer, two of the finalists from the search a year earlier. Babbitt's candidacy was appealing to Clinton. As a former governor, a presidential candidate, and now secretary of interior, Babbitt had the kind of real-world background that Clinton wanted. In addition, Babbitt's left-of-center philosophy made him attractive to party liberals.

Still, Clinton wanted to know whether Babbitt's ideology and his disagreements with senators from western states would create problems for confirmation. He called Orrin Hatch, the ranking Republican member of the Senate Judiciary Committee. Hatch told him that there would be a real fight over a Babbitt nomination. Both Hatch and Senator Alan Simpson told Clinton that they would oppose Babbitt because of his environmental views and because of their concern that, as a career politician with no judicial experience, he would be prone to legislate from the bench.[14] Senate minority leader Robert Dole also made it clear that he would oppose a Babbitt nomination, as did Senator Strom Thurmond. Clinton then consulted with Judiciary Committee Chairman Joseph Biden concerning Babbitt's confirmability. Biden told Clinton that he believed Babbitt would be confirmed with about eighty votes.[15]

Clinton, however, was concerned that if some Republicans chose to fight over a Babbitt nomination, it might impede the chances for passing a comprehensive health care bill—legislation in which the president had a major political investment. Clinton was also worried that a confirmation fight might prove politically embarrassing and could cost him crucial votes in the West in 1996. After discussing the matter with Babbitt during the night of May 12, Clinton decided that Stephen Breyer, who had strong support from Republicans as well as from Democrats, would be the safest choice.

Breyer was widely viewed by his colleagues as one of the best federal judges in the country. Moreover, he had shown an ability to forge coalitions and to avoid the kind of dissension in his court that had plagued some of the other federal courts in the country. He had displayed those same skills while serving as chief counsel to the Senate Judiciary Committee. Both Senator Hatch and Senator Kennedy thought highly of Breyer, as did other members of the Judiciary Committee. Conservatives were particularly impressed by the work he had done on Capitol Hill. As counsel to Senator Kennedy, he was one of the architects of airline deregulation and later, as chief counsel to the Senate Judiciary Committee, he took a major role in drafting the federal sentencing guidelines, which imposed a large number of stiff mandatory sentences.

Breyer was perceived as a candidate without an ideological agenda. Some of his opinions were sure to please liberals, while other opinions would give comfort to conservatives. For example, in *Massachusetts v. Secretary of HHS*,[16] he joined an opinion holding that a gag order that barred abortion counseling in federally financed clinics was unconstitutional. On the other hand, Breyer dissented from a decision which allowed plaintiffs to proceed with a lawsuit challenging the constitutionality of a Massachusetts law regulating abortion for minors.[17] Breyer believed that under existing Supreme Court decisions, the law would be constitutionally valid even if its judicial bypass provision was burdensome for most minors. Interestingly, Judge Breyer's position was not very different from Judge Arnold's view on abortion rights for minors.

After they had had an opportunity to read Breyer's opinions in *Massachusetts v. HHS* and *Planned Parenthood v. Bellotti*, abortion activists on both sides expressed some reservations. Clark Forsythe, vice president and general counsel of Americans United for Life said the Judiciary Committee "should question Judge Breyer closely on his understanding of the nature and scope of the so-called right of privacy and all it encompasses." Marcy Wilder, legal director of the National Abortion Rights Action League, remarked, "The Senate Judiciary Committee has an obligation to explore his views." And Kate Kolbert, vice president of the Center for Reproductive Law and Policy, said: "[*Bellotti*] may be the opinion of a cautious and conservative judge who felt constrained by the Supreme Court. Or it may show hostility to examination of the real burdens abortion laws impose."[18]

Liberals were heartened, however, by some of Judge Breyer's other decisions. For example, he ruled that a consent decree affording affirmative action to black Boston police officers was legally valid, despite a Supreme Court precedent limiting the use of racially based set-asides in employment.[19] Breyer wrote that consent decrees providing race-conscious remedies are valid if necessary to remedy past or present discrimination and if narrowly tailored to meet that objective. His opinion relied heavily on statistics showing that black policemen comprised 4.5 percent of the Boston police force but only .45 percent of police sergeants. He said that a racially based remedy was necessary to overcome the evils of prior discrimination in the Boston Police Department. Breyer also joined an opinion that rejected a challenge by a Boston teachers' union to the continuation of minority preferences for teachers.[20]

A few discordant notes were sounded by Senator Howard Metzenbaum and consumer activist Ralph Nader. Metzenbaum said he was concerned that Breyer had seemed to favor big business in his antitrust rulings and in his other writings. Ralph Nader criticized Judge Breyer's views on regulated industries for placing too much importance on economic efficiency and not enough on worker safety. But despite these rumblings on the left, President Clinton felt sure that Breyer's nomination would sail through the Senate and avoid the political controversy that a Babbitt nomination would have created.

The atmosphere at the confirmation hearings was as warm for Breyer as it had been for Judge Ginsburg. In part, this was because everyone expected that Breyer, as a judicial moderate, would breeze through the confirmation process. The warm atmosphere was also attributable in part to the fact that Judge Breyer once served as chief counsel for the committee and had gained the confidence and affection of senators in both parties.

Republicans like Hatch and Thurmond told Breyer that he would be confirmed. Senator Simpson remarked that President Clinton had listened to suggestions from Senator Hatch and himself that Breyer should be nominated. Since Clinton did exactly what they asked, Republicans were not about to defeat their own purpose by creating problems for the nominee. Thus when Senator Metzenbaum criticized Breyer for favoring the interests of big business, Hatch rushed to Breyer's defense, pointing out various cases in which Breyer had ruled against big business.

The most troublesome problem for Judge Breyer involved not any question of legal philosophy but the possibility of a conflict of interest. A few days before the hearings began, Long Island's *Newsday* ran a story on Breyer's holdings in insurance syndicates of Lloyd's of London and indicated that they created conflicts of interest for Breyer, which should have caused him to disqualify himself from various "Superfund" cases. Although Lloyd's was not a party to any of the lawsuits, its liability could be affected by the precedents that were established in the cases Breyer was deciding.

White House Counsel Lloyd Cutler initially argued that this posed no conflict of interest because Breyer did not know about Lloyd's potential liability under Superfund cases. However, the federal disqualification statute requires that a judge inform himself about his personal financial interests;[21] and the Supreme Court had held that a federal judge should have disqualified himself from hearing a case because, even if he did not recall his financial interest, he should have recalled it.[22] The Court found that the judge's failure to recuse himself created an *appearance* of partiality, and the same could be said of Breyer's decision not to disqualify himself in the Superfund cases. Judge Breyer showed some sensitivity to the issue in his opening statement before the Judiciary Committee, asserting that he would divest himself of his holdings in Lloyd's as quickly as possible. Breyer also said that in the future he would post all his investments for litigants or lawyers to see and would accept anonymous requests to disqualify himself.

Breyer later argued that his decision in *United States v. Ottati and Goss*[23]—the case which Senator Metzenbaum believed to pose the clearest conflict of interest—did not present a real conflict because, in Breyer's view, the decision was fact-based and established no significant precedent. However, Breyer's statement is not supported by the opinion that he wrote in the case. In the course of the opinion, Breyer did say that one major issue was fact-specific. But he also said that the other major issue involved a general question of statutory interpretation and of the availability of injunctive relief, which did set an important precedent. In fact, since *Ottati and Goss*, the Environmental Protection Agency has not even brought any other suits for injunctive relief.

Breyer also claimed that experts who had looked into the matter supported his view that he had not acted unethically. But Senator Metzenbaum pointed out that while two of the three experts consulted by the White House had taken that position, Professor Geoffrey Hazard of the Yale Law School—the third expert—said that Breyer's investment was imprudent, even though not unethical. And Monroe Freedman of Hofstra Law School opposed Breyer's confirmation because he believed that Breyer's participation in the Superfund cases was not only imprudent but also involved a clear conflict of interest.

Although Breyer's decision to participate in these cases posed a serious conflict of interest problem, no committee member except Senator Metzenbaum was willing to pursue the matter aggressively. Moreover, even Senator Metzenbaum indicated that he did not question Breyer's ethics but was only seeking to make Breyer more aware of the issue for the future. The fact that Judge Breyer was treated so gently, despite plausible arguments that he had a conflict of interest, shows how the impact of ethical issues often depends on how favorably the nominee is viewed in other respects.

The only subject that Republican senators seemed interested in pursuing was his ruling for the court of appeals that a school district's visit to a religious grade school to evaluate the quality of its teaching did not interfere with religious freedom. This issue was raised by Senators Thurmond, Hatch, and Simpson. Simpson made it clear that this was a matter of concern to some parents—particularly those involved in home schooling their children—who worried that Judge Breyer might support a state's effort to outlaw such schooling.[24] Breyer said he had no bias against home schooling. He also pointed out that in other decisions, he was more protective of religious freedom than the Supreme Court has been.

On the last day of the hearings, other interested witnesses testified on Breyer's nomination, usually with only one committee member in attendance. The ABA began the day by explaining why it found Judge Breyer to be "well qualified." Two groups had read Breyer's opinions and other writings. One group, chaired by former Solicitor General Rex Lee, consisted of ten lawyers who had argued cases before the Supreme Court. The other, chaired by Professor Nicholas S. Zeppos of Vanderbilt, consisted of twenty-six members of the Vanderbilt faculty. The first group found Breyer to be a "person of enormous intellectual ability with an outstanding ability to write clearly and persuasively." The second group called Breyer "a lawyer's lawyer and a judge's judge. He is careful, scholarly, dispassionate and objective. Furthermore, he recognizes that there are limits to his own abilities, as a jurist, to resolve every dispute engendered by the contentious press of modern life."[25]

Although most of the witnesses spoke in support of Breyer, they attracted less attention than the few who testified against him. Noteworthy among the latter was Ralph Nader, who criticized Breyer for being the biggest supporter of big business on any federal court in the country.[26] He said that in virtually all of his antitrust cases, Breyer had sided with corporate defendants—a view contradicted by Professor Robert Pitofsky of Georgetown University. Nader also criticized Breyer for relying too much on the Chicago School of economics and paying insufficient attention to the long-term cost to consumers of eliminating small businesses.

Nader asserted that in Breyer's book, *Breaking the Vicious Cycle,* the judge was too willing to accept the statistics of conservative think-tanks, which overstate the costs of regulation and underestimate its benefits. In response to questions from Senator Metzenbaum, Breyer said that the views set forth in his book were offered in the role of a policy maker rather than that of a judge. This argument helped to defuse the criticism leveled against him by Ralph Nader. Accordingly, it was no surprise when the Judiciary Committee ultimately voted 18 to 0 to approve Breyer's confirmation. Senator Metzenbaum, the committee's most vocal critic of Judge Breyer, said he was concerned that "Breyer's first priority would not be to support 'the little guy.'" He added, however, that he hoped Breyer would become more concerned with the human element in his decision making, once he reached the Supreme Court. The only other member of the committee to voice any reservations was Senator Charles Grassley, who was worried that Breyer might interpret the Constitution too broadly and find unenumerated rights that the Framers had not intended.[27]

Shortly after the hearings ended, *Newsday* ran a story showing (1) that Breyer had been a member of a three-judge panel which held the Kayser-Roth Corporation responsible for cleaning up the site of a chemical spill and (2) that Kayser-Roth subsequently sued Lloyd's of London, which had sold insurance to Kayser-Roth. Thus, contrary to his statement before the Judiciary Committee, Judge Breyer actually had ruled on a case in which Lloyd's was directly involved, although it could not be determined whether Breyer's own syndicate was involved. Joel I. Klein, deputy White House counsel, argued that Breyer could not have known that Lloyd's sold insurance to Kayser-Roth and that Breyer had decided the case contrary to his own economic interest. Nevertheless, this story helped rekindle interest in the propriety of Breyer's conduct and in whether Breyer would have to disqualify himself in the future. The *New York Times* wrote in an editorial that the Judiciary Committee had not behaved responsibly in rushing to judgment without adequately investigating the ethical issues raised by Breyer's investments. They concluded that "Judge Breyer has not been shown to deserve the prize that will be awarded him by the Senate."[28] Their sentiments were echoed by the *Arkansas Democrat-Gazette* and the *Baltimore Sun*.[29]

On July 22, 1994, Senator Richard Lugar became the first senator to announce his opposition to Breyer's confirmation. Lugar said that he would vote against confirmation because Breyer had exposed himself to so much liability at a time when the problems of Lloyd's were becoming well known. Lugar added that Breyer might be forced to disqualify himself in a large number of cases involving environmental cleanup.[30] On July 27, 1994, Senator Bob Smith joined Lugar in opposing Breyer's confirmation because "the Lloyd's investment demonstrates questionable judgment by Judge Breyer." Smith also opposed confirmation because Breyer was too "liberal" on church-state matters and, in Smith's view, advocated federal funding of abortion.[31]

On Friday, July 29, after five and a half hours of debate, the Senate voted to approve Breyer's nomination by a vote of 87 to 9. All nine negative votes came from Republicans.[32] In addition to criticizing him for his Lloyd's investment and the conflict of interest that this might pose, the senators voting against him (Conrad Burns, Daniel R. Coates, Paul Coverdell, Jesse Helms, Trent Lott, Frank H. Murkowski, Don Nickles, and Robert C. Smith) attacked Breyer for supporting abortion rights and for lacking a commitment to rights of private property.[33] Nevertheless, Breyer received broad bipartisan support. Senator Hatch defended Breyer, saying: "We cannot impose as a standard that people cannot make bad investments. People do."[34] But it was Senator Phil Gramm who made the key point for most conservative senators. Gramm said that while no Republican president would have nominated Breyer, "the chances of anyone more conservative than Judge Breyer being nominated [by President Clinton] were almost zero."[35]

24
THE BORK PRECEDENT:
A SEARCH FOR MEANING

The meaning of Judge Bork's rejection by the Senate will be a matter of debate for many years. The debate began immediately after it became apparent that at least fifty-one senators would vote against confirmation. At that point, the discussion in the Senate shifted; it was then directed toward winning the verdict of history rather than toward increasing the number of votes against Judge Bork.[1] The debate is ongoing, but some of the implications of Bork's rejection are already evident and could prove to be far reaching.

The Bork proceedings clearly established a firm precedent for ideological inquiries and for the rejection of judicial nominees, at least in some instances, on purely ideological grounds. As indicated in an earlier chapter, there was scant precedent before the Bork hearings for rejecting Supreme Court nominees because of their judicial philosophy.[2] The Bork proceedings now provide an unmistakable precedent for such rejections. The difficult question is how the Bork precedent will be limited if, indeed, it is limited.

Senator Cohen suggested during the Ginsburg hearings that judicial ideology should be used only to determine whether the nominee's philosophy is "so extreme that it might call into question" the usual confirmation prerequisites of competency and judicial temperament.[3] This was a thoughtful effort to contain the Bork precedent. But in fact Judge Bork's views, while controversial, seem well within the mainstream of constitutional scholarship. Certainly, mainstream jurists have embraced many of the positions taken by Bork, and some of the current members of the Supreme Court may embrace nearly all of those positions or take other positions that are equally controversial. Perhaps the Bork precedent for ideological rejection will be limited to Supreme Court nominees who are *perceived* to be outside the mainstream and whose views are at odds with the prevailing sentiment in the United States Senate. Of course, as the confirmation of Clarence Thomas indicates, not all of those nominees will be rejected; the point is simply that the Bork precedent provides a basis for rejecting such nominees on ideological grounds.

It is clear, in any case, that the precedent for ideological rejection will not be easily contained. Senator Orrin Hatch, who is now chairman of the Judiciary Committee, expressed that concern in the *Harvard Law Review* a year before the Bork nomination. Hatch wrote: "If blocking a nomination on ideological grounds is fair game for one president and party, it is fair game for the other as well. Such an atmosphere holds the potential for touching off a cycle of revenge and retribution which can only damage the institutional integrity of both the Senate and the judiciary."[4] Senator Hatch's comments proved to be prescient. Even before the Bork hearings had ended, Republican senators were promising that if a future president decided, for example, to nominate Professor Laurence Tribe—a vocal opponent of Judge Bork, but one who was well qualified by traditional standards for service on the Court—it should be expected that Tribe would face the same kind of onslaught that had been visited on Judge Bork.

Even if the Bork precedent is limited, the Senate's rejection of Judge Bork suggests a politicization of the confirmation process that was out of keeping with the twentieth-century tradition and that departed significantly even from the dubious confirmation practices followed during part of the nineteenth century. As was shown earlier, the Senate has rarely rejected Supreme Court nominees because of their judicial philosophy. During the nineteenth century, a number of nominees were denied confirmation because of political positions that they had taken, but no one claimed that those political matters were likely to become subjects of litigation in the Supreme Court. The Senate thus did not reject those nominees because of the way they might vote as members of the Court.[5] In Judge Bork's case, on the other hand, the Senate was asserting unequivocally that it is legitimate to reject a nominee simply because he or she cannot be counted on to "vote the right way."[6]

The rejection of judicial nominees on this basis has important implications for judicial independence and for public confidence in the federal courts. During his confirmation hearings, Judge Bork was repeatedly pressured "to make commitments regarding issues actually or potentially before the Court."[7] Often, Bork resisted, but at times, he capitulated. For example, Judge Bork assured Senator Specter that despite personal misgivings, he would accept the Court's First Amendment ruling in *Brandenburg v. Ohio*[8] as settled law.[9] And Specter himself, though often protesting that he did not seek commitments, has insisted that Bork "promised" to apply *Brandenburg* in analogous cases.[10] Commitments of this sort caused some senators to express concern that "in effect, committee members were extracting campaign promises from the nominee, who gave them under oath."[11] Bork himself clearly understood such commitments to be binding on him if his nomination were confirmed by the Senate. When asked what assurance he could offer that his testimony was an accurate indicator of his future performance on the Court, Bork said that he would be "disgraced in history" if he testified to one thing and did another.[12]

There is no doubt that the extraction of such commitments is intended to restrict the freedom of the nominee in discharging judicial duties, in the event that he or she is confirmed. But to say that a judge's freedom was restricted is clearly to admit that his judicial independence has been compromised, at least with regard to the particular issue on which a commitment was made and possibly with regard to related issues as well. Some commentators have suggested that questions should "be framed to ask for present opinions rather than for commitments."[13] However, this is likely to be a distinction without a difference, especially if the issue in question reaches the Supreme Court soon after the nominee is confirmed. "Present opinions" are essentially statements of present intention; and present intentions, when expressed to the Senate during confirmation hearings, are not easily distinguished from commitments. Perhaps for this reason, Professor Stephen Carter has said that "when senators ask questions intended to elicit information that will permit them to predict the votes that a nominee will cast if confirmed, they are engaging in an activity that represents a profound threat to judicial independence. Approving nominees who will vote the 'right way' means enshrining the politically expedient judgments of a given era as fundamental constitutional law."[14] Of course, if justices can be effectively screened out because of politically expedient judgments, there is a serious risk that constitutional protections for unpopular minorities will be weakened.[15]

In any event, the fundamental problem is that these statements of "present opinion" are extracted from a nominee by senators whose support the nominee apparently needs in order to win confirmation. Under these circumstances, concessions by the nominee are likely to take on the appearance of trading future votes in the Supreme Court for Senate votes in favor of confirmation. That appearance, which is itself pernicious, may also lead to an erosion of public confidence in the federal courts.

Public confidence can be eroded in two significant ways. First, the growing politicization of the confirmation process could cause people to believe that Supreme Court decisions are based on partisan politics rather than on any detached interpretation of the Constitution and laws of the United States. Since Supreme Court decisions are not self-enforcing, their value depends in large measure on public acceptance of judicial rulings. But public acceptance has traditionally been grounded in the belief that court decisions are based on law, not on politics. A contrary view is bound to reduce the acceptance of judicial rulings and undermine public confidence in the courts. And this loss of confidence may be exacerbated if the public believes that political groups have used the confirmation process to lock in place the earlier decisions of an unelected judiciary.

Second, the public may believe that a nominee has prejudged an issue by making commitments or even by offering his or her views on the issue. During his confirmation hearings, Judge Kennedy remarked that the main reason for judges to refuse to answer certain questions "is that the public expects that the judge will keep an open mind."[16] If instead the judge takes a firm position in advance, the public may think it will be difficult or impossible for him to remain impartial. As a result, the judge may be forced to disqualify himself from hearing cases in which he has made a commitment or, if he declines to disqualify himself, the public may believe that his commitment at the confirmation hearings will control his decision in the case.

Of course, the president, no less than the Senate, can compromise a judge's independence by demanding personal commitments as the price for an appointment. But because a nominee's statements to the president are likely to be made in private, the nominee will be less vulnerable to criticism if he does not adhere to his previously stated position. Accordingly, there may be less risk of compromising judicial independence and of eroding public confidence in the case of statements made to the president than in the case of statements made before the Senate Judiciary Committee on national television.

The politicization of the confirmation process has also created an incentive for the president to select nominees whose paper record will not excite serious opposition or who have no paper record at all. Bruce Fein, a lawyer who served in the Reagan administration, has argued that "the lesson of Bork's failed nomination has been that Republican presidents should avoid nominees who exhibit intellectual dynamism, such as federal circuit judges Richard Posner and Frank Easterbrook or Solicitor General Kenneth Starr, to avoid bitter confrontations with a Democratic Senate." Fein states that the post-Bork nominations by President Reagan and President Bush are examples of the mediocrity that the Bork controversy has produced.[17]

Ironically, a bland and undistinguished nominee may be more difficult to defeat than Judge Bork. President Bush found it easy to win confirmation for David Souter, who had no scholarly achievements or other paper trail, but was sufficiently glib to satisfy both liberal and conservative senators. And President Reagan succeeded in getting Judge Kennedy confirmed, even though Kennedy had a public record which clearly suggested that he would vote largely the same way as Judge Bork.[18] Indeed, on the major issues that have divided the Supreme Court along ideological lines, Kennedy has usually voted with the most conservative bloc on the Court.[19]

Finally, it is important to take note of the effect that the Bork precedent may have on Supreme Court nominees. In order to avoid embroiling themselves in controversy and jeopardizing their confirmation, nominees will have a strong incentive to be less than candid in answering the senators' questions. In this respect, ideological inquiries may be self-defeating and could further undermine public confidence in the courts.

Some nominees have taken pains to convince the Judiciary Committee that they are strongly committed to individual rights, a practice which prompted Justice Scalia to criticize committee hearings as "'an absurd spectacle,' with nominees asked to choose their favorite constitutional rights."[20] Other nominees may try a different tact. For example, Senator Biden indicated his frustration with the lack of responsiveness on the part of Clarence Thomas, and Biden expressed an interest in setting "new ground rules" for confirmation hearings.[21] Judge Thomas had tried to distance himself from some of his own prior statements by telling senators that many of his controversial comments were made in the role of a policy maker rather than in the role of a judge. Thomas also claimed that he had never "debated" *Roe v. Wade* and had not read, or had only skimmed, two controversial proposals—which he earlier appeared to embrace—for protection of the unborn.

Equally important is the risk that a potential nominee, who believes he will be maligned in the confirmation process, may decide to withdraw from consideration. Both the Bork hearings and the Thomas hearings suggested that a nominee's privacy may be invaded and his reputation besmirched by personal attacks against him. Judge Bork's videotape rental record was obtained by a reporter in an effort to unearth some embarrassing information. Similarly, Judge Thomas told Senator Alan Simpson that a reporter had trespassed into his garage hoping to learn what Thomas had been reading.[22] And Thomas was so outraged by the personal nature of the attacks on him that he said: "I wasn't harmed by a racist group. I was harmed by this process. This process, which accommodated these attacks on me. If someone wanted to block me from the Supreme Court of the United States because of my views on the Constitution, that's fine. If someone wanted to block me because they don't like the composition of the Court, that's fine. But to destroy me—I would have preferred an assassin's bullet to this kind of living hell that they have put me and my family through."[23] In exasperation, Thomas remarked at one point that the job is "just not worth it."[24]

To be sure, there are benefits as well as costs attendant to the Senate's new activism in judicial confirmations. The principal benefit is one that seems implicit in a system of checks and balances. The Supreme Court, initially thought to be "the least dangerous branch of government," has taken on responsibilities that were never anticipated by the Framers of the Constitution. Many factors, not least among them the adoption of the Fourteenth Amendment, have contributed to the upsurge of federal judicial power. In any event, one result of this increased power is that appointments to the Supreme Court now seem much more important than they did during earlier periods of American history. Professor Charles Black and others have stated that the Senate should be able to exercise its independent judgment to refuse to confirm a nominee "whose service on the Bench will hurt the country" and that senators should be "unencumbered by any deference to the President."[25] In light of the vast responsibilities assumed by the Court, it is hardly surprising that members of the Senate would seek an enhanced role in the process of determining who will wield this new judicial power.

It is also arguable that closer scrutiny of Supreme Court nominees by the Senate will help to educate the public on the president's nominee and, more broadly, on the exercise of federal judicial power in general. But there are alternative ways to advance these interests without incurring similar costs. For example, Professor Daniel Meador has proposed that instead of the freewheeling approach taken in the Bork hearings, senators should ask whether the nominee's views have substantial support in the legal community and whether his confirmation is endorsed by a substantial array of lawyers and scholars from diverse disciplinary and geographical backgrounds. Professor Meador's approach seems entirely consistent with the traditionally deferential attitude of the Senate toward Supreme Court nominations and, more specifically, toward matters related to the judicial philosophy of the nominee. His approach would also tend to reduce the politicization of the confirmation process and to protect the independence of federal courts.

Admittedly, the Senate has only limited power over Supreme Court appointments. Nina Totenberg, a reporter for National Public Radio, criticized Senator Biden and other committee members who held hearings on Judge Kennedy's nomination, after the defeat of Robert Bork, for lacking "the commitment to do their jobs properly a second time."[26] But Biden understood the Senate far better than critics like Totenberg. As Senator John McCain observed in commenting on Kennedy's "smooth sailing" in the Senate, virtually all of the senators were weary of fighting over Bork's confirmation: "Nobody wants to go through that again. There's just too much blood on the floor."[27]

Moreover, it would have been difficult to reconstruct the coalition that defeated Judge Bork. Some members of the coalition had political agendas that might be threatened if they attempted to defeat a second nominee. Similarly, some members of the Senate thought it was unwise to try to block another nominee. A second effort would make it appear—at least in the absence of very compelling reasons—that the senators were overreaching and were deliberately obstructing the president. In addition, a new effort to derail a nominee could divert senators from their own legislative programs and from other political responsibilities. Thus, when Judge Kennedy was nominated, two Democrats on the Judiciary Committee were in the middle of difficult re-election battles and a third, Paul Simon, was running for president.[28] Finally, there is some political risk in taking a major role against a Supreme Court nominee. Although many senators enjoy the limelight that comes from participating in televised confirmation hearings, the added exposure of a second hearing may do them more harm than good, as Senator Specter learned from the fallout that attended his cross-examination of Anita Hill during the second phase of the Thomas hearings.

For these reasons, among others, "thorough screening [of Supreme Court nominees] has been and is likely to be episodic. . . . "[29] Professor Henry Monaghan captured the key point when he noted that "it takes enormous energy for senators to unite in order to resist the President. Once undertaken, such conduct cannot easily be sustained. . . . "[30] As a result, the president will usually succeed in winning confirmation for someone who holds the views he desires in a Supreme Court nominee. Senator Simon conceded as much when he remarked, apparently with some regret, that "one thing is clear and is contrary to widely held opinion: When Presidents have tried to shape the Supreme Court through choosing someone of a particular political and philosophical bent, they have generally been successful in doing that."[31]

Nevertheless, the president will sometimes choose not to precipitate a confirmation battle, the outcome of which may be uncertain in a particular case. Furthermore, even when the outcome is clear, the president might be reluctant to risk his legislative agenda over a confirmation dispute. For example, President Clinton nominated Ruth Bader Ginsburg and Stephen Breyer after learning that Senator Hatch, then the ranking minority member on the Judiciary Committee, would support their nominations. Although Clinton might have been able to win confirmation for a somewhat more liberal nominee, he did not want to expend the political capital that would have been required to do so. Thus, the president's action on judicial nominations may be influenced by the post-Bork confirmation atmosphere, even when the prospects for confirmation are generally favorable.

NOTES
·
INDEX

NOTES

1. EXIT JUSTICE POWELL

1. Telephone Interview with Ronald Man (Oct. 8, 1990).
2. *Id.*
3. Telephone Interview with Andrew Leipold (Oct. 11, 1990).
4. G. Elsasser, *Powell Quits Supreme Court—Age, Health Force Justice to End 15 Years on Bench*, Chi. Trib., June 27, 1987, at C1.
5. J. Massaro, *Supremely Political* 40–41 (1990).
6. R. Shogun, *A Question of Judgment* 146–47 (1972); N.Y. Times, July 6, 1968.
7. W. Douglas, *The Court Years* 360–61 (1980); W. Douglas, *The Douglas Letters* 414 (D. Urofsky ed., 1987).
8. B. Woodward & S. Armstrong, *The Brethren* 367 (1979).
9. L. Cannon, *Reagan* 371 (1982).
10. Elsasser, *supra* note 4.
11. M. Minow, *The Supreme Court 1986 Term*, 101 Harv. L. Rev. 10, 303 (1987); F. I. Michelman, *The Supreme Court 1985 Term*, 100 Harv. L. Rev. 4, 305 (1986).
12. D. O'Brien, *Opinions*, L.A. Times, May 3, 1987, § 5, at 1.
13. 410 U.S. 113 (1973).
14. *Grand Rapids Sch. Dist. v. Ball*, 473 U.S. 373 (1985); *Aguilar v. Felton*, 472 U.S. 402 (1985).
15. *Lynch v. Donnelly*, 465 U.S. 668 (1984).
16. *McCleskey v. Kemp*, 481 U.S. 279 (1987) (blacks who murder whites are eleven times more likely to suffer the death penalty than whites who murder blacks).
17. D. Lauter, *Surprised Nixon; Justice Willed Power*, L.A. Times, July 26, 1987, § 1, at 1.
18. S. Taylor Jr., *Some Legal Landmarks Are Facing Reconstruction*, N.Y. Times, Oct. 13, 1985, at A5.
19. The Heritage Foundation, Policy Leader (Fall 1988).

20. D. O'Brien, *Judicial Roulette: Report of the Twentieth Century Task Force on Judicial Selection* 61 (1988).

21. *Id.*

22. S. Markman, *Judicial Selection: The Reagan Years*, in H. J. Abraham, *Judicial Selection, Merit, Ideology, and Politics* 40 (National Legal Center for the Public Interest ed., 1990).

23. O'Brien, *supra* note 20, at 62.

24. B. Fein, *The Mission: Stock Bench*, Am. Lawyer, June 1988, at 6.

25. H. Freiwald, *The Mission: Stock Bench*, Legal Times, May 1988.

26. *Id.*

27. Markman, *supra* note 22, at 38–41.

28. Telephone Interview with Melanne Verveer (April 17, 1991).

29. T. Tomasi & J. Velona, *All the President's Men? A Study of Ronald Reagan's Appointments to the U.S. Courts of Appeals*, 87 Colum. L. Rev. 766 (1987).

30. D. O'Brien, *Storm Center* 70 (1986).

31. Cannon, *supra* note 9, at 314–15.

32. Cannon, *supra* note 9, at 313; W. Murphy, *Reagan's Judicial Strategy*, in *Looking Back on the Reagan Presidency*, 211, 233 n.33 (L. Berman ed., 1990).

33. P. Huber, *Sandra Day O'Conner* 14 (1990).

34. Telephone Interview with Edwin Meese (July 17, 1990) [hereinafter Meese Interview, July 17, 1990].

35. Telephone Interview with Terry Eastland (June 19, 1990) [hereinafter Eastland Interview, June 19, 1990].

36. Meese Interview, July 17, 1990, *supra* note 34.

37. 750 F.2d 970 (D.C. Cir. 1984).

38. Eastland Interview, June 19, 1990, *supra* note 35.

39. Meese Interview, July 17, 1990, *supra* note 34.

40. D. Regan, *For the Record* 330 (1988).

41. *Id.*

42. Eastland Interview, June 19, 1990, *supra* note 35.

43. Telephone Interview with Terry Eastland (June 14, 1990) [hereinafter Eastland Interview, June 14, 1990].

44. E. Thomas, *Reagan's Mr. Right*, Time, June 30, 1986.

45. P. Noonan, *What I Saw at the Revolution: A Political Life in the Reagan Era* 213 (1990).

46. Regan, *supra* note 40, at 332.

47. Eastland Interview, June 14, 1990, *supra* note 43.

48. Telephone Interview with John Bolton, Justice Department Liaison to Congress and Assistant Attorney General (June 8, 1990).

2. ENTER JUDGE BORK

1. Telephone Interview with Edwin Meese (June 17, 1990) [hereinafter Meese Interview, June 17, 1990].

2. L. Cannon & H. Kurtz, *Senate Leaders Give List of Ten Possible Nominees; Bork Ranked Top Contender for High Court*, Wash. Post, July 1, 1987, at A1.

3. Meese Interview, June 17, 1990, *supra* note 1.

4. *Id.*

5. See Senate Judiciary Committee Initial Questionnaire (Supreme Court) prepared by Robert Bork; Telephone Interview with Terry Eastland (June 14, 1990).

6. R. Bork, *The Tempting of America: The Political Seduction of the Law* 277 (1990).

7. Telephone Interview with John Bolton (June 8, 1990).

8. Bork, *supra* note 6, at 275.

9. T. Eastland, *Bork Revisited*, Commentary, Feb. 1990, at 39–40.

10. C-Span Interview with Robert H. Bork, July 4, 1988, available in LEXIS, Nexis Library, Transcripts File [hereinafter C-Span, Bork Interview].

11. D. Russakoff & A. Kamen, *The Shaping of Robert H. Bork*, Wash. Post, July 26, 1987, at A1 (Part 1 of 3).

12. *Id.*

13. *Nomination of Robert H. Bork to Be Associate Justice of the Supreme Court of the United States: Hearings Before the Senate Comm. on the Judiciary*, 100th Cong., 1st Sess. 2977–98 (1987) [hereinafter *Bork Hearings*].

14. C-Span, Bork Interview, *supra* note 10.

15. Russakoff & Kamen, *supra* note 11.

16. *Id.*

17. C-Span, Bork Interview, *supra* note 10.

18. Russakoff & Kamen, *supra* note 11.

19. See R. Bork, *Vertical Integration and the Sherman Act: The Legal History of an Economic Misconception*, 22 U. Chi. L. Rev. 157 (1954).

20. See Senate Judiciary Committee Initial Questions of Robert H. Bork.

21. Telephone Interview with Howard Krane (Aug. 29, 1990) [hereinafter Krane Interview, Aug. 29, 1990].

22. *Bork Hearings*, *supra* note 13, at 2941.

23. Letter from Dallin H. Oaks to Scott Kains (Sept. 21, 1990) (on file with author).

24. *Bork Hearings, supra* note 13, at 2941.

25. Krane Interview, Aug. 29, 1990, *supra* note 21.

26. *Id.*

27. S. Taylor Jr., *Bork on His Evolution: Far from the New Deal,* N.Y. Times, July 8, 1987, at A1.

28. *Id.*

29. S. Taylor Jr., *Bork at Yale; Colleagues Recall a Friend but a Philosophical Foe,* N.Y. Times, July 27, 1987, at A13.

30. R. Bork, *Civil Rights—A Challenge,* The New Republic, Aug. 31, 1963, at 21–22.

31. *Nominations of Joseph T. Sneed, of North Carolina, to Be Deputy Attorney General and Robert H. Bork, of Connecticut, to Be Solicitor General: Hearings Before the Senate Comm. on the Judiciary,* 93d Cong., 1st Sess. 14–15 (1973).

32. *Bork Hearings, supra* note 13, at 153.

33. A. Kamen & D. Russakoff, *An Odyssey of Ideas: From Yale to Watergate,* Wash. Post, July 27, 1987, at A1.

34. R. Bork, *Why I Am for Nixon,* The New Republic, June 1, 1968, at 19.

35. R. Bork, *The Supreme Court Needs a New Philosophy,* Fortune, Dec. 1968, at 138.

36. See R. Bork, *Neutral Principles and Some First Amendment Problems,* 47 Ind. L.J. 1 (1971).

37. D. Russakoff & A. Kamen, *The Shaping of Robert H. Bork,* Wash. Post, July 27, 1987, at A1 (Part 2 of 3).

38. *Id.*

39. *Id.*

40. Telephone Interview with A. Raymond Randolph (June 11, 1990).

41. R. Bork, *The Problems and Pleasures of Being Solicitor General,* 42 Antitrust L.J. 701 (1972).

42. Taylor, *supra* note 29.

43. *Bork Hearings, supra* note 13, at 3332.

44. *Id.* at 3333.

45. D. Russakoff & A. Kamen, *The Shaping of Robert H. Bork,* Wash. Post, July 28, 1987, at A1 (Part 3 of 3).

46. *Id.*

47. Robert J. Bork, *The Crisis in Constitutional Theory: Back to the Future* (April 3, 1987) (address before the Philadelphia Society), reprinted in *Bork Hearings, supra* note 13, at 653, 660–62.

48. Russakoff & Kamen, *supra* note 45.

49. Bork, *supra* note 6, at 274.

3. BATTLE LINES FORM

1. D. Collin, *Hearings Set for Bork, but Date Is Drawing Fire*, Chi. Trib., July 9, 1987, at 6.

2. R. Cohen, *Byrd on the Spot*, 19 Nat'l J. 2476 (Oct. 3, 1987).

3. K. Noble, *Biden Vows to Lead Forces Against Bork's Confirmation*, N.Y. Times, July 9, 1987, at A1.

4. D. Johnston, *Reagan Hints at Bork Nomination Strategy: Stress Credentials, Not Views*, Chi. Trib., July 5, 1987, § 1, at 14.

5. H. J. Reske, UPI, July 8, 1987, available in LEXIS, Nexis Library, Wires File.

6. *Biden Plans to Oppose Bork: Hearing Set for September*, Wash. Post, July 9, 1987, at A1.

7. Reske, *supra* note 5.

8. H. J. Reske, UPI, July 9, 1987, available in LEXIS, Nexis Library, Wires File.

9. *Biden Rejects Setting Date for Vote on Bork*, Wash. Post, July 16, 1987, at A9.

10. L. Greenhouse, *Dole Suggests a Way for President to Seat Bork Before Senate Vote*, N.Y. Times, July 28, 1987, at A1.

11. T. Moran, *Conservatism Downplayed: White House Debuts New Bork Lobbying Strategy*, Legal Times, Aug. 3, 1987, at 4.

12. *Id.*

13. Memorandum to Senator Birch Bayh (on file at the Indiana University, Bloomington library).

14. *Nomination of Potter Stewart to Be Associate Justice of the Supreme Court of the United States*, Exec. Rep. No. 2, 86th Cong., 1st Sess. 2–10 (1959) (minority views).

15. S. Res. 334, 86th Cong., 2d Sess., 106 Cong. Rec. 18, 130–45 (1960).

16. L. Greenhouse, *Byrd Warns Against a Partisan Battle over Confirmation of Bork*, N.Y. Times, July 29, 1987, at A12.

17. A. Neal, UPI, July 31, 1987, available in LEXIS, Nexis Library, Wires File.

18. Telephone Interview with Kenneth Bass, adviser to Senator Biden (June 28, 1990).

19. E. Bronner, *Kennedy Tells How He Roused Opposition*, Boston Globe, Oct. 11, 1987, at A1.

20. This is exactly the effect that other restrictions on abortion, such as consent requirements, have generally had. See *Ohio v. Akron Center for Reproductive Health*, 497 U.S. 502 (1990).

21. E. Bronner, *Battle for Justice: How the Bork Nomination Shook America* (1989) [hereinafter Bronner, *Bork Nomination*].

22. *Id.* at 100.

23. Bronner, *supra* note 19.

24. Bronner, *Bork Nomination*, *supra* note 21, at 105.

25. P. McGuigan & D.Weyrich, *Ninth Justice: The Fight for Bork* 24–25 (1990).

26. Telephone Interview with Estelle Rogers (Sept. 24, 1990) [hereinafter Rogers Interview, Sept. 24, 1990].

27. Telephone Interview with Ken Kemmerling (1990).

28. *Nomination of Justice William Hubbs Rehnquist to Be Chief Justice of the Supreme Court of the United States: Hearings Before the Senate Comm. on the Judiciary*, 99th Cong., 2d Sess. 640–69 (1986).

29. L. Romano, *Leading the Charge on Bork*, Wash. Post, Sept. 15, 1987, at D1; Bronner, *Bork Nomination*, *supra* note 21, at 50.

30. Romano, *supra* note 29.

31. *Id.*

32. Telephone Interview with George Kassouf (June 11, 1990).

33. A. Kornhauser, *Working the Bork Hearings*, Legal Times, Sept. 21, 1987, at 1.

34. See 133 Cong. Rec. 10, 325 (1987).

35. A. Neal, *Bork Too Extreme*, UPI, Sept. 8, 1987, available in LEXIS, Nexis Library, Wires File.

36. R. Marcus, *Justice Department Hits Bork Critics; Agency Report Says Study Employs Spurious Techniques*, Wash. Post, Sept. 13, 1987, at A41.

37. Rogers Interview, Sept. 24, 1990, *supra* note 26.

38. *Why the United States Senate Should Not Consent to the Nomination of Robert H. Bork to Be a Justice of the Supreme Court*, Common Cause, Sept. 1987.

39. R. Marcus, *Groups Unlimber Media Campaigns over Bork*, Wash. Post, Aug. 4, 1987, at A3.

40. Telephone Interview with Mike Martinez (April 22, 1990).

41. R. Marcus, *Growing Array of Groups Fight Bork Confirmation*, Wash. Post, Aug. 25, 1987, at A16.

42. Telephone Interview with Richard Nugent (1990).

43. Marcus, *supra* note 41.

44. Romano, *supra* note 29.

45. D. Broder, *Grass Roots Activists Mobilize Against Bork*, Wash. Post, Aug. 3, 1987, at A3.

46. R. Bork, *The Tempting of America: The Political Seduction of the Law* 296 (1990).

47. *Id.* at 306.

48. Bronner, *Bork Nomination, supra* note 21, at 93.

49. Bork, *supra* note 46, at 280.

50. Telephone Interview with John Bolton (June 8, 1990) [hereinafter Bolton Interview, June 8, 1990].

51. Telephone Interview with A. Raymond Randolph (June 11, 1990) [hereinafter Randolph Interview, June 11, 1990].

52. Bronner, *Bork Nomination, supra* note 21, at 194.

53. Bolton Interview, June 8, 1990, *supra* note 50.

54. Randolph Interview, June 11, 1990, *supra* note 51.

55. Bork, *supra* note 46, at 278–79.

56. Telephone Interview with Dan Casey (Mar. 1990) [hereinafter Casey Interview, Mar. 1990].

57. Marcus, *supra* note 41.

58. Casey Interview, Mar. 1990, *supra* note 56.

59. *Id.*

60. Telephone Interview with Charles Orndorff (1990).

61. *Bork Nomination Lost by White House "Insiders,"* PR Newswire, Jan. 7, 1988, available in LEXIS, Nexis Library, Wires File; see also McGuigan & Weyrich, *supra* note 25, at 47–51 (1990).

62. Telephone Interview with Phyllis Schlafley (May 11, 1990).

63. McGuigan & Weyrich, *supra* note 25, at 79–80.

64. T. Eastland, *What's Ultra-Wrong about the Ultra-Right*, 87 Mich. L. Rev. 1450, 1459 (1989).

65. Telephone Interview with Terry Eastland (June 14, 1990).

66. Casey Interview, Mar. 1990, *supra* note 56.

67. Kornhauser, *supra* note 33.

68. S. Garment, *The War Against Robert H. Bork*, Commentary, Jan. 1988.

69. Telephone Interview with Tom Korologos (June 7, 1990) [hereinafter Korologos Interview, June 7, 1990].

70. Moran, *supra* note 11.

71. Romano, *supra* note 29.

72. Korologos Interview, June 7, 1990, *supra* note 69.

4. THE FIRST CRUCIAL ISSUE

1. B. Ackerman, *Transformative Appointments*, 101 Harv. L. Rev. 1106 (1988).

2. 133 Cong. Rec. 10, 524 (1987).

3. This is typically defined as the Senate's practice of refusing to confirm nominees who are opposed by a senator from their home state.

4. N.Y. Times, Nov. 6, 1898, at 4.

5. U.S. Congress, *Biographical Directory of the American Congress 1774–1791* (1971), at 57.

6. R. Barry, *Mr. Rutledge of South Carolina* 178–81 (1942).

7. Massey, *A History of Advice and Dissent*, Wall St. J., July 23, 1987, § 1, at 1.

8. C. Swisher, *The Documentary History of the Supreme Court of the United States*, pt. 2, at 804 (M. Marcus & J. Perry, eds., 1985).

9. *Id.* at 814.

10. *Id.* at 807–8.

11. C. Warren, *The Supreme Court in United States History* 412-13 (1923).

12. J. Harris, *The Advice & Consent of the Senate* 59 (1953).

13. C. Swisher, *The Documentary History of the Supreme Court of the United States* 220 (M. Marcus & J. Perry, eds., 1985).

14. *Id.* at 226–28.

15. *Id.* at 227.

16. Warren, *supra* note 11, at 503.

17. *Id.* at 555.

18. *Id.* at 556.

19. *Id.* at 557.

20. *Id.* at 558–59.

21. R. McElroy, *Grover Cleveland—The Man and the Statesman* 130–33 (1923).

22. *U.W.W.A. v. Red Jacket*, 18 F.2d 839 (4th Cir. 1927).

23. R. Watson Jr., *The Defeat of Judge Parker*, 50 Miss. Valley Hist. Rev. 228, 232–33 (1963).

24. R. Shogun, *A Question of Judgment* 179–80 (1972).

25. *Id.* at 154–67.

26. J. MacKenzie, *The Appearance of Justices* 78–92 (1974).

27. *Id.* at 80–92.

28. A. M. McConnell Jr., *Haynsworth and Carswell: A New Senate Standard of Excellence*, 59 Ky. L.J. 7, 22–23 (1971).

29. *Nomination of George Harrold Carswell to Be Associate Justice of the Supreme Court of the United States: Hearings Before the Senate Comm. on the Judiciary*, 91st Cong., 2d Sess. 238–54 (1970) (testimony of Louis Pollak) [hereinafter *Carswell Hearings*].

30. *Carswell Hearings*, *supra* note 29, at 276.

31. R. Harris, *Decision* 110 (1971).

32. 133 Cong. Rec. 10, 524 (1987).

33. *Id.*

34. N. Vieira & L. Gross, *The Appointments Clause*, 11 J. Legal Hist. 311 (1990).

35. C. L. Black Jr., *A Note on Senatorial Consideration of Supreme Court Nominees*, 79 Yale L.J. 657, 659 (1970); A. P. Melone, *The Senate's Confirmation Role in Supreme Court Nominations and the Politics of Ideology Versus Impartiality*, 75 Judicature 68 (1991).

36. P. Simon, *Advice & Consent* 36 (1992).

37. Black, *supra* note 35, at 660.

38. *The Federalist*, No. 76 (Alexander Hamilton). See Vieira & Gross, *supra* note 34, where we have discussed the Framers' intent and the history of judicial appointments in the United States and Great Britain in some detail.

39. See U.S. Const., Art. VI, § 3 ("No religious test shall ever be required as a qualification to any office . . . under the United States).

40. In fact, some Supreme Court appointments have been specifically aimed at maintaining a Catholic or Jewish seat on the Court, despite the prohibition against a religious test. H. Abraham, *Justices and Presidents* 57–58 (1974).

41. See *infra* chapter 24.

5. THE JUDICIARY COMMITTEE

1. G. Elsasser, *Democrats to Watch the Courts*, Chi. Trib., Nov. 6, 1986, at C8.

2. I. Molotsky & W. Weaver Jr., *Washington Talk: Briefing; Bring on the Makeup*, N.Y. Times, Nov. 17, 1986, at A18.

3. H. Kurtz, *Weighing Presidential Campaign: Biden Urged Kennedy to Chair Judiciary*, Wash. Post, Nov. 12, 1986, at A4.

4. *Id.*

5. *Id.*

6. T. Moran, *Bork Confirmation Fight Looms*, Legal Times, July 6, 1987, at 1.

7. *Bidenquiddick; Joseph R. Biden's Opposition to Robert H. Bork*, 39 Nat'l Rev. 15 (Aug. 28, 1987).

8. P. Osterlund, *An Undecided Few Will Be Crucial Factor in Bork Confirmation*, Christian Sci. Monitor, Sept. 14, 1987, at 3.

9. M. Posner, *Bork Nomination Produces Flap over Test for High Court*, Reuters, July 23, 1987, available in LEXIS, Nexis Library, Wires File.

10. P. McGuigan & D. Weyrich, *Ninth Justice: The Fight for Bork* 139–40 (1990).

11. Telephone Interview with Walter Dellinger (July 2, 1990).

12. *Nomination of Abe Fortas to Be Chief Justice of the Supreme Court of the United States*, Exec. Rep. No. 8, 90th Cong., 2d Sess. 41–44 (1968) (individual views of Senator Thurmond).

13. *Nomination of Abe Fortas to Be Chief Justice of the United States and Nomination of Homer Thornberry to Be Associate Justice of the Supreme Court of the United States: Hearings Before the Senate Comm. on the Judiciary*, 90th Cong., 2d Sess. 180 (1968).

14. *Nomination of Sandra Day O'Connor to Be Associate Justice of the Supreme Court of the United States: Hearings Before the Senate Comm. on the Judiciary*, 97th Cong., 1st Sess. 2 (1981).

15. *Nomination of Robert H. Bork to Be Associate Justice of the Supreme Court of the United States: Hearings Before the Senate Comm. on the Judiciary*, 100th Cong., 1st Sess. 30 (1987) [hereinafter *Bork Hearings*].

16. *Nomination of George Harrold Carswell to Be Associate Justice of the Supreme Court of the United States*, Exec. Rep. No. 14, 91st Cong., 2d Sess. 13 (1970).

17. *Nomination of William H. Rehnquist to Be Associate Justice of the Supreme Court of the United States*, Exec. Rep. No. 16, 92d Cong., 1st Sess. 24–25 (1971) (individual views of Senators Bayh, Hart, Kennedy, and Tunney) [hereinafter *Rehnquist Report*].

18. *Nomination of William H. Rehnquist and Lewis F. Powell, Jr. to Be Associate Justices of the Supreme Court of the United States: Hearings Before the Senate Comm. on the Judiciary*, 92d Cong., 1st Sess. 52–56 (1971) [hereinafter *Rehnquist Hearings*].

19. *Rehnquist Report, supra* note 17, at 25.

20. *Id.*

21. *Nomination of Justice William Hubbs Rehnquist to Be Chief Justice of the United States: Hearings Before the Senate Comm. on the Judiciary*, 99th Cong., 2d Sess. 16 (1986) [hereinafter *Rehnquist Hearings II*].

22. See, e.g., *Rehnquist Hearings II, supra* note 21, at 987–1039 (testimony of James Brosnahan); *Id.* at 1054–65 (testimony of Dr. Sydney Smith).

23. *Rehnquist on Civil Rights*, UPI, July 31, 1986, available in LEXIS, Nexis Library, Wires File.

24. *Rehnquist Hearings II, supra* note 21, at 229–30.

25. *Id.* at 15.

26. *Nomination of William H. Rehnquist to Be Chief Justice of the United States*, Exec. Rep. No. 18, 99th Cong., 2d Sess. 75 (1986) (supplemental views of Senator Kennedy).

27. *Id.*

28. *Id.* at 76.

29. *Senate Confirms Rehnquist, 65-33, as Chief Justice; Scalia Seated by Unanimous Vote*, Facts on File World News Dig., Sept. 19, 1986, at A2.

30. *Id.*

31. N. A. Lewis, *Orrin Hatch's Journey: Strict Conservative to Compromise Seeker*, N.Y. Times, Mar. 2, 1990, at A12.

32. *Id.*

33. *Id.*

34. *Id.*

35. S. V. Roberts, *Point Man for the Right*, N.Y. Times, Nov. 22, 1981, § 4, at 5.

36. *Bork Hearings, supra* note 15, at 40–41.

37. G. Sperling, *Down to the Wire on Judge Bork*, Christian Sci. Monitor, Sept. 29, 1987, at 11.

38. See *infra* chapter 7.

39. *Rehnquist Hearings II, supra* note 21, at 299–30.

40. *Senator Hits Way Judges Are Selected; Says Administration Has Made Process Bastion of Mediocrity*, L.A. Times, Feb. 12, 1987, § 1, at 2 (from UPI wire).

41. J. Cawley & G. De Lama, *Bork Nears Defeat, Senator Says White House Still Claims It Has Edge*, Chi. Trib., Sept. 30, 1987, at C1.

42. P. Simon, *Winners & Losers* 85 (1989).

43. UPI, July 2, 1987, available in LEXIS, Nexis Library, Wires File.

44. UPI, July 30, 1987, available in LEXIS, Nexis Library, Wires File.

45. UPI, Aug. 28, 1987, available in LEXIS, Nexis Library, Wires File.

46. C. Trueheart, *In Bork's Corner: Alan Simpson's Angry Defense; The Wyoming Senator Frustrated by Making Points at the Hearing*, Wash. Post, Oct. 2, 1987, at D1; *Bork Hearings, supra* note 15, at 671.

47. *Bork Hearings, supra* note 15, at 47.

48. R. G. Kaiser, *New Hampshire Ex-Democrat Turned Right into Senate*, Wash. Post, Mar. 3, 1979.

49. A. Neal, *Lawmakers Urge High Court to Curb Abortion*, UPI, July 10, 1985, available in LEXIS, Nexis Library, Wires File.

50. *Humphrey Likens Pro-life Fight to Anti-slavery Battle*, UPI, May 23, 1986, available in LEXIS, Nexis Library, Wires File.

51. *Gibbs Anxious to Start New Job*, UPI, July 24, 1986, available in LEXIS, Nexis Library, Wires File.

52. M. Barone & G. Ujifusa, *The Almanac of American Politics: the Senators, the Representatives — Their Records, States, and Districts*, 1990, at 734 (1989).

53. *Id.* at 429.

54. See *Bork Hearings, supra* note 15, at 1212-13.

55. T. Moran, *A Splintered Judiciary Committee,* Legal Times, Sept. 14, 1987, at 6.

56. *Engle v. Vitale,* 370 U.S. 421 (1962); *Abington School District v. Schempp,* 374 U.S. 203 (1963).

57. T. Moran, *Heflin and the Bork Question: Key Senator Gathers His Thoughts and Keeps His Own Counsel,* Legal Times, Aug. 10, 1987, at 1.

58. S. Aiges, States News Serv., July 1, 1987, available in LEXIS, Nexis Library, Wires File.

59. D. Weiss, States News Serv., June 27, 1986, available in LEXIS, Nexis Library, Wires File.

60. D. Weiss, States News Serv., June 5, 1986, available in LEXIS, Nexis Library, Wires File.

61. *Id.*

62. E. Walsh, *Publicity and Pressure Focus on an Uncommitted Senator Specter,* Wash. Post, Sept. 29, 1987, at A10.

63. *Id.*

64. D. Wisenberg, States News Serv., July 24, 1987, available in LEXIS, Nexis Library, Wires File.

65. *Id.*

6. THE ULTIMATE STAKES: CONTROLLING THE DIRECTION OF THE COURT

1. R. Bork, Address to D.C. Circuit Panel on "Interpreting the Constitution" (Mar. 31, 1987).

2. Interview with R. Bork in *Judicial Notice,* June 1986, at 17.

3. *Coppage v. Kansas,* 236 U.S. 1 (1915).

4. *Human Life Bill: Hearings on S. Bill 158 Before the Subcomm. on Separation of Powers of the Senate Judiciary Comm.,* 97th Cong., 1st Sess. 310, 315 (1982).

5. 347 U.S. 483 (1954).

7. THE RIGHT OF PRIVACY: CONTRACEPTION, ABORTION, AND STERILIZATION

1. *NOW Plans Bork Battle; New President Calls Him "a Neanderthal,"* Chi. Trib., July 21, 1987, at C4; *The Faye Wattleton Counterattack,* Wash. Post, Oct. 14, 1987, at C1.

2. Telephone Interview with Nikki Heidepriem (1990).

3. 381 U.S. 479 (1965).

4. R. Bork, *Neutral Principles and Some First Amendment Problems*, 47 Ind. L.J. 1 (1971).

5. 381 U.S. at 508 (1965).

6. See *Bowers v. Hardwick*, 478 U.S. 186 (1986).

7. N. Vieira, *Hardwick and the Right of Privacy*, 55 U. Chi. L. Rev. 1181 (1988).

8. *Nomination of Robert H. Bork to Be Associate Justice of the Supreme Court of the United States: Hearings Before the Senate Comm. on the Judiciary*, 100th Cong., 1st Sess. 330 (1987) [hereinafter *Bork Hearings*].

9. Bork, *supra* note 4, at 9.

10. *Bork Hearings, supra* note 8, at 115.

11. *Id.* at 117.

12. *Id.* at 182.

13. *Id.* at 264.

14. L. Greenhouse, *No Grass Is Growing under Judge Bork's Seat*, N.Y. Times, Aug. 4, 1987, at A18.

15. G. Will, *And the Widening Paranoia*, Wash. Post, Sept. 17, 1987, at A27.

16. L. Cutler, *Saving Bork from Both Friends and Enemies*, N.Y. Times, July 14, 1987, at A27.

17. *Bork Hearings, supra* note 8, at 184.

18. *Id.*

19. *Id.* at 293.

20. A. Allen, *Why Does Bork Have Trouble with a Right to Privacy?*, Chi. Trib., Sept. 29, 1987, at C15.

21. 316 U.S. 535 (1942).

22. *Id.* at 541.

23. Bork, *supra* note 4, at 2.

24. 741 F.2d 444 (D.C. Cir. 1984).

25. *Id.*

26. *Bork Hearings, supra* note 8, at 467.

27. *Id.* at 468.

28. *Id.*

29. *Id.* at 467–68.

30. *Id.* at 788–90.

31. J. Hanrahan, *Bork Loss Attributed to Lobbying, Other Factors*, UPI, Oct. 24, 1987, available in LEXIS, Nexis Library, Wires File.

32. See, e.g., *infra* chapter 19.

8. CIVIL RIGHTS

1. E. Walsh & A. Kamen, *Ideological Stakes High in Bork Fight; on Eve of Hearings, Both Sides Seem Eager to Keep Calm*, Wash. Post, Sept. 13, 1987, at A1.

2. *Nomination of Robert H. Bork to Be Associate Justice of the Supreme Court of the United States: Hearings Before the Senate Comm. on the Judiciary*, 100th Cong., 1st Sess. 34 (1987) [hereinafter *Bork Hearings*].

3. R. Bork, *Civil Rights—A Challenge*, The New Republic, Aug. 31, 1963, at 21, 22.

4. *Bork Hearings, supra* note 2, at 154.

5. *Id.* at 2120.

6. 334 U.S. 1 (1948).

7. 383 U.S. 663 (1966).

8. 402 U.S. 137 (1971).

9. 377 U.S. 533 (1964).

10. 14-F R. Mersky & J. Jacobstein, *The Supreme Court of the United States: Hearings and Reports on Successful and Unsuccessful Supreme Court Nominations by the Senate Judiciary Committee, 1916–1987*, at 7367, 7370 (1990).

11. *Bork Hearings, supra* note 2, at 254.

12. *Id.* at 160–61, 254–56.

13. R. Bork, *Neutral Principles and Some First Amendment Problems*, 47 Ind. L.J. 1, 11 (1971).

14. R. Bork, *Address to the Worldnet*, June 10, 1987, reprinted in N.Y. Times, Sept. 21, 1987, at B14.

15. 411 U.S. 1 (1973) (calling for close scrutiny of such classifications only when constitutionally protected interests are involved).

16. See, e.g., *McLaughlin v. Florida*, 379 U.S. 184 (1964).

17. See, e.g., *Craig v. Boren*, 429 U.S. 190 (1976).

18. *Bork Hearings, supra* note 2, at 160–61, 254–56.

19. *Id.* at 333.

20. 429 U.S. 190.

21. *Id.* at 211–14.

22. *Bork Hearings, supra* note 2, at 392.

23. *Id.* at 1518.

24. Memorandum for the United States as Amicus Curiae, *Vorchheimer v. Sch. Dist. of Philadelphia*, 430 U.S. 703 (1977) (No. 76-37).

25. *Bork Hearings, supra* note 2, at 1396, 1398–99, 1409–10 (citing *Cosgrove v. Smith*, 697 F.2d 1125, 1143, 1145–46 [D.C. Cir. 1983] [Bork, J., concurring in part and dissenting in part]).

26. 760 F.2d 1330 (D.C. Cir. 1985).
27. *Bork Hearings, supra* note 2, at 2344–53.
28. *Vinson*, 760 F.2d 1330.
29. *Meritor Sav. Bank, FSB v. Vinson*, 477 U.S. 57, 68–69 (1986).
30. *Id.* at 70–71 (an employer could have reason to know and, therefore, be liable).

9. THE REVEREND AND THE RABBI: CHURCH-STATE ISSUES

1. K. Dean, *Bork Thrives on Confrontation, Lives for the Spotlight,* Rochester Time Union, Aug. 19, 1987, at A1.
2. Telephone Interview with reporter for Rochester Democrat Chronicle (1988).
3. Telephone Interview with Melissa Nolan and other staff members for Republican minority on the Senate Judiciary Committee (Mar. 1988).
4. Telephone Interview with Reverend Kenneth Dean (Mar. 9, 1988) [hereinafter Dean Interview, Mar. 9, 1988].
5. *Id.*
6. *Id.*
7. *Id.*
8. *Nomination of Robert H. Bork to Be Associate Justice of the Supreme Court of the United States: Hearings Before the Senate Comm. on the Judiciary,* 100th Cong., 1st Sess. 2997–98 (1987) [hereinafter *Bork Hearings*].
9. Dean Interview, Mar. 9, 1988, *supra* note 4.
10. Dean, *supra* note 1.
11. *Bork Hearings, supra* note 8, at 3020.
12. *Id.*
13. *Id.* at 3020.
14. *Id.*
15. Telephone Interview with a participant at the Brookings seminar (Mar. 1988) [hereinafter Brookings Interview, Mar. 1988].
16. *Id.*
17. R. Bork, Address at the University of Chicago (Nov. 1984); R. Bork, Address at the Brookings Institution (Sept. 1985) [hereinafter Brookings Address].
18. Brookings Address, *supra* note 17.
19. Brookings Interview, Mar. 1988, *supra* note 15.
20. *Bork Hearings, supra* note 8, at 3626.
21. *Id.*

22. Telephone Interview with Diana Huffman (Mar. 1988) [hereinafter Huffman Interview, Mar. 1988].

23. *Bork Hearings, supra* note 8, at 3627–28.

24. *Id.*

25. *Id.* at 3631–32.

26. *Id.* at 3626.

27. Huffman Interview, Mar. 1988, *supra* note 22.

28. Telephone Interview with Reverend Dean Kelley (Mar. 1988).

29. *Engel v. Vitale,* 370 U.S. 421 (1962); *Abington School District v. Schempp,* 374 U.S. 203 (1963).

10. FREE SPEECH

1. R. Bork, *Neutral Principles and Some First Amendment Problems,* 47 Ind. L.J. 1 (1971).

2. 395 U.S. 444 (1969).

3. Bork, *supra* note 1, at 20.

4. *Id.* at 23.

5. *Nomination of Robert H. Bork to Be Associate Justice of the Supreme Court of the United States: Hearings Before the Senate Comm. on the Judiciary,* 100th Cong., 1st Sess. 270 (1987) [hereinafter *Bork Hearings*].

6. See, e.g., *Abrams v. United States,* 250 U.S. 606 (1919); *Gitlow v. New York,* 268 U.S. 652 (1925); *Whitney v. California,* 274 U.S. 357 (1927).

7. Bork, *supra* note 1, at 25.

8. *Id.* at 26.

9. *Bork Hearings, supra* note 5, at 270.

10. *Id.* at 269.

11. *Id.* at 271.

12. *Id.* at 282.

13. *Id.* at 283.

14. *Id.*

15. Address at University of Michigan, 1979, reprinted in *Bork Hearings, supra* note 5, at 425–26.

16. Bork, *supra* note 1, at 20.

17. *Id.* at 31.

18. *Brandenburg,* 395 U.S. 444.

19. Address at University of Michigan, *supra* note 15, at 428.

20. *Bork Hearings, supra* note 5, at 271.

21. *Id.* at 273.

22. *Id.* at 274.
23. *Id.* at 428.
24. *Id.*
25. A. Kamen, *Senators Increase Pressure over Bork's Shifting Opinions*, Wash. Post, Sept. 18, 1987, at A1.

11. ETHICAL QUESTIONS: WATERGATE REVISITED

1. M. Posner, *Long Hot Summer Seen for Bork, Confirmation Not Yet Certain*, Reuters, July 1, 1987, available in LEXIS, Nexis Library, Wires File.
2. See *infra* chapter 13.
3. *Nomination of Clement F. Haynsworth, Jr. to Be Associate Justice of the Supreme Court of the United States: Hearings Before the Senate Comm. on the Judiciary*, 91st Cong., 1st Sess. 34–37 (1969).
4. J. Frank, *Clement Haynsworth, the Senate and the Supreme Court* 119–21, 135 (1991).
5. J. MacKenzie, *The Appearance of Justice* 18–20, 23–24, 30–31 (1974); R. Shogun, *A Question of Judgment* 154, 164–67, 179–80 (1974); N. Vieira & L. Gross, *The Appointments Clause: Judge Bork and the Role of Ideology in Judicial Confirmations*, 11 J. Legal Hist. 311, 328 (1990).
6. *Nomination of Robert H. Bork to Be Associate Justice of the Supreme Court of the United States: Hearings Before the Senate Comm. on the Judiciary*, 100th Cong., 1st Sess. 3230 (1987) (testimony of Henry Ruth) [hereinafter *Bork Hearings*].
7. See Lardner Jr. & McBee, *Nixon Plans Prosecutor, Bars Access to Files*, Wash. Post, Oct. 27, 1973, at 1; *Presidential Distrust, Isolation and a Series of Miscalculations*, Wash. Post, Oct. 28, 1973, at 1.
8. S. Ervin Jr., *The Whole Truth: The Watergate Conspiracy* 237–38 (1980).
9. Telephone Interview with Elliot Richardson (Sept. 29, 1988) [hereinafter Richardson Interview, Sept. 29, 1988]; *Bork Hearings*, *supra* note 6, at 3117, 3123, 3133.
10. J. Doyle, *Not above the Law* 188 (1977).
11. Telephone Interview with Henry Ruth (Sept. 20, 1988).
12. *Id.*
13. Doyle, *supra* note 10, at 191.
14. Richardson Interview, Sept. 29, 1988, *supra* note 9.
15. *Id.*; *Bork Hearings*, *supra* note 6, at 234 (testimony of Judge Bork).
16. Doyle, *supra* note 10, at 192.

17. *Id.* at 209–10.

18. *Id.* at 191–92.

19. *Id.* at 192.

20. *Id.*

21. 2 Watergate and the White House, July–December 1973 97 (Facts on File ed., 1974).

22. *Id.*

23. Press Conference of Robert H. Bork, Acting Attorney General, Oct. 24, 1973, *in Bork Hearings, supra* note 6, at 603.

24. *Bork Hearings, supra* note 6, at 620.

25. *Id.* at 617.

26. 2 Watergate: Chronology of a Crisis 111 (Congressional Quarterly, Inc. ed., 1974) [hereinafter *Congressional Quarterly, Watergate*].

27. *Id.*

28. *Facts on File, supra* note 21, at 103.

29. *Bork Hearings, supra* note 6, 194, 235, 361–62.

30. *Nader v. Bork*, 366 F. Supp. 104 (D.D.C. 1973).

31. *Bork Hearings, supra* note 6, at 194.

32. *Id.* at 3112–13, 3117, 3123–24.

33. *Id.* at 195.

34. *Id.* at 1258 (excerpt from William Coleman's Memorandum on Robert Bork for the 1982 ABA Report on Bork's nomination to the Court of Appeals).

35. *Id.* at 615.

36. *Id.* at 230. Elliot Richardson concurred that at the time of Cox's firing, Bork had not given any thought to the appointment of a new special prosecutor. Richardson Interview, Sept. 29, 1988, *supra* note 9.

37. *Bork Hearings, supra* note 6, at 231.

38. *Congressional Quarterly, Watergate, supra* note 26, at 88.

39. *Bork Hearings, supra* note 6, at 3226 (affidavit of Ralph K. Winter).

40. *Id.* at 3216 (statement of Philip A. Lacovara).

41. Richardson Interview, Sept. 29, 1988, *supra* note 9.

42. *Bork Hearings, supra* note 6, at 3204 (testimony of Henry Ruth).

43. *Id.* at 3209 (statement of George Frampton).

44. *Id.* at 323.

45. *Id.* at 3216 (statement of Philip A. Lacovara).

46. *Id.* at 3206.

47. *Selection and Confirmation of Federal Judges: Hearings Before the Senate Comm. on the Judiciary*, 97th Cong., 2d Sess., pt. 3 (1982).

48. *Id.*

49. *Bork Hearings, supra* note 6, at 194–95, 196, 231, 234.

12. THE ABA

1. S. Vermeil, *Panel Rates Bork "Well Qualified" over Objections*, Wall St. J., Sept. 10, 1987, § 2, at 70.

2. Vermeil, *supra* note 1; S. Taylor Jr., *ABA Panel Gives Bork a Top Rating but Vote Is Split*, N.Y. Times, Sept. 10, 1987, at A1.

3. K. Noble, *Hatch Assails ABA over Vote on Bork*, N.Y. Times, Sept. 11, 1987, at A14.

4. W. Safire, *In Re: Bork Witch Hunt*, N.Y. Times, Sept. 13, 1987, § 4, at 35.

5. *Id.*

6. *Id.*

7. Telephone Interview with Estelle Rogers (June 6, 1990).

8. Telephone Interview with Ralph Lancaster (June 12, 1990).

9. See generally J. Grossman, *Lawyers and Judges* 40–81 (1965).

10. D. O'Brien, *Judicial Roulette: Report of the Twentieth Century Fund Task Force on Judicial Selection* 83 (1988).

11. See, e.g., *Lochner v. New York*, 198 U.S. 45 (1905); *Adkins v. Children's Hosp.*, 261 U.S. 525 (1923).

12. *Annual Report of the American Bar Association*, at 576 (1908).

13. O'Brien, *supra* note 10, 13.

14. A. Mason, *Brandeis: A Free Man's Life* 489 (1956).

15. A. L. Todd, *Justice on Trial: The Case of Louis D. Brandeis* 159 (1964).

16. *Id.* at 160.

17. *American Bar Association Standing Committee on Federal Judiciary: What It Is and How It Works* 2 (1988) [hereinafter *A.B.A., Committee on Federal Judiciary*].

18. I. Barth, J. Chandler, S. Hanely, & A. Miller, *Report of Committee on Judicial Selection*, 10 A.B.A. J. 820 (1924).

19. For a description of the events preceding the 1946 establishment of the ABA Special Committee on the Judiciary, see Grossman, *supra* note 9, at 165.

20. *Id.* at 50.

21. N.Y. Times, Aug. 5, 1951, at 26.

22. *Beneficial Advice or Presumptuous Veto? The ABA's Committee on Federal Judiciary Revisited*, reprinted in H. J. Abraham, *Judicial Selection: Merit, Ideology, and Politics* 64 (National Legal Center for the Public Interest ed., 1990) [hereinafter Abraham, *Judicial Selection*].

23. Grossman, *supra* note 9, at 72; *Report of the Standing Committee on Federal Judiciary*, 82 A.B.A. Reports 433 (1957).

24. Herman, *The Bar on How to Pick a Justice*, Wall St. J., Apr. 6, 1970.

25. Grossman, *supra* note 9, at 71 (quoting *Oral Reply of Nicholas Katzenbach to the House of Delegates*, Annual Meeting of the American Bar Association, San Francisco, 1962, at 3).

26. H. Abraham, *Justices and Presidents: A Political History of Appointments to the Supreme Court* 24–25 (1974) [hereinafter Abraham, *Justices and Presidents*].

27. Abraham, *Judicial Selection*, *supra* note 22, at 66.

28. Abraham, *Justices and Presidents*, *supra* note 26, at 28.

29. *Nomination of George Harrold Carswell to Be Associate Justice of the Supreme Court of the United States*, Exec. Rep. No. 14, 91st Cong., 2d Sess. 2 (1970).

30. MacKenzie, *ABA Says 2 Unfit for Court*, Wash. Post, Oct. 21, 1970.

31. Abraham, *Justices and Presidents*, *supra* note 26, at 29–30.

32. Abraham, *Judicial Selection*, *supra* note 22, at 66.

33. *Id.* at 66–67.

34. *Id.* at 69.

35. D. O'Brien, *If the Bench Becomes a Beard*, L.A. Times, Aug. 23, 1987, § 5, at 1.

36. Abraham, *Judicial Selection*, *supra* note 22, at 67.

37. S. Markman, *Judicial Selection: The Reagan Years*, reprinted in Abraham, *Judicial Selection*, *supra* note 22, at 38–41.

38. Abraham, *Judicial Selection*, *supra* note 22, at 67.

39. Telephone Interview with Edwin Meese (July 17, 1990) [hereinafter Meese Interview, July 17, 1990].

40. A.B.A., *Committee on Federal Judiciary*, *supra* note 17, at 1.

41. R. Bork, *The Tempting of America: The Political Seduction of the Law* 292 (1990).

42. Letter from Harold R. Tyler Jr., to Leonard Gross (July 26, 1990) (on file with the author) [hereinafter Tyler Letter].

43. Telephone Interview with Ralph Lancaster (June 12, 1990) [hereinafter Lancaster Interview, June 12, 1990].

44. S. Goldman, *Reagan's Second Term Judicial Appointments: The Battle at Midway*, 70 Judicature 324, 329, 334 (1987).

45. Meese Interview, July 17, 1990, *supra* note 39.

46. *Nomination of Robert H. Bork to Be Associate Justice of the Supreme Court of the United States: Hearings Before the Senate Comm. on the Judiciary*, 100th Cong., 1st Sess. 1190 (1987) [hereinafter *Bork Hearings*].

47. P. Kamenar, *The Role of the American Bar Association in the Ju-*

dicial Selection Process, reprinted in Abraham, *Judicial Selection, supra* note 22, at 94, 95.

48. M. Cogle, *ABA Clout on Judges: Too Much? Odd Couple Links Hands to Challenge Group's Power*, Nat'l L.J., Apr. 17, 1989, at 1.

49. *Id.*

50. Internal Memoranda of the Justice Department indicated that the Department believed the ABA Committee could operate under the guidelines without much difficulty.

51. Cogle, *supra* note 48, at 3.

52. *Washington Legal Foundation v. United States Dep't. of Justice*, 691 F. Supp. 483 (D.D.C. 1988).

53. 491 U.S. 440 (1989).

54. A.B.A., *Committee on Federal Judiciary, supra* note 17, at 4.

55. Lancaster Interview, June 12, 1990, *supra* note 42.

56. *Id.*

57. *Id.*

58. M. Thornton, *The ABA's Judgment on Judges; Qualifications Panel in the Spotlight*, Wash. Post, Sept. 25, 1987, at A23.

59. *Who's Who in American Law* 245 (6th ed., 1990–91).

60. P. Gigot, *ABA Panel Hides Behind Screen of Anonymity*, Wall St. J., Aug. 30, 1991, at A6.

61. Thornton, *supra* note 57.

62. *Id.*

63. A. Kornhauser, *ABA Dissenters Found Bork Too Rigid*, Legal Times, Sept. 14, 1987, at 15.

64. D. Lauter, *Pure Politics, If Politics Can Be Pure, He Says: Reagan Calls Bork Criticism "Irrational,"* L.A. Times, Sept. 12, § 1, at 2.

65. *Bork Hearings, supra* note 45, at 1189.

66. *Id.*

67. *Id.* at 1191.

68. *Id.* at 1196–97.

69. *Id.* at 1197.

70. *Id.*

71. *Id.* at 1198.

72. *Id.* at 1198–2000.

73. *Id.* at 1205.

74. *Id.* at 1208.

75. *Id.* at 1207.

76. See *Id.* at 1184–85 (statement of Harold Tyler Jr.).

77. *Id.* at 1212.

78. *Nomination of Anthony M. Kennedy to Be Associate Justice*

of the Supreme Court of the United States: Hearings Before the Senate Comm. on the Judiciary, 100th Cong., 1st Sess. 265 (1989).

79. *Id.* at 267.

80. *Id.* at 282.

81. *Id.* at 272.

82. *Id.* at 276.

83. Tyler Letter, *supra* note 41.

84. *A.B.A. Role in the Judicial Nomination Process: Hearings Before the Senate Comm. on the Judiciary Committee*, 101st Cong., 2d Sess. (June 2, 1989) [hereinafter *A.B.A. Hearings*], available in LEXIS, Nexis Library, Federal News File.

85. *Id.*

86. *Id.*

87. *Id.*

88. *Id.*

89. *Id.*

90. M. Chambers, *The Legacy of Fiske's Withdrawal*, Nat'l L.J., July 31, 1989, at 13.

91. *Bork Nomination Lost by White House "Insiders,"* PR Newswire, January 7, 1988, available in LEXIS, Nexis Library, Wires File.

92. S. Page & D. Bell, *Thornburgh Loss on Deputy Choice: Fiske Withdraws*, Newsday, July 7, 1989, at 4.

93. L. Greenhouse, *Washington Talks Justice*, N.Y. Times, July 14, 1989, at B7.

94. A. Kornhauser, *ABA's Abortion Vote Imperils Screening Process*, N.J. L.J., Mar. 8, 1990, at 4.

95. J. Sarasohn, *Lobby Talk: Korologos Picks on ABA Ratings*, Legal Times, July 2, 1990, at 15.

96. N. A. Lewis, *Bar Group Told to Stop Rating Judges*, N.Y. Times, June 4, 1994, at B3.

97. *Id.*

98. Letter from Ralph I. Lancaster to Leonard Gross (Oct. 12, 1990) (on file with the author).

99. *A.B.A. Hearings*, *supra* note 82.

100. *Id.*

101. *Id.*

102. S. Torry, *ABA Rating Panel Hunkers Down for Battle over Thomas*, Wash. Post, July 8, 1991, at F5.

103. *Id.*

104. N. A. Lewis, *Bar Association Splits on Fitness of Thomas for the Supreme Court*, N.Y. Times, Aug. 18, 1991, at A1.

105. *Id.*

106. R. Jackson, *Thomas Rated "Qualified" for Court by ABA*, L.A. Times, Aug. 28, 1991, at A1.

107. D. Ceol, *Bar Association Rates Thomas as "Qualified,"* Wash. Post, Aug. 28, 1991, at A3.

108. *Nomination of Clarence Thomas to Be Associate Justice of the Supreme Court of the United States: Hearings Before the Senate Comm. on the Judiciary*, 102d Cong., 1st Sess., pt. 1, at 537 (1991).

13. OTHER WITNESSES

1. *Nomination of Robert H. Bork to Be Associate Justice of the Supreme Court of the United States: Hearings Before the Senate Comm. on the Judiciary*, 100th Cong., 1st Sess. 918–19 (1987) [hereinafter *Bork Hearings*].

2. See *infra* chapter 14.

3. The amendment provides that no state shall "deprive any person of life, liberty, or property without due process of law."

4. 347 U.S. 483 (1954).

5. *Bork Hearings, supra* note 1, at 952–53.

6. 369 U.S. 186 (1962).

7. *Bork Hearings, supra* note 1, at 1005.

8. *Id.* at 155.

9. *Id.* at 1005.

10. *Id.* at 2122.

11. Telephone Interview with Nan Aron (Mar. 20, 1991).

12. See *Nomination of Clement F. Haynsworth, Jr. to Be Associate Justice of the Supreme Court of the United States: Hearings Before the Senate Comm. on the Judiciary*, 91st Cong., 1st Sess. 591, 602, 611 (1969).

13. See *Nomination of George Harrold Carswell of Florida to Be Associate Justice of the Supreme Court of the United States: Hearings Before the Senate Comm. on the Judiciary*, 91st Cong., 2d Sess. 111–42, 221–29, 238–54 (1970) (testimony of Professor James Moore, Professor William Van Alstyne, Professor John Lowenthal, Professor Leroy D. Clark, and Dean Louis H. Pollack).

14. See *Id.* at 108–16; *The Decline of Quality*, N.Y. Times, Nov. 2, 1980, § 6, at 38.

15. R. Harris, *Decision* 110 (1971).

16. J. Frank, *Clement Haynsworth, the Senate and the Supreme Court* 138 (1990).

17. R. Ostrow, *100 Law Professors Question Rehnquist's Ethics*, L.A. Times, Sept. 11, 1986, § 1, at 20.

18. *Bork Hearings, supra* note 1, at 3355.
19. *Id.* at 1342, 1335.
20. Telephone Interview with William Taylor (Apr. 12, 1991).
21. *Id.*
22. *Id.*
23. Telephone Interview with Melanne Verveer (Apr. 17, 1991).
24. *Bork Hearings, supra* note 1, at 408.
25. See *supra* chapter 10.
26. *Bork Hearings, supra* note 1, at 2136–37.
27. *Id.* at 2363.
28. *Id.* at 1090–1110.
29. *Id.* at 1358–63.
30. *Id.* at 1362.
31. *Id.* at 2442–43.
32. See *infra* chapter 14.
33. 699 F.2d 1166 (D.C. Cir. 1983).
34. *Bork Hearings, supra* note 1, at 138.
35. *Id.* at 136.
36. *Id.* at 145.
37. *Id.* at 146.
38. *Id.* at 727.
39. *Id.* at 730.
40. *Id.* at 770.
41. *Id.* at 776–77.
42. *Id.* at 4762–66.
43. *Id.* at 141.
44. *Id.* at 143.
45. *Id.* at 4631–32.
46. Telephone interview with Judge James F. Gordon (Sept. 20, 1988).
47. *Bork Hearings, supra* note 1, at 6063.
48. *Id.* at 6063–64.
49. *Id.*
50. *Id.* at 1209.
51. *Id.* at 3915.

14. THE MEDIA CAMPAIGN: POLLING AND ADVERTISING IN THE CONFIRMATION PROCESS

1. *55% in Poll Unaware of Bork Nomination*, L.A. Times, Aug. 7, 1987, § 1, at 22.
2. *Id.*

3. *Id.*

4. D. Lauter, *"Pure Politics, If Politics Can Be Pure," He Says: Reagan Calls Bork Criticism Irrational,* L.A. Times, Sept. 12, 1987, § 1, at 2.

5. *Id.*

6. D. Lauter & R. Ostrow, *Nominee's Strategists Overwhelmed; How Liberal Spectrum Fought to Block Bork,* L.A. Times, Oct. 8, 1987, § 1, at 1.

7. H. J. Reske, *Study: Bork Nomination—Not Just a Political Fight,* UPI, Aug. 25, 1987, available in LEXIS, Nexis Library, Wires File.

8. M. Pertschuk & W. Schaetzel, *The People Rising: The Campaign Against the Bork Nomination* 134 (1989).

9. *Id.* at 137–39.

10. R. Toner, *Poll Finds Most Undecided on Bork,* N.Y. Times, Sept. 15, 1987, at A27.

11. Telephone Interview with Nan Aron (Mar. 27, 1991) [hereinafter Aron Interview, Mar. 27, 1991].

12. P. Shenon, *The Bork Hearings: Poll Finds Public Opposition to Bork Is Growing,* N.Y. Times, Sept. 24, 1987, at A20.

13. *The Harris Survey,* Sept. 28, 1987.

14. E. Bronner, *In the 1987 Battle over Robert Bork's Nomination, Liberals Showed They Had Learned Well from Conservatives, Using Their Strategies to Keep Him off the Supreme Court,* Boston Globe Mag., Aug. 27, 1989, at 18.

15. *Harris Survey, supra* note 13.

16. *Poll: 51 Percent of Southerners Oppose Bork,* UPI, Oct. 1, 1987, available in LEXIS, Nexis Library, Wires File.

17. Aron Interview, Mar. 27, 1991, *supra* note 11.

18. E. Walsh, *Public Opposition to Bork Grows; In Shift, Plurality Objects to Confirmation, Post-ABC Poll Finds,* Wash. Post, Sept. 25, 1987, at A1.

19. See D. Lauter, *South Had Key Role in Bork Rejection; White House Misjudged Black Voting Power, Area's Senators,* L.A. Times, Oct. 24, 1987, § 1, at 30.

20. Telephone Interview with Walter Dellinger (July 2, 1990).

21. R. Bork, Address at the Federalist Society Dinner (Mar. 5, 1988).

22. Bronner, *supra* note 14.

23. Pertschuk & Schaetzel, *supra* note 8, at 167.

24. *Id.* at 151.

25. Aron Interview, Mar. 27, 1991, *supra* note 11.

26. Bronner, *supra* note 14.

27. P. McGuigan & D. Weyrich, *Ninth Justice: The Fight for Bork* 100 (1991).

28. *Id.*

29. S. Taylor Jr., *Key Senator Says Bork Improved Process of Confirming High Court Nominees*, N.Y. Times, May 27, 1988, § 1, at 10.

30. Bork, *supra* note 21.

31. Telephone Interview with Raymond Randolph (June 11, 1990) [hereinafter Randolph Interview, June 11, 1990].

32. Telephone Interview with Tom Korologos (June 7, 1990) [hereinafter Korologos Interview, June 7, 1990].

33. K. Victor, *Lobbying*, 19 Nat'l J. at 2254 (Sept. 12. 1987).

34. 133 Cong. Rec. 28, 656 (1987) (statement of Senator Biden).

35. McGuigan & Weyrich, *supra* note 28, at 77.

36. Telephone Interview with John Bolton (June 8, 1990).

37. J. Hanrahan, *Bork Loss Attributed to Lobbying, Other Factors*, UPI, Oct. 24, 1987, available in LEXIS, Nexis Library, Wires File.

38. Bork, *supra* note 21.

39. S. V. Roberts, *White House Says Bork Lacks Votes for Confirmation*, N.Y. Times, Sept. 26, 1987, § 1, at 1.

40. Bronner, *supra* note 14.

41. Randolph Interview, June 11, 1990, supra note 31.

42. Telephone Interview with Irena Natividad (June 8, 1990).

43. Bork, *supra* note 21.

44. Telephone Interview with Kenneth Bass (June 28, 1990).

45. R. Marcus, *Bork Fight: Healthy Public Debate or Dangerous Politicization*, Wash. Post, Oct. 10, 1987, § 1, at 10.

46. Aron Interview, Mar. 27, 1991, *supra* note 11.

47. Bronner, *supra* note 14.

48. Randolph Interview, June 11, 1990, *supra* note 31.

49. Hanrahan, *supra* note 37.

50. Korologos Interview, June 7, 1990, *supra* note 32.

51. T. Shales, *The Bork Turnoff: On Camera, the Judge Failed to Save Himself*, Wash. Post, Oct. 9, 1987 at B1.

15. MOUNTING PRESSURE:
THE UNCOMMITTED SENATORS

1. D. Lauter & J. Gerstenzang, *Bork in Peril as 2 Key Senators Oppose Him; Loses GOP's Specter and Democrat Johnston but Reagan Is Working to Make Sure of Victory*, L.A. Times, Oct. 2, 1987, at 1.

2. *Specter Threatened over Bork Vote*, L.A. Times, Sept. 24, 1987, at 38.

3. K. Noble, *Heflin, at Last Voting No, Weathers the Intense Heat on the Uncommitted*, N.Y. Times, Oct. 7, 1987, at B10.

4. R. McNeil, States News Serv., Sept. 29, 1987, available in LEXIS, Nexis Library, Wires File.

5. R. McNeil, States News Serv., Oct. 16, 1987, available in LEXIS, Nexis Library, Wires File.

6. R. Toner, *Saying No to Bork, Southern Democrats Echo Black Voters*, N.Y. Times, Oct. 8, 1987, § 1, at 1.

7. S. Allison, *Tennesseans Write Senators about Bork*, UPI, Sept. 28, 1987, available in LEXIS, Nexis Library, Wires File; see, e.g., E. Roth, *Bradley Comes Out Against Bork Nomination*, UPI, Sept. 29, 1987, available in LEXIS, Nexis Library, Wires File (article reports that Judge Bork's testimony concerning civil rights led Senator Bradley to vote against Bork's confirmation).

8. Toner, *supra* note 6.

9. *NAACP Statement on Opposition to Judge Robert Bork; Calls on Sam Nunn to Take a Stand*, PR Newswire, Oct. 9, 1987, available in LEXIS, Nexis Library, Wires File.

10. *Heflin, Shelby Undecided on Bork*, UPI, Oct. 1, 1987, available in LEXIS, Nexis Library, Wires File.

11. R. McNeil, States News Serv., Oct. 2, 1987, available in LEXIS, Nexis Library, Wires File.

12. A. Kopkind, *The New Voters Find Their Voice; Jesse Jackson's Political Activity in the South*, 245 The Nation 505 (1987).

13. S. Gerstel, *Bork Votes Show Power of Black Vote in South*, UPI, Nov. 2, 1987, available in LEXIS, Nexis Library, Wires File.

14. D. Lauter & R. Ostrow, *Backers Blame Bork Defeat on Lobbying by Foes*, L.A. Times, Oct. 7, 1987, § 1, at 19.

15. K. Noble, *Bid to Influence Bork Vote Is Denied*, N.Y. Times, Oct. 1, 1987, at B9.

16. M. McGrory, *Trading a Horse for a Rabbit*, Wash. Post, July 27, 1986, at D1; T. Wicker, *In the Nation: Another Such Victory*, N.Y. Times, July 25, 1986, at 32; J. Rowley, *Judgeship Confirmation Narrowly Survives Challenge*, July 23, 1986 (from the AP Newswire).

17. Telephone Interview with Tom Korologos (June 7, 1990).

18. E. Walsh, *In the End, Bork Himself Was His Own Worst Enemy; Intellectual Approach Lacked Appeal*; Wash. Post, Oct. 24, 1987, at A1.

19. 133 Cong. Rec. 26, 117 (1987).

20. D. Wisenberg, States News Serv., Sept. 30, 1987, available in LEXIS, Nexis Library, Wires File.

21. *Id.*

22. 133 Cong. Rec. 28, 905 (1987).

23. *Taking a Stand on Confirmation: Senatorial Voices for and Against Bork*, N.Y. Times, Oct. 6, 1987, at B6.

24. 133 Cong. Rec. 28, 905 (1987).

25. E. Walsh, *Bork Panel Likely to Take Neutral Stand; Undecided Senators' Options Preserved*, Wash. Post, Sept. 30, 1987, at A4.

26. *Bork Chances Called "Doomed"; Majority Leader Byrd Will Vote No*, Chi. Trib., Oct. 6, 1987, at 1.

27. *Id.*

28. *Nomination of Robert H. Bork to Be Associate Justice of the Supreme Court of the United States*, Exec. Rep. No. 7, 100th Cong., 1st Sess. 129–30 (1987).

29. See D. Russakoff, *How the South Was Swayed; Sen. Bennett Johnston Guided Freshmen's Decisions*, Wash. Post, Oct. 8, 1987, at 1; E. Bronner, *Battle for Justice* 285–87 (1989).

30. E. Lauter & J. Gerstenzang, *Byrd, & Others Join Bork Foes— DeConcini Gives Panel Majority to Opponents; Reagan Still Adamant*, L.A. Times, Oct. 6, 1987, at A1.

31. E. Walsh, *10 Senators Join Bork Opposition: GOP Conservatives Urge Nominee to Fight Growing Odds*, Wash. Post, Oct. 8, 1987, at 1.

32. B. Schiefler & G. Gates, *The Acting President* 312 (1989).

16. THE STRUGGLE OUTSIDE

1. Telephone Interview with Terry Eastland (June 14, 1990).

2. S. V. Roberts, *Bork Weighs Withdrawing Names as Reagan Aides Say Cause Is Lost*, N.Y. Times, Oct. 8, 1987, at A1.

3. *Statement on the Supreme Court Nomination of Robert H. Bork*, II Pub. Papers 1159 (1987).

4. *Remarks to Reporters on the Supreme Court Nomination of Robert H. Bork*, II Pub. Papers 1137 (1987).

5. *Address to the Nation on the Supreme Court Nomination of Robert H. Bork*, II Pub. Papers 1177 (1987).

6. Roberts, *supra* note 2, at A1.

7. J. V. Lamar Jr., *Gone with the Wind: Southern Senators May Doom the Bork Nomination*, Time, Oct. 12, 1987, at 18.

8. Telephone Interview with Edwin Meese (July 17, 1990).

9. S. V. Roberts, *Time Running Out on Votes for Bork, His Backers Admit*, N.Y. Times Oct. 3, 1987, § 1, at 1.

10. J. V. Lamar Jr., *The Road to Bork's Last Stand; How under Pres-*

sure, He Changed His Mind at the Last Minute, Time, Oct. 19, 1987, at 15.

11. *Id.*

12. *Fortas Letter*, N.Y. Times, Oct. 3, 1968, at 42; B. Murphy, *Fortas* 525 (1988).

13. N.Y. Times, Oct. 6, 1971.

14. Lamar, *supra* note 10, at 15.

15. *Id.*

16. *Bork Vows to Stay in Fight for Supreme Court Seat*, Reuters, Oct. 9, 1987, available in LEXIS, Nexis Library, Wires File.

17. *Id.*

18. R. J. Ostrow & J. Nelson, *Choice Not Easy, Ups Political Ante; Bork's Decision Seen Dictated by Principles*, L.A. Times, Oct. 10, 1987, § 1, at 1.

19. See Roberts, *supra* note 2, at A1.

20. See J. Gerstenzang, *Baker Indignant at Withdrawal Rumor; White House Frustration Grows as Bork Fades*, L.A. Times, Oct. 7, 1987, § 1, at 1.

21. S. Heilbronner, *Moderate Senator Swing Vote Discusses Bork Decision*, UPI, Oct. 23, 1987, available in LEXIS, Nexis Library, Wires File.

22. N. Sandler, UPI, Oct. 13, 1987, available in LEXIS, Nexis Library, Wires File.

23. *Id.*

24. L. Greenhouse, *Quick Senate Debate on Bork Rejected*, N.Y. Times, Oct. 15, 1987, § 1, at 15.

25. *Tough Reagan Rips Bork's Opponents*, Chi. Trib., Oct. 15, 1987, at C1.

26. *Id.*

27. *Id.*

28. R. J. Ostrow & J. Gerstenzang, *Reagan, Bork Foe in Sharp Exchange, President's Accusation of Dishonesty Hit by Sen. Sanford as "Slanderous,"* L.A. Times, Oct. 15, 1987, at 1.

17. THE SENATE DEBATE: BATTLING FOR HISTORY'S VERDICT

1. R. Bork, *The Tempting of America: The Political Seduction of the Law* 315 (1989).

2. See, e.g., 133 Cong. Rec. 26, 419 (1987) (statement of Senator Rudman).

3. *Id.* at 28, 856 (statement of Senator Grassley).

4. *Id.* at 28, 887 (statement of Senator Hatfield).

5. *Id.* at 28, 953–72 (statement of Senator Hatch).

6. *Id.* at 28, 964.

7. *Id.* at 28, 964 (quoting *Griswold v. Connecticut*, 381 U.S. 479, 508–10 [Black, J., dissenting]).

8. *Id.* at 28, 707–8 (statement of Senator Grassley, quoting former Chief Justice Burger's testimony that "[i]f Judge Bork is not in the mainstream, then neither am I and neither have I been").

9. *Id.* at 27, 068 (statement of Senator Hollings).

10. *Id.* at 26, 249 (statement of Senator Nickles).

11. *Id.* at 26, 889 (statement of Senator Sasser).

12. *Id.* at 26, 426 (statement of Senator Daschle).

13. *Id.* at 26, 818 (statement of Senator Breaux).

14. *Id.* at 26, 428 (statement of Senator Dodd).

15. *Id.* at 27, 027 (statement of Senator Mitchell).

16. *Id.* at 27, 015 (statement of Senator Sarbanes).

17. *Id.* at 28, 921 (statement of Senator Metzenbaum).

18. *Id.* at 28, 858 (statement of Senator Grassley).

19. *Id.* at 28, 901 (statement of Senator McConnell).

20. *Id.*

21. *Id.* at 28, 711 (statement of Senator Armstrong).

22. *Id.* at 28, 097 (statement of Senator Biden).

23. See, e.g., *Id.* at 28, 876 (statement of Senator Leahy).

24. *Id.* at 28, 909-10 (statement of Senator Humphrey).

25. *Id.* at 28, 918 (statement of Senator Metzenbaum).

26. *Id.* at 29, 050 (statement of Senator Danforth).

27. *Id.*

28. *Id.*

29. *Senate's Roll Call on the Bork Vote*, N.Y. Times, Oct. 24, 1987, § 1, at 10 (from the AP Newswire).

30. L. Greenhouse, *Bork's Nomination Rejected: 58-42; Reagan "Saddened,"* N.Y. Times, Oct. 24, 1987, § 1, at 1.

18. THE NEW NOMINEES: GINSBURG AND KENNEDY

1. L. Greenhouse, *Washington Talk: The Senate; New Rules of Battle, but Who Will It Help?*, N.Y. Times, Oct. 28, 1987, at B8.

2. T. Jacoby & A. McDaniel, *Spoiling for a Second Round*, Newsweek, Nov. 9, 1987, at 42.

3. T. J. McNulty & G. Elsasser, *Reagan Picks Court Nominee, Conservative Faces Fight in Senate*, Chi. Trib., Oct. 30, 1987, at C1.

4. *Id.*

5. L. Greenhouse, *Ginsburg Faces Queries over Cable T.V.*, N.Y. Times, Oct. 4, 1987, at D30.

6. UPI, Nov. 5, 1987, available in LEXIS, Nexis Library, Wires File.

7. L. Greenhouse, *High Court Nominee Admits Using Marijuana and Calls It a Mistake*, N.Y. Times, Nov. 6, 1987, at A1.

8. R. Marcus & L. Cannon, *Ginsburg Urged to Withdraw in Call Cleared with Reagan*, Wash. Post, Nov. 7, 1987, at A1.

9. S. F. Rasky, *Reagan Weighing Conflicting Advice on Court Nominee*, N.Y. Times, Nov. 9, 1987, at A1.

10. *Nomination of Anthony M. Kennedy to Be Associate Justice of the Supreme Court of the United States: Hearings Before the Senate Comm. on the Judiciary*, 100th Cong., 1st Sess. 88 (1987) [hereinafter *Kennedy Hearings*].

11. *Id.* at 121.

12. *Id.* at 164.

13. *Id.* at 165.

14. *Nomination of Anthony M. Kennedy to Be Associate Justice of the U.S. Supreme Court*, Exec. Rep. No. 13, 100th Cong., 2d Sess. 18–20 (1988) [hereinafter *Kennedy Report*].

15. *Kennedy Hearings, supra* note 10, at 170.

16. *Id.* (emphasis added).

17. *Id.* at 182.

18. *Id.*

19. *Id.* at 242.

20. *Id.*

21. *Id.*

22. 530 F.2d 247, 256 (9th Cir. 1976).

23. *Mt. View-Los Altos Union Sch. Dist. v. Sharron*, 709 F.2d 28 (9th Cir. 1983).

24. *School Comm. of Burlington v. Dept. of Educ.*, 471 U.S. 359 (1985).

25. *Kennedy Hearings, supra* note 10, at 103.

26. *Kaiser Engineers v. NLRB*, 538 F.2d 1379, 1386 (9th Cir. 1976) (Kennedy, J., dissenting).

27. *Eastex v. NLRB*, 437 U.S. 556 (1978).

28. *Kennedy Hearings, supra* note 10, at 162.

29. *Topic v. Circle Realty*, 532 F.2d 1273 (9th Cir. 1976).

30. *Gladstone Realtors v. Bellwood*, 441 U.S. 91 (1979).

31. *Kennedy Hearings, supra* note 10, at 101.

32. *Pavlac v. Church*, 681 F.2d 617 (9th Cir. 1982), vacated 463 U.S. 1201 (1983).

33. *Kennedy Hearings, supra* note 10, at 196.

34. *Kennedy Report, supra* note 14, at 10.

35. *Kennedy Hearings, supra* note 10, at 149.

36. *Id.* at 192.

37. Of course, no one would expect Kennedy and Bork—or any other judges—to vote alike in every case.

19. JUDGE SOUTER: A STEALTH NOMINEE

1. A. Devroy, *In the End, Souter Fit Politically*, Wash. Post, July 25, 1990, at A1.

2. S. Wermeil & D. Shribman, *Bush's Choice: High Court Nominee Is Conservative but Isn't Seen as an Idealogue*, Wall St. J., July 24, 1990, at A1.

3. R. Cohen, *No Paper Trail*, Wash. Post, July 26, 1990, at A27.

4. N. A. Lewis, *Hearings Near, White House Makes It Clear: Souter Is No Bork*, N.Y. Times, Sept. 12, 1990, at A15.

5. N. A. Lewis, *Souter Deflects Senators' Queries on Abortion Views*, N.Y. Times, Sept. 14, 1990, at A13.

6. *Nomination of David H. Souter to Be Associate Justice of the United States Supreme Court: Hearings Before the Senate Comm. on the Judiciary*, 101st Cong., 2d Sess. 115, 116 (1990) [hereinafter *Souter Hearings*].

7. 410 U.S. 113 (1973).

8. *Souter Hearings, supra* note 6, at 59.

9. *Id.* at 182.

10. *Id.* at 182–83.

11. See, e.g., L. P. Campbell, *Souter Unscathed as Testimony Ends*, Chi. Trib., Sept. 18, 1990, at C1.

12. *Souter Hearings, supra* note 6, at 184.

13. S. Chapman, *Souter Provided Plenty of Replies and No Answers*, Chi. Trib., Sept. 20, 1990, at C29.

14. *In re Estate of Dionne*, 518 A.2d 178, 181 (N.H. 1986).

15. *Nomination of David H. Souter to Be an Associate Justice of the United States Supreme Court*, Exec. Rep. No. 32., 101st Cong., 2d Sess. 7 (1990).

16. *Souter Hearings, supra* note 6, at 303.

17. See A. Bickel, *The Original Understanding and the Segregation Decision*, 69 Harv. L. Rev. 1 (1955).

18. *Souter Hearings, supra* note 6, at 235.

19. Chapman, *supra* note 13.

20. CLARENCE THOMAS: ROUND ONE

1. P. Bedard, *The Supreme Court Nominee*, Wash. Times, July 2, 1991, at A7.

2. D. Savage, *Turning Right: The Making of the Rehnquist Supreme Court* 350 (1992).

3. *The McLaughlin Group*, Fed. Information Sys. Corp., Fed. News Serv., July 5, 1991, available in LEXIS, Nexis Library, Transcripts File (comments of Pat Buchanan).

4. J. Germond and J. Witcover, *Inside Politics: Sham Fight over Thomas Nomination?*, 23 Nat'l J. 1702, (1991).

5. T. Phelps & H. Winternitz, *Capitol Games* 12 (1992).

6. A. Devroy, *Danforth's Backing Was Key to President's Choice of Thomas*, Wash. Post, July 3, 1991, at A1.

7. See T. Eastland, *Bush and the Politics of Race*, N.Y. Times, July 3, 1991, at A19.

8. J. Mayer & J. Abramson, *Strange Justice* 30 (1994) (Thomas's supporters "knew that the safest and best strategy was to bury ideology and sell biography.").

9. A. Willette, *Strategist Learned from Bork How to Fight for Thomas*, Gannett News Serv., Oct. 7, 1991, available in LEXIS, Nexis Library, Wires File.

10. R. Marcus, *Making the Case for Thomas: Lessons of Failed Bork Nomination at Play*, Wash. Post, July 19, 1991, at A1.

11. W. J. Eaton, *Thomas Backers Adopting Policy of Instant Rebuttals; Judiciary: Strategists See Nominations to the Supreme Court as Political Campaigns. They Move Quickly to Fight Potentially Explosive Charges*, L.A. Times, July 20, 1991, at A18.

12. Marcus, *supra* note 10.

13. Phelps & Winternitz, *supra* note 5, at 133–36.

14. *The McLaughlin Group*, Fed. Information Sys. Corp., Fed. News Serv., Aug. 30, 1991, available in LEXIS, Nexis Library, Transcripts File.

15. Phelps & Winternitz, *supra* note 5, at 143.

16. See Press Conference of Citizens United, Conservative Victory Committee, and Citizens Committee to Confirm Clarence Thomas, Fed. Information Sys. Corp., Fed. News Serv., Sept. 4, 1991, at 8, available in LEXIS, Nexis Library, Transcripts Files (statement of Gary Bauer).

17. P. Applebome, *Dr. King's Rights Group Backs Court Nominee*, N.Y. Times, Sept. 26, 1991, at A15.

18. R. A. Taylor, *Democrats Heflin, Kohl to vote Against Thomas*, Wash. Times, Sept. 27, 1991, at A1.

19. R. L. Burke, *Black Caucus Votes to Oppose Thomas for High Court Seat*, N.Y. Times, July 12, 1991, at A1.

20. W. R. Mears, *Unlike Solid Front v. Bork, This One Has Cracks*, Chi. Daily Law Bull., Aug. 29, 1991, at 1; M. Garrett, *Moderate Democrats Seen Backing Thomas*, Wash. Times, Sept. 16, 1991, at A3.

21. It was only when allegations of sexual harassment began to surface that some of these senators found enough political cover to vote against Thomas's confirmation. See *infra* chapter 21.

22. R. Suro, *Thomas's Foes, Off to Slow Start, Say Swaying Public Will Be Hard*, N.Y. Times, Sept. 8, 1991, § 1, at 1.

23. 410 U.S. 113 (1973).

24. *Nomination of Clarence Thomas to Be Associate Justice of the Supreme Court of the United States: Hearings Before the Senate Comm. on the Judiciary*, 102d Cong., 1st Sess., pt. 1, at 222 (1991) [hereinafter *Thomas Hearings*].

25. Phelps & Winternitz, *supra* note 5, at 194–95.

26. *Id.*

27. See *Thomas Hearings*, *supra* note 24, pt. 1, at 218–21 (Senator Leahy questioning Judge Thomas about his comments concerning the Lehrman article).

28. *Id.*, pt. 1, at 353–54.

29. P. Simon, *Advice & Consent* 91 (1992).

30. See W. J. Moore, *Like Souter, Thomas Left Few Ripples*, 23 Nat'l J. 2274 (1991).

31. See generally *Thomas Hearings*, *supra* note 24, pt. 1, at 227–36, 354–61.

32. *Supreme Mystery*, Newsweek, Sept. 16, 1991, at 18, 26.

33. *Thomas Hearings*, *supra* note 24, pt. 1, at 360–61.

34. *Id.*, pt. 1, at 363.

35. 958 F.2d 382 (D.C. Cir. 1992).

36. See, e.g., R. L. Berke, *Two Democrats on Senate Panel Say They Will Oppose Thomas*, N.Y. Times, Sept. 27, 1991, at A1; R. Marcus, *Split Committee Seen Possible on Thomas Court Nomination; Heflin Joins Opposition; Panel to Vote Today*, Wash. Post, Sept. 27, 1991, at A1.

37. A. Kamen, *Specter Says Thomas Didn't Hold Decision in Preference Case*, Wash. Post., Sept. 28, 1991, at A5.

38. *Id.*

39. C. Thomas, *The Higher Law Background of the Privileges or Immunities Clause of the Fourteenth Amendment*, 12 Harv. J.L. & Pub. Pol'y 63, 68 (1989); *Thomas Hearings, supra* note 24, pt. 1, at 178.

40. *Thomas Hearings, supra* note 24, pt. 1, at 274.

41. *Id.*, pt. 1, at 274.

42. *Id.*, pt. 2, at 29 (prepared statement of Professor Lawrence).

43. N. A. Lewis, *Thomas Is Unsuitable, 4 Academics Say*, N.Y. Times, Sept. 17, 1991, at A16.

44. *Id.*

45. 137 Cong. Rec. S13, 737–38 (daily ed., Sept. 26, 1991) (statement of Senator Kohl).

46. 137 Cong. Rec. S13, 738–39 (daily ed., Sept. 26, 1991) (statement of Senator Heflin).

21. CLARENCE THOMAS: ENTER ANITA HILL

1. See T. Phelps, *Sexual Harassment Claim on Thomas Surfaces*, reprinted in *Report of Temporary Special Independent Counsel, Pursuant to S. Res. 202*, S. Doc. No. 20, pt. 2, 102d Cong., 2d Sess. 54 (1992) [hereinafter *Report of Special Counsel*].

2. Telephone Interview with Nan Aron (Nov. 19, 1991).

3. *Report of Special Counsel, supra* note 1, at 11.

4. *Id.* at 13.

5. *Id.*

6. *Id.* at 14.

7. *Id.*

8. *Id.* at 15.

9. *Id.*

10. *Id.* at 16.

11. *Id.* at 17.

12. *Id.* at 18.

13. *Id.*

14. R. J. Ostrow, *Doubts Raised on Quality of Thomas Investigation; Court: Harassment Charge Became Public Late in the Confirmation Process, but Panel's Staff Knew for Weeks*, L.A. Times, Oct. 9, 1991, at A1.

15. *Report of Special Counsel, supra* note 1, at 18.

16. M. Wines, *The Thomas Nomination: How the Senators Handled the Professor's Accusations*, N.Y. Times, Oct. 8, 1991, at A22.

17. A. L. Bardouh, *Nina Totenberg's Queen of Leaks*, Vanity Fair, Jan. 1992, at 46.

18. *Id.* at 26, 29.

19. *Id.* at 40.

20. *Report of Special Counsel, supra* note 1, at 38.

21. *The Report on the Thomas Leak, Part I,* Commentary; Editorial, Wash. Times, May 6, 1992, at G2.

22. *Report of Special Counsel, supra* note 1, at 38–39; Hill had refused to discuss her charges with Nina Totenberg unless Totenberg could first convince her that she already had a copy of Hill's statement; *Id.* at 29.

23. P. Gigot, *Tracing the Hand That Leaked Anita Hill's Tale,* Wall. St. J., May 15, 1992, at A14.

24. *Report of Special Counsel, supra* note 1, at 46. Brudney had originally asked Hill for a written description of her allegations for use in a memorandum on sexual harassment that he was preparing for Senator Metzenbaum; *Id.*

25. H. Dewar, *Senate Probe Fails to Identify Leakers; Sources in Hill-Thomas, "Keating Five" Cases Elude Special Counsel,* Wash. Post, May 6, 1992, at A3.

26. 137 Cong. Rec. S14, 527 (daily ed., Oct. 8, 1991) (statement of Senator Hatch).

27. *Id.* at S14, 538–39, S14, 566–67 (statements of Senator Hatch).

28. *Id.* at S14, 566–67 (statement of Senator Dole).

29. *Id.* at S14, 570 (statement of Senator Mitchell).

30. *McNeil-Lehrer,* PBS Broadcast, Oct. 8, 1991, available in LEXIS, Nexis Library, Transcript File.

31. 137 Cong. Rec. S14, 567–68 (daily ed., Oct. 8, 1991) (statement of Senator Biden).

32. See T. Phelps and H. Winternitz, *Capitol Games* 274 (1992) (arguing that these procedural decisions effectively "sealed the fate" of Anita Hill).

33. *Nomination of Clarence Thomas to Be Associate Justice of the Supreme Court of the United States: Hearings Before the Senate Comm. on the Judiciary,* 102d Cong., 1st Sess., pt. 4, at 8–9 (1991) [hereinafter *Thomas Hearings*].

34. *Id.,* pt. 4, at 27.

35. *Id.,* pt. 4, at 37.

36. *Id.,* pt. 4, at 38.

37. *Id.,* pt. 4, at 56.

38. *Id.,* pt. 4, at 52.

39. *Id.,* pt. 4, at 104.

40. *Id.,* pt. 4, at 157–58.

41. *Id.,* pt. 4, at 160.

42. *Id.*, pt. 4, at 201, 202.

43. *Id.*, pt. 4, at 165.

44. E. Chen, *Stung by Attack, Hill Legal Team Uses Lie Detector; Tactics: Risk Is Taken after Thomas Backers Score Point after Point*, L.A. Times, Oct. 14, 1991, at A12.

45. M. Tolchin, *The Thomas Nomination; Hill Said to Pass a Polygraph Test*, N.Y. Times, Oct. 14, 1991, at A10.

46. *Thomas Hearings*, *supra* note 33, pt. 4, at 368–69.

47. *Id.*, pt. 4, at 370.

48. *Id.*, pt. 4, at 275.

49. *Id.*, pt. 4, at 278.

50. *Id.*, pt. 4, at 277.

51. *Id.*, pt. 4, at 296.

52. *Id.*, pt. 4, at 341.

53. *Id.*, pt. 4, at 354–55.

54. *Id.*, pt. 4, at 363.

55. *Id.*, pt. 4, at 574.

56. See generally *Id.*, pt. 4, at 554–573.

57. *Id.*, pt. 4, at 554–55.

58. *Id.*, pt. 4, at 563.

59. For example, Anna Jenkins, who had been Thomas's secretary, testified that Anita Hill was very excited about moving to the EEOC and that she never appeared to be uncomfortable around Thomas; *Id.*, pt. 4, at 594.

60. J. Mayer & J. Abramson, *Strange Justice: The Selling of Clarence Thomas* 336 (1994).

61. 137 Cong. Rec. S14, 641 (Oct. 15, 1991) (statement of Senator Kennedy).

62. P. Houston, *Senators' Phone Lines Sizzle with Public Comment; Constituents: Depending on Office Nominee Receives Strong Support or Stiff Opposition. Committee Members Admit They Are Sensitive to Mood of Voters*, L.A. Times, Oct. 13, 1991, at A14.

63. R. Brownstein, *The Times Poll; Public Tends to Believe Thomas by 48% to 35%*, L.A. Times, Oct. 14, 1991, at A1.

64. Professor Hill had already experienced a backlash. According to one writer, "Anita Hill put her private business in the street, and she downgraded a black man to a room filled with white men who might alter his fate—surely a large enough betrayal for her to be read out of the race." R. Bray, *Thomas Hill Hearing Raised Deeply Buried Issues*, N.Y. Times Mag., Nov. 17, 1991, at 56.

65. P. Simon, *Advice & Consent* 125–26 (1992).

22. JUDGE GINSBURG: A DEMOCRAT
FACES THE CONFIRMATION PROCESS

1. T. L. Friedman, *The Supreme Court; Clinton Expected to Pick Moderate for High Court*, N.Y. Times, Mar. 20, 1993, at A9.

2. *Id.*

3. *Id.*

4. Although President Clinton could undoubtedly secure the confirmation of some judicial liberals (just as Reagan and Bush had succeeded in appointing judicial conservatives), Clinton could not do so without risk to his legislative agenda.

5. See C. Bolick, *Clinton's Quota Queens*, Wall St. J., Apr. 30, 1993, at A12.

6. R. L. Berke, *Republicans Oppose Naming Babbitt to Court*, N.Y. Times, June 9, 1993, at A17.

7. *Id.*

8. B. Nichols, *Little Backlash So Far for Breyer; Nominees Win, Lose, Ante Up after Run-Ins with Law*, USA Today, June 14, 1993, at A4.

9. R. L. Berke, *Judge's Friends Try to Save Candidacy for High Court*, N.Y. Times, June 14, 1993, at A11.

10. D. Drehle, *Conventional Roles Hid a Revolutionary Intellect; Discrimination Helped Spawn a Crusade*, Wash. Post, July 18, 1993, at A1.

11. Nat'l. Pub. Radio Broadcast, July 6, 1993, available in LEXIS, Nexis Library, Transcripts File (Nina Totenberg reporting).

12. R. L. Berke, *The Supreme Court: The Overview; Clinton Names Ruth Ginsburg, Advocate for Women, to Court*, N.Y. Times, June 15, 1993, at A1.

13. *All Things Considered: Clinton Nominates Ruth Bader Ginsburg to High Court*, Nat'l. Pub. Radio Broadcast, June 13, 1993, available in LEXIS, Nexis Library, Transcripts File.

14. S. Blumenthal, *A Beautiful Friendship*, The New Yorker, July 5, 1993, at 34, 37–38.

15. *Id.*

16. E. M. Rodriguez, *The Ginsburg Nomination: On Bench, in Life Her Tiny Steps Lead to Big Gains*, Legal Times, June 21, 1993, at 1, 16–17.

17. *Transcript of President's Announcement and Judge Ginsburg's Remarks*, N.Y. Times, June 15, 1993, at A13.

18. *Id.*

19. *Id.*

20. *Id.*

21. *Nomination of Ruth Bader Ginsburg to Be Associate Justice of*

the Supreme Court of the United States: Hearings Before the Senate Comm. on the Judiciary, 103d Cong., 1st Sess. 1 (1993) [hereinafter *Ginsburg Hearings*].

22. *Id.* at 32.

23. *Specter Seeks More Scrutiny of Ginsburg*, St. Louis Post-Dispatch, July 20, 1993, at 13B.

24. *Ginsburg Hearings, supra* note 21, at 139.

25. *Id.* at 172.

26. 60 U.S. (19 How.) 393 (1857).

27. *Ginsburg Hearings, supra* note 21, at 269–73.

28. See R. Bader Ginsburg, *Speaking in a Judicial Voice*, 67 N.Y.U. L. Rev. 1185 (1992). The publication date of this article is misleading. Justice Ginsburg originally delivered her observations in a lecture on Mar. 9, 1993.

29. *Id.* at 1208.

30. *Id.* at 1199.

31. *Ginsburg Hearings, supra* note 21, at 52.

32. *Id.* at 219.

33. *Id.* at 275–76.

34. *Id.* at 264–65.

35. *Id.* at 322.

36. *Id.* at 323.

37. *Id.* at 546, 547.

38. *Id.* at 345–46.

39. *Id.* at 349.

40. N. A. Lewis, *Judge Ruth Bader Ginsburg: Her Life and Her Law*, N.Y. Times, June 27, 1993, § 1, at 20 (in cases of divided opinion in 1987, Judge Ginsburg voted with Judge Bork 85 percent of the time and with Judge Wald only 38 percent of the time).

23. JUDGE BREYER REVISITED

1. 505 U.S. 833 (1992).

2. U.S. Const. Art. I, § 6, cl. 2.

3. D. Klaidman, *Sitting Out the Supreme Court Search*, Legal Times, Apr. 11, 1994, at 7.

4. M. Jacoby, *A Mitchell Nomination Could Get Complicated*, Roll Call, Apr. 11, 1994.

5. M. Locin & E. S. Povich, *Once Again, President Searches for New Nominee*, Chi. Trib., Apr. 13, 1994, at N1.

6. D. Jehl, *Mitchell Rejects President's Offer of Seat on Court*, N.Y. Times, Apr. 13, 1994, at A1.

7. G. Ifill, *White House Memo: Mitchell's Rebuff Touches Off Scramble for Court Nominee*, N.Y. Times, Apr. 16, 1994, § 1, at 1; N. Lewis, *No Apparent Front-Runner to Fill Supreme Court Seat*, N.Y. Times, Apr. 27, 1994, at B10.

8. See A. L. Todd, *Justice on Trial* 133–39 (1964).

9. *Bertrand v. Sava*, 684 F.2d 204 (8th Cir. 1982).

10. *United States Jaycees v. McClure*, 709 F.2d 1560 (8th Cir. 1983).

11. *Roberts v. United States Jaycees*, 468 U.S. 609 (1984).

12. *Hodgson v. Minnesota*, 853 F.2d 1452 (8th Cir. 1988).

13. See, e.g., *Forbes v. Arkansas Educ. Television Communication Network Found.*, 22 F.3d 1423 (8th Cir. 1994) (upholding the right of an antiabortion independent candidate to have his ad aired on public television); *Gay & Lesbian Students Ass'n v. Gohn*, 850 F.2d 361 (8th Cir. 1988) (upholding the right of gay rights activists to speak at the University of Arkansas).

14. G. Ifill, *Babbitt Waits as Clinton Ponders Successor*, N.Y. Times, May 11, 1994, at A16.

15. *Washington Week in Review*, Fed. Information Sys. Corp., Fed. News Serv., July 15, 1994, available in LEXIS, Nexis Library, Transcripts File (statement of Ken Bode).

16. 899 F.2d 53 (1st Cir. 1990).

17. *Planned Parenthood League of Massachusetts v. Bellotti*, 868 F.2d 459 (1st Cir. 1989).

18. *Activists Fear Breyer's Abortion Position*, S. Illinoisan, May 23, 1994, at 2C (from AP wire).

19. *Stuart v. Roache*, 951 F.2d 446 (1st Cir. 1991).

20. *Morgan v. Burke*, 926 F.2d 86 (1st Cir. 1991).

21. 28 U.S.C. § 455(c).

22. *Liljberg v. Health Serv. Acquisition Corp.*, 486 U.S. 847 (1988).

23. 900 F.3d 429 (1st Cir. 1990).

24. *Nomination of Stephen G. Breyer to Be Associate Justice of the Supreme Court of the United States: Hearings Before the Senate Comm. on the Judiciary*, 103d Cong., 2d Sess. 154–56 (1994) [hereinafter *Breyer Hearings*].

25. *Id.* at 400 (statement of Robert P. Watkins, chair, American Bar Association Standing Committee on the Federal Judiciary).

26. *Id.* at 469, 471–86, 558.

27. Robert L. Jackson, *Senate Panel Unanimously OK'S Breyer Nomination*, L.A. Times, July 20, 1994, at A19.

28. *A Cloud on the Breyer Nomination*, N.Y. Times, July 26, 1994, at A1.

29. *Supreme Court: A "Conservative Shift" and Ethical Trouble*, Am. Pol. Network Abortion Rep., July 27, 1994, vol. 6, no. 6 (discussing editorials in the Arkansas Democratic-Gazette and the Baltimore Sun).

30. M. Ingwerson, *U.S. Senate's Lone Voice of Dissent on Breyer Sees Potential Conflicts*, Christian Sci. Monitor, July 27, 1994, at 3.

31. *Second Senator, Citing Lloyd's Tangle, Opposes Breyer*, Reuters, July 27, 1994, available in LEXIS, Nexis Library, Wires File.

32. *The Clinton Administration Supreme Court: Senate Confirms Breyer by 87-9 Vote*, Am. Pol. Network Abortion Rep., Aug. 1, 1994, vol. 6, no. 9.; H. Dewar, *Breyer Wins Senate Confirmation to Top Court, 87 to 9*, Wash. Post, July 30, 1994, at A9; L. Greenhouse, *Plaudits Drown Out Critics as Senate Confirms Breyer*, N.Y. Times, July 30, 1994, § 1, at 6.

33. Greenhouse, *supra* note 32; Dewar, *supra* note 32.

34. Greenhouse, *supra* note 32, at 5.

35. M. Sandalow, *Breyer Confirmed for Court: Boston Judge Approved by Senate 87-9*, S.F. Chron., July 30, 1994 at A1.

24. THE BORK PRECEDENT: A SEARCH FOR MEANING

1. See *supra* chapter 17.

2. See *supra* chapter 4.

3. *Nomination of Ruth Bader Ginsburg to Be Associate Justice of the Supreme of the United States: Hearings Before the Senate Comm. on the Judiciary*, 103d Cong., 1st Sess. 219 (1994).

4. O. Hatch, *Save the Court from What?*, 99 Harv. L. Rev., 1347, 1352–53 (1986) (reviewing L. H. Tribe, *God Save This Honorable Court* [1985]).

5. See *supra* chapter 4.

6. S. L. Carter, *The Confirmation Mess*, 101 Harv. L. Rev. 1185, 1193 (1988).

7. P. A. Freund, *Appointment of Justices: Some Historical Perspectives*, 101 Harv. L. Rev. 1146, 1163 (1988).

8. 395 U.S. 444 (1968).

9. See *supra* chapter 10.

10. A. Specter, *Concluding Address: On the Confirmation of a Supreme Court Justice*, 84 Nw. U. L. Rev. 1037, 1044 (1990).

11. 133 Cong. Rec. 28, 858 (1987) (statement of Senator Roth).

12. *Nomination of Robert H. Bork to Be Associate Justice of the Su-*

preme Court of the United States: Hearings Before the Senate Comm. on the Judiciary, 100th Cong., 1st Sess. 262 (1987).

13. G. Rees III, *Questions for Supreme Court Nominees at Confirmation Hearings: Excluding the Constitution,* 17 Ga. L. Rev. 913, 962 (1983).

14. S. L. Carter, *The Confirmation Mess, Revisited,* 84 Nw. U. L. Rev. 962, 965 (1990).

15. See Carter, *supra* note 6, at 1193.

16. *Nomination of Anthony M. Kennedy to Be Associate Justice of the Supreme Court of the United States: Hearings Before the Senate Comm. on the Judiciary,* 100th Cong., 1st Sess. 217 (1987).

17. B. Fein, *It's Been All Downhill since Bork,* A.B.A. J., Oct. 1991, at 75, 76.

18. See *supra* chapter 18.

19. See, e.g., *Adarand Constructors, Inc. v. Pena,* 115 S. Ct. 2097 (1995); *United States v. Lopez,* 115 S. Ct. 1624 (1995); *Shaw v. Reno,* 509 U.S. 630 (1993); *Employment Div. v. Smith,* 494 U.S. 872 (1990); but see *Planned Parenthood v. Casey,* 505 U.S. 833 (1992) (plurality opinion).

20. *Scalia: Hearings "an Absurd Spectacle,"* Wash. Times, Feb. 5, 1992, at A2.

21. R. Marcus, *As Thomas Hearings Wrap Up, Democrats Question the Process; Biden Vows to Examine "Ground Rules" for Confirmation Sessions,* Wash. Post, Sept. 21, 1991, at A7.

22. News Conference with Senator Alan Simpson, *Nomination of Clarence Thomas to the Supreme Court,* Fed. Information Sys. Corp., Fed. News Serv., July 18, 1991, available in LEXIS, Nexis Library, Transcripts File; D. Ceol, *Thomas Potshots Fail to Yield "Smoking Gun,"* Wash. Times, July 19, 1991, at A4.

23. D. G. Savage, *Thomas Backers Try to Make Him Seem Victim; Strategy: The Issue Is Pressed So Relentlessly That They Appear to Have Taken the Steam Out of Accuser's Charges,* L.A. Times, Oct. 13, 1991, at A1.

24. *Nomination of Clarence Thomas to Be Associate Justice of the Supreme Court of the United States: Hearings Before the Senate Comm. on the Judiciary,* 102d Cong., 1st Sess., pt. 4, at 252 (1991).

25. See C. L. Black Jr., *A Note on Senatorial Consideration of Supreme Court Nominees,* 79 Yale L.J. 657, 663–64 (1970); see also R. F. Nagel, *Advice, Consent, and Influence,* 84 Nw. U. L. Rev. 858, 861 (1990).

26. N. Totenberg, *The Confirmation Process and the Public: To Know or Not to Know?,* 101 Harv. L. Rev. 1213, 1224 (1988).

27. See H. P. Monaghan, *The Confirmation Process: Law or Politics?*, 101 Harv. L. Rev. 1202, 1209 (1988).

28. Totenberg, *supra* note 26, at 1226 n.84 (1988).

29. Nagel, *supra* note 25, at 869.

30. Monaghan, *supra* note 27, at 1209.

31. P. Simon, *Advice & Consent* 35 (1992).

INDEX

Norman Vieira is a graduate of Columbia University and the University of Chicago Law School. He is a professor in the Southern Illinois University School of Law, where he teaches constitutional law and civil rights. He taught previously at UCLA and the University of Idaho and is the author of *Constitutional Civil Rights*.

Leonard Gross is a graduate of the State University of New York at Binghamton and Boston University Law School. He teaches a course on the legal profession at Southern Illinois University School of Law, where he has been teaching since 1983. He is the coauthor of *Organizing Corporations and Other Business Enterprises* (6th ed.).